CW00926693

steal my heart

Rosewood River
Book One

laura pavlov

Copyright:
Rosewood River, Book 1
Copyright © 2025 by Laura Pavlov
All rights reserved.
No part of this book may be reproduced or transmitted in any form or by any
means, electronic or mechanical, including photocopying, recording, or by any
information storage and retrieval system without the written permission of the
author, except for the use of brief quotations in a book review.
This is a work of fiction. Names, characters, places, brands, media, and incidents
are either the product of the author's imagination or are used fictitiously. Any
resemblance to actual persons, living or dead, events, or locales is entirely
coincidental.

Laura Pavlov
https://www.laurapavlov.com

Cover Design: Hang Le

Sometimes there is no way to avoid a storm.
Sometimes you just have to open the door and go through it.

one

. . .

Easton

"HI, EASTON." Laney flashed me the smile of a sixteen-year-old girl who didn't have a care in the world outside of getting off work at the end of the day and heading down to the river to meet her friends.

"Morning," I said, as I tapped the counter twice at Rosewood Brew. "I'll take the iced mocha, tall, please."

"You know, we're running a special on our Taylor Teas today. Buy one, get one free."

"I'll stick with my usual. I'm actually surprised that you guys would name a drink after that ridiculous 'Taylor Tea' column." As far as I was concerned, it was a crock of shit that the *Rosewood River Review*, our local newspaper, had started some anonymous gossip column and called it "The Taylor Tea." And now everyone in town was acting like it was the best thing they'd ever read—when it was a bunch of horseshit served up on an alluring small-town platter.

The Taylor family owned the newspaper, and most people were convinced that the column was penned by their daughter, Emilia Taylor. At this point, nothing would surprise me.

"Are you kidding! I hear there's a new lady in town starting work at your law office today. Where do you think I found that out? 'The Taylor Tea.'" She squealed, far too loud for seven o'clock in the morning, and I winced. "Everyone loves getting the scoop on what's happening in town. Best thing to happen to Rosewood River in a long time."

"Interesting, seeing as we have a new health clinic that opened last year, a newly expanded law office, and a top-tier veterinarian hospital, and this is what you consider the best thing to happen to Rosewood River? You know it's all gossip, right?" I raised a brow as she poured the coffee over the ice in my cup.

"Um… yes. That's why we love it. All my friends are actually reading it now, and we haven't read anything that hasn't been school assigned in years. We wait for it to come out every Saturday."

The world has gone to shit if this is their idea of reading.

I took my cup from her and pulled out some cash. "Laney, there are much more interesting things to read about other than gossip in Rosewood River. You do remember that the first column that went to print was about Emerson's wedding disaster. Does that seem like something everyone should be reading?"

My twin sister had almost walked down the aisle with an asshole, and I was happy she'd ended up calling off the wedding. Now she was engaged to Nash Heart in Magnolia Falls, and everything had worked out. But that still didn't mean that her heartache should have gone to print and been talked about by everyone in town.

It was her personal life, for fuck's sake.

"Listen, with social media today, everything is out there anyway. Everyone would have found out that the wedding was canceled eventually because they'd invited everyone in Rosewood River to that wedding. It was all everyone was talking about. At least this is just news that's spread through our small town." She thought about her next words, and I bit my tongue before biting her head off and telling her that was a lame defense. I was a goddamn lawyer—I knew what a good argument looked like, and this wasn't it. "Think about it, Easton. If they hadn't printed that juicy gossip about the wedding being called off, Emerson might have come home, and then she wouldn't have met Nash and become a mama to little Cutler."

Yes. They'd gone on to print another story about my twin sister finding love after heartbreak, as well.

"It's shit and you know it. People are entitled to a private life. The Taylors have a reputable newspaper; they should keep it that way." I dropped a couple of bucks in the tip jar and turned to leave.

"Well, how do you think I know that Henley Holloway just moved to town?" she said over a fit of giggles like this was huge news.

I pushed the door open with my shoulder and turned to look at her one last time. "There are much more interesting things than a new lawyer moving to town. Be a normal teenager and go have fun with your friends and stop reading that trash."

She giggled some more and nodded, as I let the door close before walking the short distance to the office.

We had two locations, and I ran the law office here, which worked out great as many of the employees preferred to live just outside of Rosewood River and avoid the madness of commuting to the city. We were only thirty minutes outside of San Francisco, and I made the drive when I had to be in court, but I preferred to work out of our satellite office here.

I rounded the corner, taking in the large brick building I'd convinced the partners to invest in when we'd expanded. The sign hanging above the door was my daily motivation to put my head down and keep working.

Holloway, Jones, and Waterman.

Our firm was one of the longest-standing law firms in the state of California. My boss, Charles Holloway, had hired me four years ago. I'd fought hard to get my foot in the door of such a prestigious law firm, and I'd been the youngest attorney they'd taken on in the history of the firm—up until today, of course.

Charles's daughter, Henley Holloway, was starting at the firm this morning fresh out of law school.

I was assigned to being her mentor, which was a fancy term for babysitting the boss's daughter. She'd graduated from Harvard Law a few months ago. And sure, it was Harvard, but she'd probably cruised through the program as a longtime legacy, since her great-grandfather, her grandfather, and her father had all attended. Then she'd spent the summer in the south of France with her mother, living a life of leisure.

Because that's what you did when you had a rich daddy who saved you a spot at the firm.

Birthright had gotten her this position—not her credentials.

And that shit pissed me off.

I was determined to get my name on the door.

Holloway, Jones, Waterman, and Chadwick.

And the little princess was the only thing standing in my way.

My final task.

Take her under my wing. Show her the ropes. Let her shadow me for a few months to show her how it's done. I was an arrogant prick, no doubt about it. But I had the track record to back it —so I made no apologies for knowing that I was the best at my job.

I knew how to win cases, and I didn't quit until I had every juror convinced that I was right.

When I came around the corner, the sound of the alarm had me moving quickly. I pulled the door open to my building, only to see the backside of a woman wearing a pink fitted skirt and matching jacket with long blonde waves trailing down her back. My eyes scanned her lean, tan legs all the way down to the nude heels on her feet. She frantically typed a code into the alarm system and was having a full fucking conversation over the loud ringing coming through the walls.

"Stop! Oh my gosh! Please, stop!" she shrieked.

For fuck's sake.

"Move." I slid in beside her, and she gasped at my presence before stepping aside.

I typed in the code quickly, and the noise came to a stop.

"I'm so sorry. I—er, my dad clearly gave me the wrong code," she said, shaking her head, her sapphire blue eyes locked with mine. Her skin was flawless, even though she barely wore a stitch of makeup, and her plump, pink lips turned up the slightest bit in a forced smile.

She was gorgeous.

I'd seen photos, so I'd expected as much.

But in person—she was quite possibly the most stunning woman I'd ever laid eyes on.

Which meant she'd be a big fucking distraction in the office.

"Do you always decide to show up earlier than your boss on your first day?"

"My boss?" She quirked a brow and smirked, as if the idea were comical.

"I run this office, in case you weren't informed. Your last name might be Holloway, but you're new here, and even if you get to start out in a posh office—that doesn't change the fact that you answer to me." Her father told me to treat her like I'd treat anyone else, even if he clearly wasn't going to take his own advice.

"I prefer the word mentor over boss." She tipped her chin up in challenge.

"And I prefer not to start my day with a blasting alarm going off in my ear."

She sighed. "It won't happen again. I'll get the correct code from you today."

She followed me inside, and I directed her to the staff lounge before pointing in the direction of her new office. "Yours is at the end of the hall. Get yourself settled and give me half an hour. We'll meet in my office."

"I'll see you there."

She marched down the hall, and I turned in the opposite

direction toward my office. I dropped my briefcase onto my desk and opened my laptop before turning on my monitor.

I made my way down to the staff lounge to top off my coffee, because my assistant, Rosie, wouldn't be in until later this morning, as she had an appointment. The woman spoiled me. She was quite possibly the best executive assistant on the planet, and I wouldn't function well without her.

But today, I'd get my own coffee.

As I turned the corner, scalding hot liquid collided with my chest as Henley Holloway let out a deafening squeal.

Motherfucker.

I stepped back, tugging my dress shirt away from my skin, which was burning like a bitch.

"Oh, my gosh," she said as I stormed past her. "I was bringing you a cup of coffee as an apology for the alarm."

I tossed my suit coat onto the chair and hurried to the sink, unbuttoning my dress shirt as I went. I was fairly certain she'd had hot lava in that mug, and it was currently eating through my flesh.

I reached for a towel and ran it under the cold water before pressing it to my chest.

"How about you don't do me any favors, and just do your fucking job," I hissed. The words came out harsher than I meant them to, but my fucking skin was on fucking fire.

"I can do that."

"One would hope so with a Harvard degree." I turned off the water. "I need to go change my shirt. I'll see you in my office at the scheduled time."

She nodded and walked away.

I'd most likely hurt her feelings, and I was fine with it. This was not an easy career or firm to work for. No one had held my hand when I'd started, and I wouldn't be doing her any favors by giving her special treatment.

Hell, she was already given an office, which was going to be noticed by everyone who worked here.

Carver Thomas had just moved into a small office after two years of working his ass off. Joey Barker, who was a junior associate, just like Henley, sat in a cubicle with the other junior associates nine months after being hired.

She was already receiving special treatment.

And this day was off to a shit start.

She'd set off the alarm and spilled scalding hot coffee on me, and it wasn't even seven thirty in the morning yet.

This woman was going to be my shadow for the next six months, and I was already on edge.

And that was never a good thing.

two

. . .

Henley

I WENT to the restroom to wash my coffee-stained hands. I shouldn't be surprised that my father would hire a pretentious prick to run the office. Easton had been highly annoyed by me when I'd set off the alarm, and then I'd spilled hot coffee all over him. Not like I'd done *either* on purpose!

Off to a great start, Henley.

I tried to apologize for the alarm, and he'd ripped my head off.

I'd made matters worse with the coffee, but I'd apologized for that, as well.

But did he need to be so harsh about it?

Was I mortified that I'd started off the day like this? Of course.

I'd thought that working out of this office instead of the office in the city with my father would give me a chance to make a name for myself.

Obviously, my last name preceded me. It was painted on the door. I was Charles Holloway's daughter, so there'd already be people who hated me here.

I get it.

Birthright could be a blessing and a curse.

I'd been born into a family with a ridiculous amount of money. I'd attended the best schools, traveled the world, and wanted for nothing.

That, by design, makes me a spoiled brat in the eyes of many.

But there was more to my story. So much more.

I'd worked hard at everything I'd ever done from as early as I could remember.

I'd always been a straight-A student, and I'd just graduated first in my class at Harvard Law.

That had nothing to do with my name.

I'd played collegiate tennis all through undergrad and considered playing professionally for a brief period of time.

My point was—I worked hard to get here.

But very few people ever considered that. I'd walked through these doors today with a big target on my back. It was the reason I'd considered staying back east and working for a firm that didn't have my name on the building.

But my father and my grandfather dreamed of me eventually taking over this firm that they'd built.

And I wouldn't avoid it just because people would judge me and think it had been handed to me.

I'd just have to prove myself.

Clearly, I hadn't started off on the best foot, but I was determined to show Easton Chadwick that I wasn't a burden. I had a lot to offer, and I just needed some time to show him.

I'd dealt with assholes like Easton before.

He was supposed to be a coworker and a mentor. Yes, he was my senior, and he had several years' experience over me, but he didn't need to act like I was an inexperienced intern.

I'd worked with some of the greatest legal minds out there during my internships in law school. I did not require a babysitter, which was how he was acting.

I'd actually been looking forward to working with Easton Chadwick. He had a reputation of being arrogant, but it was justified if you looked at what he'd already accomplished.

Which, of course, I'd done.

I'd read about his cases, and I admired what he'd already accomplished at a young age.

But at the end of the day, I was here to do my job. If he didn't like it, he could pass me on to someone else.

Or just leave me alone.

I was a resourceful girl. I knew how to take care of myself. I knew how to do my job. I knew how to win cases.

I stared in the mirror for a few seconds, giving myself a silent pep talk.

You've got this. You've earned this. You've worked your ass off. Hold your head high and pull it together.

It was a mantra I'd been saying since I was in high school.

I blew out a breath and stopped in my office to grab my notebook and pen and made my way to Easton's office.

I knocked on the door, and he barked at me to come in.

Once I pushed the door open, he gestured for me to take the seat across from him.

His office was large. Much larger than mine, thankfully. I hadn't asked for my own office. My father had just insisted I take it.

Dad and I were close, but he'd always been a workaholic. So gifts were his love language. Time wasn't something he had a lot of, so I'd always soaked up those moments that we'd had together from a young age, and Sunday mornings had been our thing when I was young. It was the time that was set aside for the two of us. It had been my favorite day of the week up until the time I left for boarding school.

I shook off the memory.

I sat down and noted the crisp white dress shirt that Easton was now wearing. This one was not covered in coffee.

"You keep a spare here at the office?" I asked, trying to lighten the mood.

"Yes. You aren't the first person to startle in my presence." His tone was dry and lacked any emotion.

"I wouldn't say I startled in your presence." I tried to hide my irritation by the insinuation. "We just sort of slammed into one another."

He was staring at his monitor before he looked up at me. "It's the staff lounge. It shouldn't be surprising that people are coming and going."

"Can I pay to have your shirt dry-cleaned as a peace offering?" It was my olive branch. I'd offer it once, and it was up to him if he wanted to start fresh. We'd be working together; no sense starting off as enemies.

He narrowed his gaze. "How about you just focus on doing your job."

"That's what I'm here to do." I cleared my throat.

"Great. Because I've got a heavy caseload, so I guess we'll see if that Harvard law degree was worth it."

So much for the olive branch.

I let out a strained breath and folded my hands together, looking down to see my knuckles turn stark white. I needed to be professional. I wanted this to work, after all.

"Listen, I get it. This is a hassle for you. But I assure you that I can handle whatever you throw at me. My Harvard law degree was not handed to me. I earned it."

He raised a brow and nodded. "Your father attended Harvard, didn't he? And your grandfather?" he said, and I knew what he was insinuating, so I finished the next statement for him.

"Correct. And my great-grandfather also graduated from Harvard Law. I'm a legacy. It's public knowledge." I glared at him, trying hard to control my voice so it didn't shake. "But if you did your homework and bothered to read my résumé, you'd know that I scored a 180 on my LSAT, so I believe that receiving a perfect score helped me get into Harvard, too. It wasn't only my name."

His eyes widened, and he sat back in his chair. "Your father didn't mention that."

"Maybe he assumes you would have done your research, especially with that sterling reputation you have in the courtroom. But it appears you just made assumptions before looking beyond my last name."

He nodded slowly as the door opened, and a woman walked inside with a coffee mug in her hand. "Good morning. You must be Ms. Holloway. I'm Rosie, Easton's assistant."

She was probably in her forties, short dark hair cut in a blunt bob style just beneath her ears.

"Yes, I'm Henley. It's nice to meet you." I extended my arm after she set the coffee down on Easton's desk, and she shook my hand.

"Can I get you a coffee?"

I glanced over at Easton, and he raised a brow as if the idea of me holding a hot cup of coffee in his presence was not a good idea.

"I'm okay. I got in early, so I've already had a healthy dose of caffeine this morning. But thank you for the offer."

"Of course. And if you need anything, just let me know."

"Henley already has a corner office. She doesn't get to add in an administrative assistant when she's just starting out," Easton hissed, and Rosie raised a brow. I didn't miss the questioning look that she gave him before leaving his office.

So clearly, he wasn't always an asshole.

He must be reserving this attitude especially for me.

Once the door closed, he tossed a stack of files in my direction, and they landed on the desk in front of me. "Get to work on these. They aren't big cases, but that's not what matters. We want to win as many as we can. Big and small. So cut your teeth on these. See what you can come up with, and you can present your findings to me at lunch."

I looked down at the four files now in my hands. He expected me to research all of these by lunchtime?

"Not a problem," I said, clenching my teeth hard as I pushed to my feet.

"Henley," he barked, just as my hand wrapped around the door handle, and I turned around to face him.

"Yes."

"I wasn't being a dick when I said that you didn't have access to Rosie. I was actually trying to help you."

My hand fell from the door handle, and I stared at him. "You were trying to help me?"

"Correct."

"Which part? The part where you said that I only got into law school because of my last name? Or the part where you insinuated that I only got this job because of my last name? Or the part where you acted like I wasn't capable of doing my job?"

"All of those, Princess." He leaned back in his chair, his dark hair longer in the front and shorter on the sides. His eyes were a deep gray and intense. My gaze moved lower, where the fabric strained against his muscled arms that were crossed. I tried to forget about the six-pack abs that were on full display when he'd unbuttoned his dress shirt to place a cold cloth there just a few minutes ago. "Listen, if this is what I'm thinking, trust me, it's what everyone else is thinking, too. So accessing Rosie just makes you less likable than you already are."

"So, you're basically saying everyone hates me before they've even met me?"

He shrugged. "The boss's daughter moves to town and buys a big house on the river, gets a corner office, and wants her own admin? You're the youngest hire at this firm. That wouldn't happen to anyone else."

"I'm a year younger than you were when you got hired."

"Yeah. And I sat in a cubicle and worked my ass off the first year. I didn't have an office or an admin. But they still hated me for being young. For being smarter than they were. So I put my head down, and I worked. I worked hard, and I made a name for myself. And it sure as shit isn't Holloway. So, yeah, you've got your work cut out for you."

"I can't change my last name." I tucked my lips between my

teeth, determined not to get upset, as I pushed the lump from my throat.

"I'm aware of that. So don't take any more perks if you want this to work. They'll hate you for it. Let your work do the talking. If you're as smart as you say you are, it shouldn't be a problem. And I gave you plenty to work with, so how about you start proving yourself right now." He reached for his coffee.

The pompous ass.

"Not a problem, Mr. Chadwick." I turned toward the door and walked out.

"His bark is bigger than his bite," Rosie whispered. "But if you tell him I said that, I'll deny it."

"I won't say a word." I stopped at her desk and glanced over my shoulder to make sure I'd pulled his office door closed behind me. "Hey, is one of those cubicles open over there?"

She followed my gaze to the open room, where three rows of cubicles were lined up.

"Yes, the two at the end are open." She quirked a brow curiously.

"Great. I'm setting up there. I don't need an office. I just need a desk to set my laptop on."

"I like you already," Rosie said with a chuckle.

"That makes you the first one today. Let's hope everyone else gives me a chance before they presume I'm the devil, like my mentor just did."

"No one else will be hard to win over. Easton is going to be the most challenging. They don't call him the shark for no reason."

"The shark?" I groaned.

"Yes. That's what they call Easton. He got the nickname because he works harder than anyone in the industry, and he never backs down. He always finds an angle, and that's how he continues to win cases."

"Great. The guy I answer to is called the shark," I said, before shaking my head in disbelief. "Isn't his ego already big enough?"

"You have no idea." She chuckled. "But he's actually a great guy beneath all that intensity. If you can survive working under him, he'll make you the best. Because he won't settle for anything less."

I nodded. "Great. I have a high threshold for suffering. He can put me through as much as he wants to; I'm not going anywhere."

"Buckle up, because he's going to test you."

"Got it. Thanks for the heads-up. I'm going to go get my stuff, and I'll set up out here."

"Looks like you're up for the challenge," she said, taking a sip of her coffee.

"Always."

And that was the truth.

An insufferable boss would be a minor hurdle.

Easton Chadwick was not going to run me off.

I was going to show him that my last name had nothing to do with the reason that I was here.

three

. . .

Easton

ONE WEEK.

One week of Henley Holloway winning over every single person in the office.

That had not been expected.

First, she'd moved herself out to the cubicles with the others.

Then she'd brought donuts to work the following day.

I'd expected everyone to be tough on her, but a goddamn cake donut with a few sprinkles on it had won these bastards over.

Joey Barker was all over her. The dude's cubie was right beside hers, and he was an ass-kisser by nature. Add in the fact that she was fucking gorgeous, and he was putty in her hands. It pissed me the hell off.

I'd fact-checked her LSAT score, and she'd told the truth.

She'd received a perfect fucking score on that test. I ended up looking over her résumé, and her bar exam was equally impressive. She'd been in the top one percent.

Our scores had been similar, but she'd edged me out on the LSAT, while I'd edged her out on the bar exam. I wasn't used to anyone scoring higher than me. I was intrigued. There was no way that her last name could have helped her score on either of those exams.

The woman was clearly smart, as she'd crushed everything that I'd thrown at her these last few days. And I'd thrown a lot at her.

Cases that didn't appear to have loopholes, she'd found them.

Cases that seemed to be dead ends, she'd see something no one else saw.

Cases that had no business going to court, she'd found a reason to fight for the client.

Henley Holloway had not gone to Harvard because of her last name. She hadn't graduated first in her class because she was the granddaughter of a man who donated a ton of money to that school.

She was a brilliant attorney. One who'd barely begun her career.

A career that I was mentoring at the moment.

So, I'd push her, because she had the potential to be better than she probably even realized.

I glanced out the glass walls of my office to see Joey Barker's chair pulled over on the edge of her cubicle. Again. That shit annoyed me for reasons that I couldn't explain.

I picked up my office phone and called Rosie. "Tell Henley I need to see her."

"She's helping Joey with a case that he's struggling with."

The dude was following her around like a puppy, and it bugged the fuck out of me. She had that kind of light around her, and people in the office had quickly assessed that she was smarter than them, so they were going to try to ride her coattails.

"Is Joey her mentor? Does she answer to him?"

Rosie chuckled. "Nope."

"Great. Then we're on the same page. Send her in now."

"You got it, boss."

"You know I hate when you call me that."

"I thought you hated being called Shark?" She chuckled.

I rolled my eyes. "I prefer you just call me by my actual name. I don't need a handle to prove that I'm the best."

"Spoken like the cocky bastard you are."

"Hey, if the shoe fits." I paused.

"Fair enough, Mr. Chadwick."

I rolled my eyes because she knew I preferred her to call me Easton, and I groaned into the phone. "Just send her in, Rosie."

She laughed, and I ended the call. I looked over the files that Henley had left for me this morning. She arrived early every single day. So early, that now I was coming to the office earlier because I was always the first one here.

I liked it that way.

The knock on the door came quickly, and I called for her to come in.

"You beckoned?" She smirked because she was a smartass, even when she clearly tried to tamp down her irritation with me.

My gaze moved over her cream-colored dress that ended just below her knees. There shouldn't be anything sexy about this outfit. It was perfectly professional. In fact, if anyone else had worn it, I wouldn't have taken a second glance.

But Henley Holloway could be wearing a paper sack, and she'd manage to look like a fucking runway model. And that shit pissed me off, too. I was here to work. I didn't have time to be distracted by my understudy.

My boss's daughter.

"Take a seat."

She sat down in the chair on the other side of my desk, crossing one long, tan leg over the other.

Is she fucking with me?

I sat back in my chair and looked up to meet her sapphire blue gaze. She had a little speckle of freckles over her nose, she wore very little makeup, and her plump lips were hard not to stare at.

But I was a man who could handle a challenge.

"What's up? I was helping Joey with something, but Rosie said it was urgent."

I raised a brow. "You don't work for Joey."

"I'm aware. But we're coworkers."

"I think you've made your point by leaving your office and working in the cubicles."

"Made my point?" She raised a brow.

"Yes. You're one with the people. I get it. They get it. But you don't owe Joey or any of them anything. He has been here for months, and he works with Carver Thomas. He needs to figure it out on his own or go to the man he answers to," I said.

I'd been shocked when she'd decided to forgo the office and work out of a cubie. Like I said, the woman was full of surprises.

"I thought we were a team here."

"To an extent. You and I are on the same team. Joey is on a team with Carver. That's who he should be going to for help."

She shifted in her chair the slightest bit, and her dress rode up, exposing more of her lean leg, and I reached for my coffee. I needed to do something with my hands because I had the sudden urge to run my fingers over the skin of her silky thigh.

"Well, we all work for the same firm." She quirked a brow. "But I'll be more conscientious."

"Listen, if I'm not giving you enough work, I'm happy to give you more." I set my mug down.

"You give me plenty," she said. "And I've finished everything you've asked of me, yet you've given very little feedback. As my mentor, aren't you supposed to tell me how I'm doing?"

"Do you need to have your ego stroked, Princess? Didn't you get a perfect fucking score on your LSAT? I would guess your ego is just fine." I leaned forward, rolling up the sleeves of my dress shirt and resting my forearms on the desk. Her eyes flicked there before moving back up to meet my gaze.

"I don't need my ego stroked," she said, her eyes on mine, and for whatever reason, my dick thought that was sexy as shit and sprung to life.

I cleared my throat and shifted in my seat. "What is it that you need to hear from me?"

"I just want to know if I'm meeting your standards."

She was fucking exceeding my standards. But telling her that wouldn't do her any favors.

"You're doing well, Henley. You have a good eye."

Her teeth sank into her bottom lip, and the move was so sexy I nearly came right there.

What the fuck is this about?

I didn't lose control around women.

I obviously hadn't been out in a while, as I'd been working ridiculous hours.

"Thank you."

I needed her out of my office. Now.

"You can leave."

She startled the slightest bit. "Oh. Okay. I thought you called me in here."

I turned my attention back to my monitor. She was a distraction, and I didn't have time for distractions.

"I wanted to make sure that you knew we had work to do. You don't have time to be helping Joey with his job. I just emailed you a few things that I need you to research for me."

She didn't leave, and I could feel her watching me. "You called me in here to tell me that I shouldn't be helping Joey?"

I glanced over at her. "Correct."

"You could have just called."

"I wanted to grace you with my presence," I said, motioning for her to leave.

She was so goddamn beautiful, and I hated that I noticed. I'd been around beautiful women more times than I could count— what was it about this one that had me all twisted up?

She shook her head and huffed before storming to the door.

She was irritated?

Good. Because whatever was going on with me could not be reciprocated. I needed to get laid and fast because I was a busy man, and I didn't have time to deal with this shit, nor could I continue suffering from a bad case of blue balls.

I had work to do and this woman was so far under my skin, I couldn't see straight.

She left my office, and I picked up my cell phone when it vibrated on my desk. There was a text from my sister, Emerson, that I opened first. There was a photo of her and Cutler, her fiancé Nash's son, whom she was currently in the process of adopting. She sent a photo of the two of them sitting in the grass with their pup, Winnie.

I hearted the photo before opening my ongoing group text with my brothers and cousins. The six of us, seven with Emerson, had grown up together. My cousins had lived in the ranch house next door, and we were more like siblings.

> League starts tonight. Be on time.

BRIDGER

You take this far too seriously. It's fucking pickleball.

CLARK

I have this short break from official practice, but I'll be there because I can't handle seeing you have one of your pickleball meltdowns.

AXEL

Dude. None of us want to do this. You know we only do it for you. Are you sure you don't want to retire the Chad-Six after our win last season?

> That's what they want us to do. We're playing. I got us new shirts, too.

Laura Pavlov

RAFE

Great. Matching fucking shirts. That's reason enough to leave work early and get screamed at by Easton for an hour and a half on the courts.

A win will make it all worth it.

BRIDGER

No one cares, asshole. We're doing it because you're a whiney little bitch when we don't do it.

ARCHER

Dude. Melody is sick. I was just about to text you. I can't make it.

My cousin was a single father of the sweetest little girl on the planet. We were all crazy about her. It was the only excuse I'd ever tolerate for missing pickleball. Because Melody was my favorite girl.

Fuck. I'm sorry she's sick. I'll find a replacement. Give her a kiss from me. I'll see all you other assholes at the club at 6:00 p.m. Bring your A-game.

A slew of middle finger emojis followed, and I laughed before getting back to work.

I rarely left work before six p.m.

There were only three things that I enjoyed outside of work.

Sex.

Time with my family.

And pickleball.

I spent the rest of the day buried in work. I ate lunch at my desk, had three conference calls, and I'd just wrapped up a phone call with a prospective client.

I glanced up to see Joey and Carver standing at Henley's cubicle, laughing.

Do these fuckers not have work to do?

I picked up the file on my desk and made my way through my office as I yanked the door open.

Rosie's head whipped up, and she started to speak, probably ready to say something snarky, but I stormed past her.

Joey turned to look at me as I approached, and he quickly shuffled his feet and moved around me. I didn't say a word. Didn't need to. The disdain in my gaze seemed to say plenty.

Carver raised his head and looked at me. "Hey, Easton. Just checking on our new girl. Making sure she's enjoying her time here."

"Ah, I forgot you got promoted to camp director. Let me know how that's working out for you."

He chuckled, but it was forced, and he didn't hide his irritation. "Very funny. Just one lawyer being friendly to another. I'm on my way out. I'll see you tomorrow, Henley." He turned to glare at me as he walked away.

Her eyes widened as Joey held his hand up. "See you both tomorrow."

"Bye," she said, and I just crossed my arms over my chest and stared at her.

"Are you pleased with yourself?" she whisper-hissed.

"Well, they're both gone, so yes, I am."

Everyone else was slowly trickling out of the office and saying goodbye just as Rosie rounded out the group.

"See you tomorrow, boss," she said, and I groaned at her choice of words again. She patted me on the back and winked.

"Bye. See you tomorrow," Henley said as she turned back to her computer.

"Let's call it a day," I said, and she pivoted in her chair and faced me.

"Call it a day?"

"Yes."

"I was going to keep working," she said, looking at me like I had three heads. "You always stay late."

"Not tonight. You're coming with me. It'll be good for you."

"What will be good for me?"

"Getting out of this place. Come on. You'll love it," I said, heading toward my office to grab my keys and turn off the lights.

"Where is it that you think I'm going?" she asked, as she pushed to her feet and grabbed her purse and briefcase.

"The happiest place in Rosewood River," I said, motioning for her to walk out ahead of me.

"I thought you said *this* was the happiest place in Rosewood River?"

I followed her outside. "This is one of them, but where I'm taking you gives it a run for its money."

"You're taking me somewhere?" She gaped at me.

I had been short with her all week. But we were working together, and she had proved herself and worked hard.

"Consider it a reward for a great first week."

"Well, I walked to work today, so my car isn't here." She shrugged.

"Lucky for you, mine is. Get in, Princess." I pulled the passenger door open, and she slipped inside my Tesla.

And for whatever reason, I was suddenly elated that Henley Holloway was coming with me.

I'd spent most of the week burying her in work and trying to avoid her, and now I didn't want her to leave.

four

. . .

Henley

THE MAN WAS GOING to give me whiplash.

One minute, he hated me. The next, he was bossing me around. Then he'd insisted I come to his office immediately, only to finally rush me out of his office like he couldn't stand the sight of me.

And now he was driving me somewhere?

He pulled into the parking lot, and I realized we were at the Rosewood River Country Club.

"This is the happiest place in Rosewood River?" I asked, unable to cover my laugh.

"Hey, don't mock it till you try it. Do you know what today is?"

I unbuckled myself, but we didn't get out of the car. "Friday?"

"Such a smartass." He shook his head. "It's the first day of league play."

"League play? Are we talking about golf? Tennis?"

He smirked. "Better than golf and better than tennis. And you're looking at the reigning champion."

"Of what? The greatest legal mind on the planet?"

"Thank you for that. If that were an actual award, I'd take it. But I'm talking about pickleball."

My head fell back in laughter. This was not what I'd expected. "Pickleball?"

He just stared at me. His eyes hard. Lips flat. Dead serious.

"Oh. You're serious? You play pickleball?"

"Is the pope Catholic? Is the sky blue? Is Carver Thomas a dickhead?"

"I'm guessing the answer you're looking for is yes?" I chuckled. "I just wouldn't have guessed you a pickleball player."

"Henley."

"Easton."

"Pickleball is the fastest-growing sport in America," he said, and his dark gray eyes locked with mine. He was ridiculously good-looking, and he knew it. Tall, broad shoulders, chiseled jaw, and thick dark hair.

"Good to know. So why am I here?"

"Because you've worked hard this week, and I've kind of been a dick to you. Yet you didn't complain."

"Let me get this straight. You admit that you were a dick to me, and I didn't complain. So now I'm at the Rosewood River Country Club?"

"Correct. It's like a dick tax. I tested you, and you passed your first test. So I thought you should get out and have some fun."

"A dick tax?" I chuckled. "Well, for the record, you may control my work life for the next six months, but my personal life is sort of off-limits."

"From where I'm sitting, you don't have one."

My jaw fell open. "Excuse me? You know nothing about me."

"I know that you work crazy long hours, because I do, too. You arrive when I do, and you leave when I leave. You can't have much of a social life working those hours, unless you're just trying to impress me this first week, and next week you'll start slacking?"

"You really do think the world revolves around you, don't you?" I rolled my eyes.

"No. I call it as I see it. I'm your mentor. You answer to me. It would be normal to want to impress me."

"Well, you're wrong there. The hours I've worked this week are typical hours for me. I worked and studied my way through law school while juggling an intense internship. I don't require a lot of sleep."

"Neither do I." He smiled, like that made us both special.

"So you're saying that *you* don't have much of a social life, then? Because I assume you aren't trying to impress me, so these must be the hours you normally work?"

"Correct. My social life is my work. I squeeze in time for my family where I can."

"No wife? No girlfriend?" I asked. I knew he wasn't married, because half the women in the office were trying to win his attention, and they'd mentioned that he was single. He was the unattainable golden boy at the office, and I knew the type.

Charming. Handsome. Workaholic.

The type of man I made a point to avoid.

"Nope." He clapped his hands together.

"So you're just alone all the time? Seems lonely for a man your age."

"Look at you, Princess. Trying to figure me out, are you?"

"Not really. Just having a conversation. It's what humans do, or didn't your alien leaders teach you that?" I said, as I covered my smile with my hand.

He barked out a laugh. "You can ask me whatever you want. We're off the clock, and I'm a straight shooter. I work a lot, and I'll be a managing partner in the next year. That's my focus. My social life is spending time with my family and going out with the guys when I need to blow off steam."

"Blow off steam?" I raised a brow.

He leaned forward. His face was so close, I stopped breathing temporarily. "Get laid, Princess. I enjoy sex as much as the next dude. Is that what you're asking?"

Is it hot in here?

I blew out a breath when he pulled back.

"That wasn't what I was asking, but thanks. Glad to know you like your job, pickleball, and sex."

"You're a quick learner. How about you? Do you have a secret lover hidden away in your big house? Does he wait for you to come home at night from your long day at the office so he can strip you down and have his way with you?"

I shook my head in disbelief but couldn't help but laugh. "You're insane."

"No argument there. Answer the question." His tone was serious now.

Like I said. The man was going to give me whiplash.

"Nope. I had a boyfriend in law school, but we broke up a few months ago. And I don't really know anyone here in Rose-wood River. My best friend lives in San Francisco, and I'm trying to get her to move here. So, for now, I just work."

"Hmmm… well, you're about to meet my brothers and my cousins, so prepare yourself. They'll probably all hit on you, and you'd be smart to stay away from them."

"Well, if they're as charming as you, it shouldn't be a prob-lem." I oozed sarcasm, and he smiled before his tongue moved along his bottom lip. The move was so sexy, I squeezed my thighs together in response.

"So, what exactly am I doing here?"

"My cousin Archer canceled. You're going to stand in for him today. We need six players to show up. We can't look weak."

"I'm in a dress!"

"They have a shop. I'll buy you an outfit and some shoes, and you can just stand there and pretend that you know what you're doing. I'll do all the work." He pushed out of the car.

I wasn't going to mention the fact that I'd played collegiate tennis. I'd let my actions speak for me.

"This day just keeps getting better," I said, feigning irritation when I was actually happy to be here. My evenings had been pretty boring since I'd arrived in town, and I hadn't met anyone yet, so maybe it would be good for me to get out a little.

"Are Joey and Carver bothering you?" Easton asked as we walked toward the clubhouse.

"What? No. And for the record, I can take care of myself," I said, my tone hard. I'd been taking care of myself for a very long time. I certainly wouldn't be relying on any man to do that for me.

He pulled the door open and motioned me inside. "I wasn't suggesting that you couldn't take care of yourself. I was asking if they're bothering you."

"Well, they aren't. I like them."

He paused at the front desk, and the woman behind the counter lit up when she saw him. "Hey, Easton. How are you doing, handsome?"

"I'm doing well, Samantha. I was hoping you could do me a favor."

"Sure. Name it."

"This is my friend, Henley. I'm going to take her down to the golf shop and get her some clothes for pickleball. Can you grab us two burgers and fries and have them brought out to the tables by the courts?" He turned to me. "What would you like to drink?"

I was startled by him ordering dinner for me. "Um. A Coke would be great."

Samantha, who was sweet as sugar to the man beside me, turned a little icy when she faced me. "Sure."

"Thanks for that. Let's go," Easton bossed, hurrying me toward the stairs as we made our way down to the floor below.

"How did you know I would want a burger?"

"I saw you eat one at your desk a few days ago."

"Are you spying on me?" I chuckled.

"I'm observant, Princess."

Within the next twenty minutes, he'd purchased an outfit, socks, shoes, and a visor for me. He led me to the locker rooms, and I quickly changed and made my way back out. I couldn't even believe that I was here.

Not because I hadn't been to my fair share of country clubs. I grew up going to the country club in the city. My father liked the finest things, and we'd attended holidays there when I was young.

But I didn't know why Easton was suddenly being friendly. The man had only talked about work up until now.

Maybe this was just his way.

His gaze moved from my head down to my feet when I found him outside, sitting at a table.

"Sit. Eat. I'll tell you the basics," he demanded.

"Are you always this bossy?"

He bit off the top of a french fry. "Yes. Get used to it."

I spent the next fifteen minutes eating and listening as he told me the basic rules about pickleball. Rules I was more than aware of. But the man was so passionate when he was into something that I enjoyed watching him get all animated. This was how he appeared when he spoke about the law. I'd studied a bunch of his cases, and I loved that he fought hard for his clients.

He believed in them, and it showed.

He didn't cut corners, and I respected it.

He worked hard.

But I'd never been with him outside of work, and it was nice to see this side of him. He was lighter, even with his intensity about pickleball. He wore a black tee and black athletic shorts. His legs were long, and his thighs were thick.

"Well, well, well… what do we have here?" A man approached the table, and my eyes widened when I recognized him.

"You're Clark Chadwick," I said, before I could stop myself.

Easton groaned. "You're a fucking hockey fan?"

"I am. I heard you're going to come play for San Francisco," I said, pushing to my feet and extending my arm. "I can't believe you didn't tell me that you were related to Clark Chadwick."

I was a huge sports fan. I loved hockey, amongst many other sports.

"Yes, ma'am. I start training here with the new team next month."

"I'm Henley. It's nice to meet you." My hand was still in his, and Easton shocked me when he karate chopped his brother's forearm, causing him to drop my hand.

Clark's head fell back in laughter. "You're Henley Holloway. My brother speaks highly of you. How's he been treating you? Working you to the bone?"

"He's fine. Bossy. Moody. A little needy at times." I sat back down, and Easton raised a brow.

"Bossy and moody are spot on. Needy? Never."

Clark was laughing hysterically as three more men approached the table. I was introduced to his other brothers, Rafe and Bridger, and their cousin, Axel. They were all ridiculously good-looking.

"So what you're telling me is that I need to have a kid who pukes in order to get out of this," Rafe said over his laughter, before turning to wink at me.

"Do you play?" Bridger asked, and he'd been the least animated in the group. He struck me as more of an observer.

"Yes. I've played."

Easton narrowed his gaze. "You laughed at me when I told you I played pickleball."

"I laughed because I didn't expect *you* to be into pickleball. I never said that *I* didn't play."

He snatched a french fry from my plate because he'd finished his. "You're suspect, Holloway."

He had no idea.

But he was about to find out.

five

. . .

Easton

WE BROKE INTO DOUBLES TEAMS, and seeing as Archer was normally my partner, I told Henley she would sub out for him.

I needed to focus. Her legs in that cute-as-fuck pickleball skirt made it hard to look anywhere else.

I shook it off. We worked together. She was Charles's daughter, and as a good mentor, I was just trying to get her out of the office to have a little fun.

Today was our first day of league play. We would be playing other doubles teams from the club to get a feel for the teams this year. The scores didn't count today.

I was a competitive asshole, so where everyone else thought today would be fun, it was anything but for me. I knew the Wilcox brothers were out for blood this year, and from the minute we stepped onto the courts, they were watching us.

"These two fuckers are going to act like they don't take this seriously, but trust me when I tell you, Barry Wilcox would sell a kidney for the club trophy," I said as I leaned close to Henley's ear.

She smelled like roses and jasmine, and it was fucking with my focus.

Agreeing to partner with an amateur was probably not my best move. Clark offered to team up with her, but for whatever reason, that didn't sit well with me.

Maybe it was the way she giggled and looked at him with stars in her eyes. It pissed me off.

I'd just have to overcompensate for her lack of skill and up my game. I could beat the Wilcox brothers by myself if I had to.

"Wow. You take your pickleball pretty seriously." She chuckled.

"Buckle up, Princess. Things are about to get real."

"What do we have here?" Barry asked, as he sauntered over like the slimeball he was. "Did you bring a beautiful woman to sub out for Archer to try to distract us?"

There was no need to distract this bastard. I didn't need any help crushing him.

"Your tactics never cease to amaze me, Chadwick, or should I say, *Chad-Six*," Steven Wilcox barked out a laugh at our team name as his gaze landed on Henley, who stood beside me. "Catchy name. I see you chose not to change it up. Same name for three years seems a little boring."

"If it ain't broken, why fix it? Am I right, fellas? What did you guys go with this year? Cocks-R-Us? Or is it Little Cocks, Big Game again?"

Henley used her hand to cover her laugh, and the Wilcox brothers glared at me.

"Last year's name was actually Big *Will-Cox*, Big Game." Barry winked at the woman beside me.

"But I'm quite sure you've looked at the roster and already know that we went with *Win*-Cox," Steven said, his eyes still on Henley.

"Keep dreaming. How about you stop staring at my coworker like she's your next meal and start playing," I growled.

Steven laughed. "Anywhere. Anytime."

"Well, that's now and here, genius. So get your paddle." I reached for Henley's hand and led her away.

"You need to take it down a notch, Chad-Six." Henley laughed as we bent down to grab our paddles.

"This is no joke. You can hang out up front and just let the balls come back to me, unless you're sure you can hit one and keep it in. You've played a little, right?"

"I never said I played *a little*. I said I've played." She bent over and touched her toes before doing a few leg stretches. My gaze moved around to see every dude within a two-hundred-yard vicinity staring at her.

"Stop stretching," I hissed. "These fuckers are watching you."

She stood up and looked around. "You need to calm down, Chadwick. It's not a weakness if the competition sees you stretching."

She didn't get it at all. I wasn't worried about looking weak. They were checking her out, and I didn't like it.

She was Charles's daughter, for fuck's sake.

"Let's go," I grumped.

"I can't believe Easton Chadwick is playing with a sub. I thought you were all business when you were on the court," Barry said, as he bounced the ball a few times.

"How about you just play the game and stop running your mouth?" I hissed, before moving toward Henley. "This is the kitchen. You stay up here. You can let the balls go right by you. I've got it."

"How about you take care of your balls, and I'll take care of mine." She winked like this was some kind of joke.

I shook my head and moved to the back of the court. Steven served the ball, and I moved to the right immediately, swung my paddle back, and then gaped as Henley returned it with such a force that both Barry and Steven startled as it surged past them, just bouncing inside the line as they both watched it go by.

What the fuck was that?

She turned around and held her paddle up for me to tap mine against in celebration.

"Was that a lucky hit?" I whispered.

"I guess we'll find out, won't we?"

She moved back into position. Standing behind her wasn't the best choice. Her ass was out, legs on full display, as she bent forward, ready to go.

The next forty minutes were mind-boggling.

Henley fucking Holloway is a pickleball goddess.

She moved like a gazelle on the court.

She didn't miss a single return.

She was a natural.

We played like we'd been playing together for years. We absolutely crushed the Wilcox brothers. Archer and I would have destroyed them, but not quite like this.

We continued to dominate when we played Mary and Bob Johnson, but we toned our game down, and Henley definitely pulled back on her skills when we played them.

Like a goddamn pro.

She adjusted to the competition.

"What the fuck was that?" I leaned down, speaking close to her ear.

"What do you mean?"

"You know exactly what I mean," I said, falling in stride beside her when she started walking toward the table, where the guys were sitting and waving us over.

"Well, well, well… leave it to E-money to bring a ringer to pickleball." Axel handed Henley a bottle of water.

"A ringer is a bit dramatic." She smirked.

"We were watching. You smoked the Cock-brothers. You're as good as Easton," Clark said over his laughter. "Did he screen you at the office?"

I scrubbed a hand over the back of my neck. "I had no idea she could play."

"Right. You expect us to believe you just brought her to league play with no clue that she could play professional pickleball?"

"Wait. Does professional pickleball pay well? Because my

new mentor at the office is a real broody guy, so maybe I should spend my days on the court." She waggled her brows.

I rolled my eyes. "You acted like you knew nothing about the sport."

"Oh, you mean when you told me to stay in the kitchen and let the balls go to you?" Her voice was all tease. "It shouldn't be such a shock. There are 48 million pickleball players in the US. You just assumed I wasn't one of them."

"Have you played in a league before?" Clark asked.

"I played collegiate tennis at Stanford during my undergrad and then started playing pickleball recreationally with my grandfather." She smiled, and her sapphire blues locked with mine.

"You could have told me so I didn't spend all that time explaining the game." I took a long sip from my water bottle. The sun was just going down, and the lights on the court flickered on.

"You were enjoying sharing all your pickleball wisdom with me, and I didn't want to rain on your parade." Her lips turned up in the corners, and the guys all laughed.

She was charming and beautiful, and she definitely had everyone's attention.

"He sure does like to share his wisdom," Bridger grumped. "I need a beer. Who wants to head to Booze & Brews?"

Henley looked up at me, and I realized in that moment that mixing booze with my boss's daughter was not a good idea. I'd already crossed a line by bringing her here. I needed to keep things professional. "I'll drop Henley off at home, then grab a shower and meet you there."

"Hey. Maybe she wants to come with us," Clark said, his gaze moving to her.

My brother was a wicked flirt. Hell, I'd noticed the way they'd all been checking her out.

"Oh, thank you. This was fun, but I've got some work to do.

My best friend is coming to town tomorrow morning, so I need to go get some more unpacking done at my house."

"You bought the brick house on the river, right?" Rafe asked. "Easton lives a few houses down from you."

She turned to look at me with surprise. I hadn't said anything. I wasn't a fucking creeper. Sure, I'd seen her going for runs on the trail beside the water early every morning, but I wasn't about to tell her that.

"You do? I didn't know that." She studied me.

"Yeah. I didn't realize you bought that house," I lied.

Axel coughed over the sip of water he'd just taken. "It's Rosewood River, asshole. Everyone knows what house she bought."

"I don't read 'The Taylor Tea,' so I don't keep up with town gossip." It was true. I hated that fucking column, but you didn't need to read it to know that Henley Holloway had bought the Paxon house on one of the most beautiful lots on the water.

"What's 'The Taylor Tea?'" she asked, as we all started walking toward the parking lot.

"The bane of our existence," Bridger grumped.

"Some bullshit column where they print everyone's business, and the Chadwicks make for good content," I said.

"It's town gossip. And people eat that shit up." Rafe paused at his car.

"You were a topic the day you moved to town," Axel said.

"You're kidding me." Henley laughed. "It's like reality TV in Rosewood River, but in print."

"It's stupid," I said, as each of the guys hugged Henley goodbye and walked toward their cars. "I'll see you at the bar. I'm going to grab a shower, and I'll walk over."

They waved, and I led her to my car, opening the passenger door and watching as she slipped inside, dropping her bag of clothes at her feet.

I drove toward her house, only a few doors down from mine, and pulled into the driveway.

"Thanks for tonight." She shrugged. "Thanks for this week, actually. It's been a good first week here."

"Sure." I cleared my throat and glanced over at her. The light from the moon was flooding my car, and her lips parted the slightest bit. And, for whatever reason, it was sexy as hell. I definitely needed to get laid. I was horny, and my boss's daughter was driving me mad. "Your best friend is coming to town tomorrow? That'll be nice."

"Yeah, Lulu lives in the city. I'm trying to convince her to move here, but she's running a business, and she's been traveling a lot lately." She chuckled.

I nodded. "Do you go home often?"

"To the city?"

"Yes, isn't that home?"

She glanced out the window before turning back to look at me. "Yeah, it's definitely home. I went to school back east for high school but then came back for my undergrad before leaving again for law school. So home feels like it's been a lot of places, too, I guess. My parents aren't together, and my mom and her husband live in France, which is why I spent the summer there," she said. "And I just don't come to the city all that often because my father usually comes to see me if he can take time off. If he's in the city, he's working."

"You and your father are close, huh? He was so excited for you to come work for the firm," I said.

She smiled. "Yeah, he's always been my favorite person. But I didn't have the traditional upbringing that you probably had."

"Meaning?"

"Meaning I can tell how close you are with your family. I was an only child. I was raised by the people who worked for my father most of the time." She shook her head. "I'm not complaining. I know I'm fortunate to be born into a family like mine, with so many opportunities afforded to me."

Henley Holloway was like a riddle that I was dying to solve. "Did your parents divorce when you were young?"

"They divorced when I was four years old. My father had an affair, and then my mother went on to fall in love with the tennis pro at the club, and that's who she lives with in France to this day. I stayed with my father, as my grandparents lived nearby, and I'd see them on the weekends. I spent summers with my mother. And then I left for boarding school when I was fifteen."

There was a sadness there that I hadn't noticed before. "That couldn't have been easy on you as a kid."

"I mean, I didn't know any different. I've gone to the best schools that money can afford. I've traveled the world. I'm hardly someone you need to pity." She tipped her chin up.

"I wasn't pitying you. I was just saying it was probably hard."

"It was fine." She reached for the door handle and glanced over at me. "I'm guessing you need to get to that bar. Your day is almost complete."

"Almost?"

"You said that you enjoy your job, pickleball, and sex. You've got one more thing to check off your list tonight." She chuckled as she pushed the door open. "Have fun with that."

My dick jumped to attention at the mention of sex. I internally cursed myself for sharing that with her earlier.

I jumped out of the car. "I always do, Princess."

She rolled her eyes as she pulled her keys out of her purse. "You don't need to walk me to the door. I'm a big girl, Easton."

"My mother trained me well. Go inside and lock up."

"I'm off the clock. You can stop bossing me around now."

"That wouldn't be any fun, would it?" I asked, as she unlocked the door and pushed the door open before turning around to face me.

"See you Monday." She closed the door, and I jogged down to my car, wondering why the fuck I missed her already.

Time to head to the bar and get Henley Holloway out of my system.

six

• • •

Henley

I FINISHED my run and grabbed a quick shower before Lulu was due to arrive. My bestie and I were more like sisters. We'd met at boarding school, Westcliff Academy, in Pennsylvania, when we'd found out we were rooming together.

I ran a brush through my wet hair and slipped my bikini beneath my cover-up. This house had a gorgeous pool, with the river just a few feet in the distance. It really was beautiful here.

Peaceful and serene.

I'd craved a slower pace when I'd graduated from law school. My father had given me the option of working out of the office in the city or the office in Rosewood River, and I'd jumped at the idea of living in a small town.

I was exhausted.

I'd been working so hard for so long that I didn't know what to do with myself now that I'd actually accomplished everything I'd set out to do.

The doorbell rang, and I made my way to the front door, pulling it open to find Lulu Sonnet on the other side. She wore a pink and turquoise silk bandana tied around her head, a denim jumpsuit, and a pair of heels, and she was holding two bottles of champagne in her hands.

"Is there a hen in the house?" she shouted, as she waggled the bottles of bubbly in front of her. This was her favorite saying whenever we saw one another.

I held my arms open, beyond happy to see her. "I missed you, Lulu girl."

"Damn you, Henley Holloway. Why do you always make me cry? My makeup was pristine." She sniffed as her arms wrapped around me, and the two bottles clanked at my back.

"We're going swimming. Why are you wearing makeup?" I laughed as she pulled back and set the two bottles on the table before walking through the house and whistling.

"Because there are all sorts of handsome cowboys in this town, right? You never know if you're going to break down on the side of the road and need rescuing."

I chuckled. My best friend was born into a very wealthy family. Her father's side of the family was in politics, and they were often compared to the Kennedys. Lulu's great-grandfather was the Vice President of the United States back in his day. She had uncles who were senators and governors. Her mother's side of the family was in the fashion industry, and their brand, named Laredo, was one of the most well-known luxury brands in the world. They made purses and shoes and were considered similar to brands like Gucci and Louis Vuitton.

"Ahhh… we're into cowboys now. We're over the boy banders?" I asked.

Lulu had dated a guy she'd met at Juilliard, Beckett Bane, on and off for years. He was the lead singer of a band called Tier One, which had blown up into one of the most famous groups in the world in the last two years. Lulu and Beckett had a tumultuous relationship that was highly covered by the press, as he was considered an international bad boy musician, and she was a wealthy socialite born into a very prestigious family whom the media loved.

"We are so over the arrogant boy banders. That fucker tried to call me last night, knowing that I'd seen those photos of him and his backup singer making out in some nightclub in London. I'm so over him."

I hoped she was, because as much as I knew Beckett was crazy about her, he'd caused her enough pain for a lifetime.

"I'm sure your father will be pleased."

"Yes. He keeps encouraging me to get into a stable relationship because every time the press prints anything about me, it has to do with Beckett and his madness." She rolled her eyes as she walked around the great room, smiling as she took in all the details.

"And I'm sure your mom is still trying to play matchmaker."

"Oh, yes. That last dude was a real prize. He sat on his phone the entire time we were at dinner." She paused and cleared her throat, doing her best impression. "Babe. I'm a dealmaker. These clothes. This watch. I make the magic happen."

I was laughing hysterically, just like I did the night she'd phoned me to tell me about it a few weeks ago.

"I was like, *yeah, babe,* please make some magic and let this horrible date come to an end. My mother is no longer allowed to set me up with anyone." She chuckled. "Anyway, I like playing the field. I want to be single for a while. All these years with Beckett have been filled with drama and the press following us everywhere. I'm just ready for a break."

"That's why you need to move here," I reminded her. Lulu could use some time in a small town. She was constantly in the spotlight, and I knew it had been taking a toll lately.

"Trust me. The idea is intriguing. I'm thinking about it. Maybe I'll rent a place for a few months and try it out. But I have a few shows I'm doing over the next couple of weeks, and then things will slow down," she said, following me to the kitchen. Lulu had wanted to make a name for herself, and she'd started a jewelry line, MSL, short for My Silver Lining, which was booming. She glanced around the kitchen and the family room. "It feels like you've lived here for years. You're all unpacked."

"You know I like to be settled." I'd always been that way. Craved a home base. That comfort of creating a home for myself.

"Yes. I remember. Our dorm room at Westcliff was like a Pinterest board. What did you call your style back then?"

"Cozy, college chic, and you loved it. Stop giving me shit and let's get some food and have a mimosa."

"You're speaking my love language." She watched as I pulled the charcuterie board I'd made this morning from the refrigerator. "I can't get over how gorgeous this place is. And it was all done before you even moved in, right?"

"Yep. A developer came in and fully renovated the place, and I fell in love with it when I saw the pictures online," I admitted, as she popped a bottle of champagne and I pulled the orange juice from the fridge.

I reached for two champagne flutes before glancing over at her and seeing her making a face at me.

"We're going to need a larger glass than that." She chuckled.

I found two tall glasses, and she poured a very healthy helping of the finest champagne and then added a splash of orange juice. I waited for her to run down the hall and change into her swimsuit.

We settled on the lounge chairs outside by the pool and spent the next three hours talking and laughing and catching up.

"I'm so happy to be here with you. I've missed you," she said, as she glanced over at me under her oversized sunglasses. "And you need a break from work."

"I played pickleball yesterday," I said, as her head fell back in laughter.

"You are one wild twenty-five-year-old woman."

"Hey, we smoked everyone. It was a good time." I reached for my water bottle.

"Well, I'm glad you got to put your Wimbledon skills to good use." She chuckled. "By the way, who is *we*?"

"My boss made me go."

"The arrogant prick? He plays pickleball, and he actually left the office?" She raised a brow.

"Yep. And I met his brothers and cousin. They all grew up here."

"Are they hot?" she pressed.

"Yes. Ralph Lauren underwear model meets rugged rancher, kind of hot," I said with a laugh. "One of his brothers is Clark Chadwick, the professional hockey player. But they were all ridiculously good-looking. But Easton's my boss and they're his family, so I wasn't really looking."

She sat forward and scrolled on her phone. "I just looked up your boss. He's a very well-known attorney, and he's fucking hot, Hen. You failed to mention that before now."

"Because he's literally been a tyrant, and I hadn't noticed."

"Bullshit." She shot me a look. "You noticed."

"He's not my type. And I don't mix work and pleasure. I'm not my father." My tone came out harsher than I'd expected.

"Yes. Daddy Holloway loves an office fling, doesn't he?"

I moved over to the pool and walked into the water before Lulu did the same. "I'm guessing it's because he works so much, so it's the most likely place to meet someone. I'm definitely not going to follow in his footsteps."

My father had a track record for dating women that worked for him, clients he represented, and young socialites. I'd always hated it. I'd come to town and go to dinner with him and the women he dated, who were normally closer to my age than his own. The man went through executive assistants as quickly as he went through women he dated. He was noncommittal.

I knew he had tried hard with me. I was the one relationship in his life that had remained consistent, aside from his relationship with my grandparents.

But he didn't make much time for them either.

I knew he had tried his best with me.

So even though most of the time it felt like it wasn't enough, it was the most he could give, and I tried to be grateful for that.

"So you're not interested in your sexy boss, then?"

"You know I prefer my men to be artsy. I'm not looking for a workaholic with a wandering eye." I chuckled.

"Yes. Speaking of artsy, is Pete still calling?"

Pete Powers and I had dated for almost a year. He was the best. Easygoing. Sweet. He played guitar in an indie band in Boston. We fell in love, and I wanted him to be the one. I really did. But as much as I loved the way he sang to me in bed on Saturdays and he enjoyed getting high and reading me poetry, it was a fun way to spend the day after an intense week of work and studying. But Pete enjoyed doing that exact thing every single day. He wanted to play music, have sex, and get high.

That was it for him.

I hated the way he'd cried when I'd ended things before I left for France for the summer. Turns out, I wanted a man with a bit more drive than that.

"Yes. He still calls me every couple of weeks."

"When he's high and lying in bed?" She chuckled.

"Yep." I pushed out of the water and to my feet and wrapped a towel around myself. "Apparently, the band broke up, so he's collecting unemployment and writing music and trying to go out on the road solo."

"He was so pretty to look at." She hopped out of the water, striding toward me as I tossed her a towel.

"He was. But I'm enjoying being single at the moment."

"You know, you could have a fling for once in your life. Find some small-town cowboy and ride him like a stallion." She waggled her brows.

"I love that I moved to a small town, and now you're all about the cowboys and the horses."

"Hey, you're trying to convince me to come here, so of course, I did my research. There are all kinds of farms and ranches in Rosewood River." She dropped to sit on the lounge chair and fell back, letting the sun beat down on her. "You've been working hard for so long. Why not have some fun?"

"I do have fun. I just played pickleball last night and spent the day drinking mimosas and swimming with you."

She sprung forward. "You know what we need to do?"

"Take showers, order takeout, and watch *Bridgerton*?"

She groaned. "Let's put on some sexy clothes and go to the local bar and dance our asses off tonight. Come on, Hen, when was the last time we went out dancing?"

"Ummm… two weeks ago in the city before I moved here."

"That doesn't count. It was a nightclub. I brought two cowboy hats with me, too. So if we don't go out, we're having a dance party here." She waggled her brows. "Ohhhh… I almost forgot. When I stopped to get gas in town, I picked up the local paper because the girl who worked at the mini-mart told me to read the gossip column that comes out every Saturday for all the local scoop."

"'The Taylor Tea?'"

"Yes, I think that's what she called it… let's read it. I'll be right back."

She jogged into the house, and I lay back in the sun, loving the feel of the heat on my face. Lulu returned to her chair and started reading all the latest headlines to me as she searched for the gossip column.

"There's a cookout at the Honey Biscuit Café on Sunday afternoon, and it's karaoke night at Booze and Brews," she said with a chuckle as she flipped the page. "Ooohh, there's a river rafting trip every Sunday morning if you want to go rafting tomorrow."

"Yes. I signed us up to try that tomorrow. I've been dying to get out on the river."

"Fine. But when we did it a few years ago, it was a lot of work," she groaned.

I laughed as she continued flipping the pages.

"Here we go. 'The Taylor Tea,'" she purred. "It says the author is anonymous. This is so very *Gossip Girl*. Are you ready?"

My eyes were closed, and I was starting to doze off. "Do I have a choice?"

"Hey, Roses. It's time to spill the tea in Rosewood River," Lulu read, and I could hear the excitement in her voice. *"Looks like Rosewood River's golden couple, who shall remain unnamed... You know the ones... They've been together since middle school and got busted for skinny dipping in Mr. Hanson's pool in high school. Wink. Wink. Well, they might not be heading to the altar, after all. Word on Main Street is our groom got caught with his pants down at his bachelor party in the city. But 'The Taylor Tea' has eyes everywhere, and let's just say, our bride was sent some very questionable photos from someone that was at said bachelor party. We've heard from a very reliable source that she packed her bags and moved out of their home this week. Apparently, our jilted bride was seen at Booze and Brews last night, having several cocktails and grinding up against one of the Chadwick boys, who we shall also not name. Not a bad place to rebound, am I right, ladies?"* Lulu paused, and I opened one eye, squinting against the sunlight. "This is freaking gold. Like *Gossip Girl* meets small-town drama."

I laughed. "Does it say which Chadwick boy?"

Why did I care? It didn't matter if it was Easton, did it?

So why was I sitting forward now and tugging the newspaper from her hands?

I continued reading. *"You know those Chadwick boys can be a little litigious, so we'll play it safe, and we won't name which one took this runaway bride home last night, but let's just say that he's a 'shark' in the courtroom. We'll leave that to your imagination."* I shook my head in disbelief. "How do they get away with printing this? It's obviously Easton. He's the attorney."

"They're practicing their second amendment rights. Freedom of speech." She reached for the charcuterie board and popped a grape into her mouth.

"The second amendment is the right to bear arms. The first amendment is freedom of speech."

"Ahhh... you're such an attention-to-detail person," she said over her laughter. "But I'll bet some of these ranchers in Rose-wood River are packing more than just firearms."

I rolled my eyes and fell back in laughter.

It felt so good to have Lulu here.

Maybe it was having my best friend here, or the relaxing day by the pool, or the last week finding my footing at the office.

But Rosewood River was starting to feel like home.

And it had been a long time since I'd felt that way.

seven

. . .

Easton

"THAT WAS AMAZING," Henley whispered as we walked side by side out of the courtroom.

Once we were out in the hallway, Sadie Walker turned to face me. "Easton, I owe you everything. I never thought I had a chance of winning this case until you agreed to take it."

Sadie wasn't lying. She was going up against a big chain restaurant, and they knew how to intimidate people who attempted to fight them tooth and nail for fair compensation after being let go from a job she'd given her heart and soul to.

"What they did to you was wrong. You gave them twenty-eight years, and you should have gotten a goddamn ticker tape parade." Instead, they'd fired her unfairly and unjustly. And the court had agreed with me.

"Thank you." Her weathered face showed the distress this had caused her, and I was hoping the large check she'd receive very soon would help alleviate some of that stress. "You were the only one who stepped up and offered to help me."

"Don't give me more credit than I deserve," I said.

Sadie leaned forward and whispered to Henley. "He did it pro bono. I couldn't afford a fancy lawyer."

Sadie could barely afford to stay afloat and keep a roof over her head. But sometimes, you met people who you knew deserved a break.

And Sadie Walker deserved a break.

She deserved someone to stand up for her in a forum where others would listen.

These were the days that I really loved my job.

"He's clearly softer than he lets on," Henley said as her gaze locked with mine.

"All right, Sadie. You go celebrate with your family. I'll follow up with you next week on what you can expect moving forward."

The older woman threw herself into my arms, and I patted her back before giving her a nod and watching her walk away.

Henley studied me for a few beats. "The ruthless Easton Chadwick, AKA…*the Shark*, has a heart?"

"Don't offend me." I motioned for her to walk outside, and we paused when a few reporters asked if we were happy with the settlement. I stopped to make a very brief statement, letting them know we were pleased that justice was served today, before guiding Henley toward the waiting car. We'd left my car at the office when we'd arrived in the city this morning and used the company car service so we didn't have to deal with the press and parking.

Our driver, Walt, opened the back door, and Henley slipped inside first, before I moved in beside her. The woman distracted me to no end. I'd avoided her these last few weeks, bogging her down with cases and then deciding last minute to bring her to court with me after she'd all but begged.

Roses and jasmine were my new kryptonite.

Her scent was fucking everywhere.

It was like some sort of curse, having this woman as my mentee. I'd tried to get laid after pickleball a few weeks ago, and when I was about to close the deal with Valerie Lennox, a woman I'd spent some time with on and off over the years, I just wasn't feeling it.

So, I'd fucked my fist more times than I could count to thoughts of my boss's daughter over the last few weeks.

A woman I was mentoring.

I blamed her goddamn scent for all of it.

Her sapphire eyes.

Her plump lips that I imagined wrapped around my dick.

Her sexy-as-hell legs, which were currently on display in this SUV.

The space was small.

Too small.

And Henley was—everywhere.

I didn't get distracted by women. At least, I hadn't for a very long time.

And I didn't fucking like it.

So, most of the time, I barked at her, and she'd clearly tried her best to keep busy and stay away.

And then I'd invited her to court. Today of all days. This was the one day a year that I preferred to be alone, at least while I wasn't working. I had my reasons, and most people in my life just accepted it. Yet, I'd made the offer to bring her. We'd spent thirty minutes in the car alone as we drove to the city this morning, and we'd barely said two words to one another. She'd claimed she was reading over the notes for the case, but I think she just didn't want to make small talk after the way I'd acted ever since I'd brought her to pickleball.

And now we were sitting beside one another, heading to meet her father for lunch.

"I'm glad you came today. It's good for you to get experience in the courtroom."

"Thanks. I wasn't sure if I was going to get to go, seeing as you insisted you weren't bringing me, and then did a one-eighty. It seems to be your thing." She smirked.

I narrowed my gaze and then snapped my fingers a few times. "Things are always changing in the legal world, Princess. You have to be ready to pivot at all times."

"Sure. Law and pivoting go hand in hand," she said with a chuckle.

Is she mocking me?

"Listen, I'm your mentor. I'm not here to hold your hand. I'm here to show you what you're getting into."

"I appreciate it," she said dryly, as if she were completely annoyed by me.

"Something bothering you? Because this would be the time to tell me. We're about to be at lunch with your father, so I'd rather clear the air now. If I'm pushing you too hard, you need to tell me."

She gasped as her head whipped in my direction. "Pushing me too hard? You have no idea how hard I can be pushed."

Why was she so pissed all of a sudden?

"Okay." I smirked, holding her gaze. "I can push you harder if you'd like."

"How about you just treat me like you'd treat anyone else. I swear you're giving me whiplash, Chadwick."

"Whiplash? I thought you just said I could push you harder, Princess." I quirked a brow, and I could see the anger in her eyes.

And I liked it.

Why the fuck do I like it so much?

"One minute, you're inviting me to pickleball and acting like a normal human, and the next, you can't seem to stand the sight of me, and you're kicking me out of your office and yelling at me. I can't figure you out."

"Perhaps you shouldn't try. I'm a complicated man."

She leaned forward, keeping her voice low. "Maybe you need to… what did you call it? *Blow off some steam.* But according to 'The Taylor Tea,' you already did that with a certain local. Yet, you're still snapping at me all the time."

Of course, she'd read the ridiculous column. And they'd kept that narrative going for the last two weeks because, apparently, there was nothing new to share in Rosewood River.

"First of all, you attended Harvard Law School. I can't

believe you're reading that shit. You probably lost brain cells on that one." I shook my head in disgust. "Desiree Carson grew up next door to me, and she's barely twenty-one years old. The insinuation is offensive. She's a family friend. She was upset, and I walked her home. And for the record, she and Grant are back together. She never moved out. He never cheated. They'd had a fight, and some nosy-ass deviant decided to run with it. But I'm wondering why you appear so concerned with my sex life, anyway?"

Her cheeks flushed, and she quickly straightened her features. "I'm not. My best friend came to town for a visit, and the column was right up her alley. I guessed it was you that they were referencing."

"It's ridiculous that they're allowed to print that bullshit."

"Why are you so bothered by it if it isn't true? Who even writes it, and why is it called 'The Taylor Tea?'"

"The Taylor family owns the paper. A lot of people assume their daughter, Emilia, writes the column, though she's denied it."

"The anonymity probably makes it more exciting. Why are you so worked up about it?" she asked, her voice completely calm, yet I was pissed off now.

"They wrote all sorts of shit about my sister when her wedding blew up, and I tried to intimidate them with some legal jargon, but it's hard to stop someone from printing what they want to print nowadays."

"It's not that big of a deal. You're single, right? So it's not like it's offending anyone."

She was awfully concerned with my dating status.

We pulled up in front of the restaurant in downtown San Francisco, and Walt opened the back door, allowing me to slip out first, before I helped Henley out of the car.

She startled when a passing car laid on their horn, and I chuckled. "It's hard not to be surprised by the noise when you've been living in a peaceful place for the last few weeks."

She nodded, and I guided her toward the front door of the restaurant, maneuvering through the people who were walking down the street, on a mission to get wherever they were going.

Charles was sitting at the back table with another managing partner, Dick Jones. I couldn't stand the guy. He was a weasel. He took shortcuts at his job, but he was a close friend of Charles's, so they were often together at work lunches.

They both stood as we approached the table.

"There's my girl. You look beautiful, sweetheart," Charles said as he pulled his daughter in for a hug before shaking my hand.

"Well, look at you, Henley. You look all grown up, like a real lawyer." Dick chuckled before wrapping his arms around her.

Who the fuck says that?

She didn't seem fazed, as she was obviously used to dealing with assholes in a male-dominant profession. I pulled out the chair beside her father and motioned for her to sit down. Then I settled in the seat on the other side of her.

The waiter came by and took our drink orders as he set down the brie appetizer, and we all dove in.

"I heard that you crushed it in court today. Another win for the team," Charles said, and I nodded.

"Thank you. The client deserved it, so I'm glad the court sided with us." I reached for my Pellegrino and took a sip.

"He's being humble. He owned that courtroom." Henley shrugged.

I puffed my chest up but tried to act unaffected.

"Wow. That's a high compliment. My girl is a tough critic." Charles held his whiskey glass up for the waiter to bring him another.

"He's young, so he's still hungry. Some of us don't need to hunt anymore. We can sit back and reap the fruits of our labor," Dick said, and I fought the urge to roll my eyes. He'd never been an impressive trial attorney. He'd had one really strong gift, and that was to surround himself with the right people. He'd latched onto Charles, and I'd credit him for recognizing talent there. Charles Holloway was one of the best I'd ever met. I'd seen him in action when I first graduated law school, and I'd made a conscious decision that I wanted to be just like him.

"I think that if you love the law, you don't ever want to sit back and be lazy, *Dick*," I said, purposely accentuating the name. I knew it bugged him, but he was pretentious and demeaning to others, so I liked to kick him down a few notches when I could. He'd been the one who fought me on taking this case for Sadie Walker. He didn't like to take on anything that didn't bring in the big bucks. A pro bono case had been risky, and he never did anything that was for the greater good.

Hence the reason I called him Dick.

He paused, his rocks glass at his lips, and he stared at me. "I've told you multiple times that Rick is short for Richard."

"Oh, my apologies. I guess you'd have to take that up with medieval England. That's where I must be getting it," I said, and Henley chuckled, which caused Dick to shoot her a warning look.

"Luckily, we aren't living in medieval times, Easton. So, I'd prefer we go with Rick moving forward."

I nodded, even though we'd had this conversation multiple times over the years, and we both knew I wasn't going to listen to anything that he said.

"Anyway, court went great, and Henley did a lot of the research for this case. So she deserves a big pat on the back."

She raised a brow as if she were surprised. "Thank you. But that was all you today."

"It's good you recognize the strengths you each bring to the table. I definitely teamed you up with the right mentor," Charles said. "You can't work at this firm if you aren't winning cases, Henley. So, learn from the best, and be the best."

This was fucking lunch; he needed to relax.

"Agreed. And you are the youngest female that we've hired

at the firm," Dick added, giving her a pointed look as if he'd done her a huge favor.

Like I said, he just rubbed me wrong every time he spoke.

"She's the youngest *attorney* at our firm. Male or female. Not sure why you left the attorney part out of your statement, *Dick*."

The asshole just glared at me and ordered another cocktail.

"Being my daughter means that you've got a lot to prove. And I'm counting on you to help her get there, Easton." Charles paused when the waiter set our food down.

"I'm happy to prove myself. I've made that clear." Henley reached for her fork and started eating her salad.

"I believe Henley is the only one at this table who got a perfect score on her LSAT, and I'm fairly certain that the only person with a higher score on their bar exam at this table is me. And it was by only one point. Not to mention the fact that she graduated number one in her Harvard Law class. So, I think you gentlemen can relax. She's way ahead of where you were when you first started, isn't she?"

Charles barked out a laugh. He was a brilliant guy, and he pushed those who worked for him hard, but he never minded when you argued with him, as long as you made your point.

Especially if you were right.

"Yes, my girl is a superstar." He popped a scallop into his mouth and then winked at her.

"She really is," Dick said, setting his glass down on the table. "The only time I ever saw Charles disappointed in her was at the NCAA tennis championships. He'd flown us all out to that tournament, bragging about how he was sure you would win. We tried reminding your father that you can't win them all."

"That's true." Henley reached for her water and took a sip. "However, my team won. It was still a win."

"Yes, sweetheart. And you did your best. You know I feel badly that I was hard on you about that. It's that Holloway spirit in me." Charles looked at his daughter, and she forced a smile and nodded.

I looked between them, unsure what the fuck was going on.

"Henley was favored to win the individual title, and she took second. It was still a very good showing," Dick said, as he forked a piece of steak. "You almost pulled it off."

Henley sighed. "I was pleased with how I finished, considering the fact that I had a 102 degree fever."

Charles winced. "You showed a lot of fight that day. Your coach wasn't too happy with me pushing you to play."

"Yeah. He wanted to pull me, but you wanted me to play. I don't regret finishing, Dad. I had to really dig deep, and I did. So, I think that speaks to my point that I don't back down from a challenge, and I'm willing to do the work."

"I was very proud of you that you didn't let him pull you, and you finished your last tournament like a champion." Charles smiled at his daughter.

"Well, you sure weren't acting like that on the plane ride home." Dick barked out a laugh, and I had the sudden urge to put my fist through his face. "Your dad is a competitive guy, Henley. He wanted that win."

"Thank you for the reminder." Henley oozed sarcasm. "Anyway, it was a long time ago, so let's celebrate the win we got today in the courtroom."

But I could feel her shutting down beside me.

A maniacal chuckle left my mouth unexpectedly, and everyone turned to look at me. "I'm just picturing either one of you on the court with her. I'm guessing she'd smoke both of you easily, even in your prime. So, glass fucking houses, gentlemen."

How fucking dare they call her out.

And why did I feel this intense need to defend her?

It didn't really matter why I felt this way. I always trusted my gut.

And my gut wanted to burn these bastards to the ground right now.

eight

· · ·

Henley

IT HAD BEEN A DAY. I'd loved being in the courtroom. I couldn't wait to have my own cases and fight for my clients like Easton had done today.

He was different from my father. His passion didn't just come from the accolades of winning. It came from his love for the law and the way he cared for his clients. My father had always been a workaholic, and he wanted to build something that people talked about.

His passion came from the win.

Whether it was a good win or a bad win, it didn't matter.

But the world wasn't always black and white. There were many shades of gray. My father had been the reason that I even went into law. He was passionate and brilliant, and I'd always admired that side of him. He was the most driven man I'd ever known, but he had no balance.

He wanted me to be the best at everything that I did. It was instilled in me at a young age. When I started playing tennis at just seven years old, he'd hired a private coach for me. He was never there to see the work that went into the training, but he would show up to all of my tournaments. And I pushed myself hard, even from a young age, knowing that he'd be there to watch.

If I won, he'd tell me how proud he was of me, and he'd take me home.

If I lost, he wouldn't wait to bring me home. He'd go back to the office and have Darleen, our house manager, who was basically my nanny, bring me home.

Later, he'd tell me that he'd had to get back to work, but I knew he'd been disappointed.

I knew it even as a little girl.

So, I tried hard not to disappoint him for many years. And when I left for boarding school, I found my confidence.

I found more balance.

Lulu was a big part of that.

And yes, I still won many tennis tournaments, even being the individual state champion in my last three years of high school. But when I lost, I didn't shut down. I used those moments to figure out what I needed to do to get better.

My father and I were different that way.

And I'd been proud as hell of finishing second in the NCAA championships in college and helping my team get the win.

My father was disappointed that I'd gotten second place.

That's all he could see at that time.

He wasn't an easy man.

But I knew that he loved me, and he did his best.

There was a teddy bear with a big heart beneath the over-achieving attorney, and I saw glimpses of that over the years.

"You all right?" Easton asked as he merged onto the freeway to head back to Rosewood River.

"Yes. I'm fine," I said, glancing over at him and keeping my tone light and laced with humor. "Thanks for defending my tennis skills."

"I shouldn't have to," he said. "Your dad can be a stubborn man, and Dick is just—well, he's a dick. The fact that you played in that game sick is crazy."

"Yeah, it was rough. It took me a long time to heal after."

"What happened after?"

"My coach took me to the hospital, and I ended up having pneumonia and bronchitis, so I was admitted for almost a week."

"Jesus. Did your dad feel bad after he realized you were that sick?"

I chuckled. Easton clearly came from a very different style of parenting than I did. "My father left to catch their private plane home immediately following the match and made it known that he was disappointed in my performance. So, Coach Blackstone took me to the hospital. But yes, I think he felt terrible once he realized I was admitted for several days. He sent flowers. My best friend, Lulu, was there. My grandparents flew out. It all worked out."

He was quiet for a long moment. "I'm sorry. That was really shitty. What about your mom?"

"She lives in France."

"They have planes in France, don't they? She wasn't there for the tournament? Isn't her husband a tennis pro?" he asked, not hiding his irritation.

I sighed. "It's not a big deal. This is the way I grew up, Easton. My mother hates my father. He was unfaithful with his secretary. She won't attend anything if he's going to be there, so she doesn't do tennis tournaments or graduations."

He cleared his throat and glanced over at me as his car phone rang, and the Bluetooth announced an incoming call from his mother. "I'm sorry. Do you mind if I grab this? She's called a few times."

"Of course not."

He pushed the button as he continued to drive down the freeway. The sun was just going down, and I glanced out the window to see the sky was a mix of pinks and oranges.

"Hey, Mom."

"Is that my birthday boy?" Her voice oozed that motherly love everyone yearned for. He glanced over at me, and my mouth fell open as she started singing into the phone, and a man's voice joined in.

It was his birthday?

"Hey, Dad. Thanks for that, guys. We're celebrating my birthday at Sunday dinner, remember?"

"We were just checking on you because we know you work so hard, Easton. Did you call your sister today?"

I remembered he was a twin and wondered what it was like to not only have a big family, but someone you shared a birthday with.

Someone you shared a womb with.

I'd always longed for a family like that.

I'd spent a lot of time alone growing up, and I'd always wanted siblings.

And then I'd met Lulu and learned what it meant to have a sister.

"I didn't get a chance because she called the minute I woke up. She and Nash and Cutler sang to me."

"She told me you sent her that new KitchenAid they just came out with," his mother said, and you could hear the pride in her voice.

"Well, she loves to bake." He cleared his throat. "Hey, Mom, Dad, I appreciate the call, even if it's the third time I've talked to you today." He chuckled.

"You're such a smartass. I feel like there is a *but* in there... Is this you rushing me off the phone?" his mother asked, and his father just laughed and then said he had to go check the steaks on the grill. "Because I just wanted to make sure you were doing okay today?"

Was he that bothered by his birthday?

"Mom. There's someone in the car, so can I call you later?" His voice was deep and gruff.

"Ohhhh. Someone is in the car," she said, her voice completely changing into this curious, mischievous tone. "I thought you were working, and that's why we couldn't have dinner tonight."

"I was in court today, and I am working. We're driving back from the city. Henley's in the car," he said. "Charles's daughter."

"I know who Henley is, Easton. Clark told me she was quite the impressive pickleball player."

I laughed. "Hi, Mr. and Mrs. Chadwick. It's lovely to meet you."

"Oh, sweetheart, you have no idea." She paused, and Easton started to speak just as she gasped and interrupted. "Wait. Why don't you join us for Sunday dinner?"

"Mom."

"Easton," she said in a deep voice, clearly trying to mimic her son, and I chuckled.

"It's inappropriate. You're putting her on the spot. Not everyone wants to go to Sunday dinner." He exited the freeway.

"You dragged her to pickleball. This is dinner. And we're having cake," she said. "How about you let her answer?"

He glanced over at me, and I didn't miss the way the corners of his lips turned up.

"Thank you for the invite. I'd love to come. I don't really know anyone here outside of the office, so it sounds like fun. And it's the big guy's birthday, right?" I said over my laughter as his mother joined in.

"Oh, that's so wonderful. I can't wait to meet you in person, Henley."

"Don't forget whose birthday it is." Easton feigned irritation.

"Never. Love you, my boy. I can't wait to see you both on Sunday."

"Love you. I'll call you later." He ended the call.

"You guys are close, huh?"

"Yeah. There's a lot of us, and my mom lives for birthdays and holidays and Sunday dinners," he said.

"I can't believe you didn't tell me it was your birthday."

"Listen. I care more about it being Emerson's birthday than mine. I did exactly what I wanted to do today. And I got to call Richard a dick multiple times. That's the gift that keeps on giving."

I laughed as he pulled down my driveway. Why was I bummed that we were already home? It had been a long day.

My father had acted like a jackass by bringing up that damn tennis tournament, and normally, it would weigh heavily on me, but having Easton call him out—it meant something to me.

I'd stood up to him many times, but today, I just hadn't had the energy.

But I hated that he'd brought it up in front of Easton.

My mentor.

A man I respected.

A man I was ridiculously attracted to.

"It was a good day," I said, as I unbuckled my seat belt when he put the car in park.

"Yeah? You liked being in court?"

"I'm going to say something to you, and if you use it against me, I'll deny it," I said over my laughter.

"Oh, boy. That bad, huh?" His tongue swiped out along his bottom lip. "Let's hear it."

"Seeing you in court today," I said, glancing out the window before looking back at him. "It was inspiring. It was—magic. It made me realize that I want to be the kind of attorney that makes a difference in people's lives, just like you did today."

His eyes searched mine before the corners of his lips turned up in a full-blown smile. My stomach fluttered in response.

"You're in awe of me," he said, his tone completely dry before he chuckled.

"I am not!" My head fell back in hysterical laughter. "I knew you'd make it a big deal."

"Admit it, Princess. You think I'm sexy when I'm in the courtroom."

Laura Pavlov

I shook my head, feeling my cheeks heat. "Please. You're fine, but sexy is a bit much."

"You sure about that?"

Why aren't I getting out of the car?

"I'm sure, boss."

"I'm not your boss. I'm your coworker, right?" he teased.

I sighed. I couldn't get out of the car because I didn't want this to end.

"I suppose that's true." My teeth sank into my bottom lip. "So, what are you going to do for the rest of your birthday? Are you going out? You can't be home alone on your birthday."

"No?" He smiled, and I swear my heart raced so fast I could hear it in my ears. Nothing had happened, but he was flirting with me, and I liked it. "What do you think I should do?"

"I don't know. You could go to Booze and Brews and *blow off some steam*," I said, but for whatever reason my words were breathy now. "Isn't that your thing?"

"Usually. But it's not what I feel like doing tonight."

"What do you feel like doing?" I asked.

He tilted his head to the side and moved closer. "What are you going to do the rest of the night?"

"I'll probably make some pasta and take a dip in the pool." My chest was rising and falling rapidly, and I didn't know why, but I couldn't stop it.

"I like pasta, and I'm all about taking a night swim. I'd join you, but I don't have my swim trunks."

Oh. My. God.

What were we even doing?

"You could swim in your underwear. It is your birthday, after all," I said, with a forced chuckle.

Because thoughts of Easton in just his briefs in the pool with me… there wouldn't be anything funny about it.

"I could do that." He smiled. "But it would be rude to make the birthday boy do that alone."

"Is this your birthday wish, Chadwick? To eat pasta and

64

swim in your underpants with your coworker? Do you think it's a good idea to do that?"

"Most of the best things in life are not good ideas, Princess," he said. "But I think any chance to swim in a pool with you is never a bad idea."

"I mean, this doesn't even have to be weird. We're two professionals who had a long day and are celebrating your birthday."

"Exactly. We're grown-ups. It's almost dark, so we'll barely see anything."

"Let's set some ground rules," I said.

"I hate ground rules. But tell me what they are."

"No touching." I raised a brow.

"Well, that's a buzz kill, but okay. What else?"

"We don't talk about it at the office. I don't need people to think I'm messing around with Easton Chadwick. Everyone there is kind of afraid of you. I have a reputation to protect," I said over my laughter.

"You make a good point. You'll be a fabulous attorney when you get into the courtroom, Ms. Holloway. And I wouldn't want to tarnish your reputation by anyone thinking we're friends. I agree to your terms."

"Should we start with the pasta?" I asked.

"Fuck the pasta. I say we start with the night swim and work up an appetite."

I chuckled. "You're ridiculous."

"I've been called worse." He reached forward and tucked the hair behind my ear. "Relax. We're just going swimming. We're not running naked through town."

"Good point," I said.

"Just think about how sexy I was in that courtroom, and now you get me in my briefs in the water."

"I'll barely notice. And this is a professional swim, right?" My voice was all tease. "It's the least I can do, seeing as it's your birthday."

"My birthday just got a hell of a lot better." He pushed the door open and came around the car just as I started to step out.

"Happy Birthday, Chadwick."

"It's about to be." He winked, and I laughed as we walked toward the water.

We were really doing this.

nine

. . .

Easton

SHE INSISTED we go inside her house first so she could drop off her purse and I could leave my keys there.

Henley went to grab a couple of beach towels as I took in her place. It was not what I'd expected. It was completely decorated, as if she'd lived here for months. Her style was relaxed and warm.

"Okay, I'm ready, birthday boy." She waggled her brows, and I laughed.

Why the fuck was I doing this?

We worked together. She was the managing partner's daughter. This couldn't go anywhere.

It was inappropriate for a multitude of reasons.

Yet, I couldn't stop myself from getting out of the car.

I wanted to be around her.

Needed to be around her.

Hell, I wasn't even mad that my mom had invited her to Sunday dinner. Normally, I would have lost my shit when she extended the invitation to a woman without running it by me.

But I was happy she'd invited her.

I'd always liked to be alone on my birthday. I'd go to work and then head home, where I drowned myself in booze and tried to get through the night without being haunted by the memories.

But here I was, going for a night swim with my mentee.

Maybe we could be friends. I'd never had many female friends, so this wasn't really my field of expertise.

But something about Henley was different.

I dropped my keys, my phone, and my wallet on her counter, before slipping my dress coat off and leaving my shoes and socks inside, as well.

She was barefoot as she padded by me to step outside, and she flipped on the lights on the patio, as the sky was completely dark now.

"I thought you'd cheat and go put on a swimsuit." I followed her over to the pool.

"A deal's a deal, Chadwick. Swim in our undies and then make you some pasta," she said as she stopped at the lawn chair near the shallow end. The pool was a decent size and set about forty feet from the river.

The view was unbelievable.

Similar to mine, but I didn't have a swimming pool.

I slowly unbuttoned my dress shirt. "Good to know you don't back down from a deal."

Her eyes scanned my chest before she unbuttoned her white blouse, exposing a peach-colored bra. My mouth watered at the sight. I'd imagined what she'd look like beneath her clothes at work hundreds of times.

Her tits were works of art.

Perky.

A perfect handful.

Two hard peaks pointed through the lace, taunting me.

"You're staring," she said, as she raised a brow.

"You didn't say staring wasn't allowed."

She let out a breath as I dropped my shirt on the chair and lowered my pants. Now it was her turn to gape at me. I looked down to see that my dick had decided to make a grand entrance by standing tall and proud beneath the black cotton fabric of my briefs.

"What? Have you never seen an erection?" I quirked a brow.

Her cheeks flushed as she unzipped her skirt and let it fall to the ground. She wore purple lace panties, which surprised me, because I was sure they'd match her bra.

"Of course, I have. But not normally when I'm going for a professional swim with my mentor." She covered her mouth with her hand, an attempt to muffle her laughter.

"I've got news for you, Princess. HR would not approve of this. There's nothing professional about swimming with your coworker after hours in your underwear."

She walked toward the steps and dipped her foot into the water. I stayed back, enjoying the view. Her ass was pure perfection, even covered by the layer of lace hugging her cheeks. Round and toned and everything an ass should be.

"So, if we were in swimsuits, would that make the difference?" she asked, as she dropped all the way into the water and turned around, her shoulders and head the only thing exposed.

I walked around to the side of the pool, before picking up speed and launching myself into a cannonball. I wanted to be in there with her now. Regardless of whether I got to touch her. I wanted to be closer to her.

How the fuck could I want to be close to her today, of all days?

I pushed the thought away.

She squealed, and her head fell back in laughter when I surged up from the water and shook my head like a dog. My feet touched the bottom of the pool, and this was where being six foot four inches tall always came in handy. She was treading water, and I ran my hands through my hair, pushing it away from my face.

"I don't think the bathing suits are the problem here." I smirked.

"What's the problem?"

"Well, for starters, your panties don't match your bra. That's offensive."

"Oh, I see. You have a problem with my mismatched set?"

"I'm just saying, I think HR would have a problem with it. Though your ass and tits are pure perfection."

"Thank you. But for the record, I cheated a little on our agreement."

"How so?"

"When I went to get the beach towels, I changed my panties. They originally matched my bra, and that felt... inappropriate, seeing as this is a professional swim. Plus, I was wearing a thong, and I wanted a little more coverage."

I barked out a laugh as I moved closer to her. "Are you shitting me, or are you serious?"

"About what part?"

"Did you change your panties, Princess?"

"Yes."

"But you didn't put on a swimsuit."

"No. I wouldn't break our deal. But you never said anything about what panties I had to wear."

"Maybe I wanted the thong. It is my birthday, after all." I was standing right in front of her, and she was still treading water, her breaths coming faster now.

"I think you'll live."

"You getting tired of treading water over there?" I held out my hand. "All you have to do is ask."

"We said no touching," she said.

"That was a stupid rule, wasn't it?" I moved so close that the tip of our noses were almost touching. The water moved between us as she continued moving her arms and legs beneath the surface.

"I think it was probably a smart rule." She pulled back and swam toward the shallow end, where she could stand. "Tell me why you got defensive about my dad calling me out for getting second in a tennis match years ago. I'm no longer offended by it, so why were you?"

"Because he was being an asshole."

"He's your boss. You don't want to piss him off."

I moved toward her before swimming in a circle around her. "I don't give a fuck. If someone's being an asshole, I'm going to call them out."

"Even if it's the man who gets to decide if your name is on the door?"

I came to a stop and floated on my back. "Yep."

"That's bold." She copied my movements by flipping onto her back and floating beside me. "But he clearly likes you because he didn't lose his shit on you."

"Your father may get to decide if my name goes on that wall, but the truth is, he needs me as much as I need him. The managing partners don't have near the trial wins that I do, nor did they in their prime. And now, they don't want to work eighty hours a week. He knows how dedicated I am to this job, and he knows that I'm good for the firm. Why do you think he asked me to take you under my wing?"

"Makes sense." She was quiet for a bit as she floated beside me. "Tell me something that I don't know about you."

I used my hands to slide back beside her as we started to float in different directions. "I don't know what you know about me. So, ask me whatever you want."

"You're an open book?" she asked, the back of her hand grazing mine as we stared up at the stars.

When was the last time I was this relaxed?

"Not even fucking close. I'm a fairly private guy."

"Then why did you just say that I can ask you anything?"

"How about you just take the win. I trust my gut. If you want to know something, ask me," I said.

"Why didn't you make plans tonight for your birthday?"

Of course, that was what she wanted to know. It was the one

thing I wouldn't answer. "I told you that I have a twin sister. She's the only girl in the family, so our birthday was always a big fucking deal. And I'm happy to celebrate with her. But with her living in Magnolia Falls now, I don't really give a shit to celebrate. I'd rather work. And trust me, my mom will go overboard on Sunday."

"All right. Seems like a fair answer. Can I keep going?"

"Yep. So far, this is painless." My hand brushed against hers again as we both floated on the surface of the water. The warm summer air kept us comfortable, and a light breeze off the river moved the branches on the trees in the distance.

"So, I know you have this big, wonderful family. And you're the best at your job, *according to you*," she said over her laughter, before I splashed water at her. "You didn't let me finish. Everyone at the office thinks you're a god, and my father allowed you to call him out at the table, so clearly, you're fabulous at your job."

"Is that the question? Because the answer is yes. I'm fabulous at my job."

"That wasn't the question, oh, humble one." She laughed, and I pointed at the star moving across the sky, and we both stared before she spoke again. "So you said you don't have a girlfriend. When was your last relationship?"

I didn't mind the question coming from her for some reason.

"College. Undergrad."

"How long did you date?"

"Three years." I cleared my throat.

She rolled onto her stomach, and her jaw fell open. "Three years? I wasn't expecting that."

"Don't be so dramatic. It's not that shocking."

Her teeth sank into her bottom lip, and she studied me. "Fine. It's no surprise at all. But you've been out of college a long time. You went on to law school and have been practicing law for years. You've never had a relationship since…" She raised a brow as if she were curious about the woman I'd dated.

"Jilly." I rolled over and stood abruptly. "And no. It was a one and done."

"Interesting. Why'd you break up?"

"How about you take a turn in the hot seat." I moved closer to her. "When was your last relationship?"

"Sure. I dated Pete Powers for about a year. He played guitar in a band. He's a super-talented musician. We ended things a few months ago."

"Why'd you break up?"

"We had no future. Pete is fabulous. We're still friends. But we want different things."

"What did he want?"

"Well, if you must know, Chadwick..." She tucked a loose strand of hair that had fallen free behind her ear as she stood in the shallow end, looking up at me. "He wanted to basically get high and have sex all day, every day."

"Ah... not a horrible plan."

"Correct. And every Saturday for a year, it was intriguing. I'd work all week and spend one weekend day with him. I'm not going to lie, it was nice, you know, being wanted all the time. No pressure. No hurry to do anything or go anywhere. Being with Pete was like being on vacation. But for a year. And I was ready to end the vacation and go back to living my regular life." She chuckled.

"I get that. And before the pothead sex fiend, who did you date? A strip club owner or a pimp?"

She used both hands and sent a gush of water in my direction. "Not even close. I dated Houston Callen for three and a half years. Most of my undergrad years, actually."

"Houston. He sounds like a bore."

She laughed, and the sound trickled around us like a song in the breeze.

"Houston was anything but a bore. He was driven and very similar to me when it came to working hard and studying. He was also on the tennis team with me, and he was determined to go to law school, as well."

"It sounds like a match made in Division I sports heaven," I hissed, because I hated the dude, and I had no idea why. Henley chuckled at my tone.

"It was. And I loved his parents and his sister. They were sweet and down to earth. I'd go home with him on the weekends often, and a part of me thinks I was more into his family than him."

"So you dumped him?" I asked.

"No. He dumped me." She looked up at the sky, as if she didn't want to see my reaction.

"That dickhead."

She chuckled and looked at me. "We both applied to Harvard Law. He didn't get in. And he decided that I only got in because I was a legacy."

"Are you fucking kidding me? You had a perfect score on your LSAT. Your legacy had nothing to do with it," I growled. Sure, I'd thought it before I knew her. But this was her fucking boyfriend.

"My grandfather and my father both wrote a letter of recommendation for him, too. But he didn't score well on the LSAT, and he was hungover when he interviewed there, so apparently, he didn't make a great impression."

"And then what? He just broke up with you for getting into Harvard?"

She tipped her head to the side. "No. He broke up with me when he asked me not to go to Harvard, and I let him know that I was going. He then told me that he wanted to be with a woman who didn't have my professional aspirations."

"What a fucking joke. He was jealous of his own girlfriend."

"I don't know. After all was said and done, I packed up and left for Boston and never looked back."

"You never spoke again?" Why was I so fucking curious?

"He reached out a year into law school to tell me that he was engaged. I wished him well, and that was it."

"Did it bother you when he got engaged?"

"Nope. After everything he'd said before I left, I didn't look at him the same way. I was relieved it wasn't me that he'd proposed to." She shrugged. "So tell me why you and Jilly broke up."

I glanced out at the river and then turned back to her. "If I tell you, can we make a deal that you won't ask any questions about it?"

Her gaze softened. "Of course."

"Jilly and I never broke up. She was killed in a car accident."

It was as if the universe had heard me say it aloud. A gust of wind came off the river, and Henley shivered.

"I'm so sorry." She shook her head and studied me.

"Come on. Let's get out of the pool."

And just like that, the mood shifted.

Memories of my past bringing me back to that time in my life.

Bringing me back to this specific day.

To all the reasons I liked my life exactly how it was.

What in the fuck was I even doing here?

ten

. . .

Henley

"SO THAT WAS IT? He just sent a text saying he'd see you there?" Lulu asked, as I talked to my bestie through my earbuds while walking the short distance to Easton's parents' house. He'd texted me the address yesterday and said he'd see me there.

I had a bouquet of flowers and a bottle of wine in my bag for his mother, as well as a birthday gift for Easton.

"I mean, his mom invited me to the dinner. He didn't. He probably just felt obligated to text me the address."

"No way. He wants you there. You had all that flirty banter in the pool—I mean, until he dropped that bomb," she said.

"It probably wasn't flirty at all, and I just built it up in my head."

"Come on! He had a boner pointing at you like he was picking you out of a lineup. The man was flirting his ass off, and you know it," she said over a fit of laughter.

"I knew I shouldn't have told you that," I grumped. I'd pulled out a bottle of wine after Easton had gone completely quiet on me when we'd gotten out of the pool. He'd said that he would take a raincheck on the pasta because it had been a long day.

And then he'd just left.

"Can we not analyze this, please? It's not like it could go anywhere anyway."

"Give me three reasons why it can't go anywhere. Because from where I'm sitting, he's hot. You're hot. He's single. You're single. You're both clearly attracted to one another. So why not throw caution to the wind and at least have a fling with that legal eagle bad boy."

I groaned. "Hmmm… I can give you plenty, but here are a few to start with. He's my mentor and my coworker. He works for my dad. And he doesn't do relationships."

"Those are so lame."

"Stop. I don't want to talk about this anymore," I groaned.

"Fine. But I want an update after the birthday dinner."

"Deal. Now, tell me how Beckett reached you when you'd blocked him."

"He did what a typical man does. He sent me flowers and apologized for being caught in a compromising position with Anastasia. This is exactly why we aren't together. He's untrustworthy. I just can't do it anymore. And then, he had the florist write that on the card, which you can guess is going to end up in the press because an employee at the florist will most likely sell the story within twenty-four hours. So, he's going to fuck me over once again. And then he called me from another number, and I picked up without thinking about it."

"I'm so glad you ended things with him."

"Yeah, well, he's not letting me go very gracefully. And when he pulls this shit and makes a scene in public, my family gets dragged into it. I can't handle one more call from my father shouting about what an embarrassment this is."

"I'm sorry, Lu. You've done your part. You've ended it. You can't help what he does in response." I stopped in front of the beautiful ranch house. There were several cars parked out front, and I was suddenly nervous.

"It's fine. I'm just not going to take any calls from unknown numbers. He'll get over it soon. I mean, at the rate he's hooking up with other women, I don't know how he finds the time to keep bothering me." She chuckled, but I heard the hurt beneath it.

"I love you. If you want to come hide out here with me, you can stay with me as long as you want."

"I know. I've got a few big trips for work, and then I'll be back. Are you there yet?"

"Yes. I'm standing out front."

"You sound a little nervous." My phone rang while I was on with her, and I saw the incoming FaceTime call from her.

I chuckled as I answered, and she came into view. "Why are you FaceTiming me? I need to go inside."

"Because you're nervous and seeing my face always helps." She smirked. "Listen to me. You've got this. You're Henley Freaking Holloway. Rock star lawyer. Superstar tennis player. And the world's greatest best friend. Go in there and let that man see you in that dress. His boner will spring right to life."

I gaped at the phone before looking over my shoulder and gritting through my teeth. "Stooop."

"You stop. Own that shit, Hen. Even if he's your coworker, or whatever excuse you keep coming up with, he's hot. Go torture the man a little bit. It is a birthday party, after all." She winked.

"I thought you told me that I needed to trust my gut? My gut tells me that this man is trouble. Not that he even likes me half the time we're together. He's so hot and cold, he's impossible to read."

"You misunderstood me. I meant to say, trust *my* gut. And my gut says that you should have a hot office fling with the sexy lawyer."

"I'm hanging up now."

"Fine. Call me later. Love you big."

"Love you bigger." I ended the call and made my way up the flower-lined pathway to the front door.

I knocked lightly, shifting on my feet, as I didn't know what to expect.

"You were brave enough to come to Sunday night dinner at the Chadwicks'?" Rafe's voice was all tease as he pulled the door open and motioned me inside.

"Well, I live alone, so I can use some entertainment."

"I promise you that you're about to experience it in spades."

A gorgeous woman came walking around the corner, her hair tied back in a neat chignon and a wide smile spread across her face. "You must be Henley. I'm Ellie Chadwick. It's so lovely to meet you. Thank you for joining us."

"Of course. I appreciate the invite." I handed Easton's mother the flowers and wine, and the gift bag for Easton dangled in my hand.

His mother pulled me in for a hug.

She hugged me like she'd known me my entire life.

She smelled like roses and sunshine and goodness.

"I love your dress," she said, as she squeezed one of my hands in hers and took me in. I didn't know what one should wear to Sunday dinner, so I went with a white floral maxi dress and my cowboy booties. Everyone in Rosewood River wore boots, and I'd always been a fan. They were so much more comfortable than heels. Easton had also mentioned they had a stable on their property, and I was dying to see the horses.

We'd had horses at Westcliff, and Lulu and I used to ride every chance we got. She'd grown up riding and introduced me to it my freshman year, and it had become a passion. An escape.

"Thank you so much. You look lovely, as well." I smiled, admiring the white wrap dress she wore.

"Is anyone going to say anything about my outfit?" Rafe asked with a laugh, and his mother shook her head and chuckled.

"You're wearing jeans and a tee." Ellie dropped my hand and pushed up on her tiptoes to kiss his cheek. "But you look very handsome."

I'd barely stepped inside this home, but I could feel the love already.

"Are you keeping her hostage in the entryway?" Clark stood at the end of the hallway, holding a beer bottle in his hand.

Rafe led the way toward his brother, flipping him the bird as he did so.

The next twenty minutes were spent meeting the family. My eyes kept connecting with Easton, who watched me from the far side of the room as he sipped his beer.

They were a large crew. Each one bigger than life. And in the short time it took for introductions, I'd gathered a ton of information.

Easton's parents, Keaton and Ellie, had raised their family in this home. They were both warm and kind. Ellie was the quintessential mother, looking at her children with so much love every time they spoke.

Keaton was funny and liked to razz his boys. They made jokes that Easton's twin sister, Emerson, was the only one their father was soft on. It was clear they all missed her being at dinner.

I'd met his brothers and cousin at the club when I'd played pickleball, aside from Archer and his adorable daughter, Melody, who was the cutest toddler I'd ever laid eyes on. Archer and Axel's parents, Isabelle and Carlisle, lived in the house next door, and they were fawning over their granddaughter, even though Archer reminded them that they see her almost daily.

It was a lot to take in, in the best way.

I'd never had a family gathering like this, so it was new for me. But I liked it.

I liked the energy and the laughter and the warmth. It was impossible to miss.

It smelled like barbecue and honey, and my stomach growled in response.

The kitchen was attached to a giant family room, making for one large entertaining space. The kitchen cabinets were painted a French blue, and there was an oversized oak island in the middle that looked more like a vintage piece of furniture that they'd brought in.

Keaton handed me a glass of chardonnay just as Easton walked over for the first time and leaned down to whisper in my ear as chaos swirled around us. "Are you ready to run for the hills?"

"No." I shook my head and chuckled. "This is great."

"We'll see if you're singing that tune in a few hours."

"I'll be just fine." I held up the gift bag. "Happy Birthday. It's nothing big, as I didn't have much notice, but I just wanted to get you a little something, seeing as it's a birthday party."

"So proper, Princess." He smirked, and his cheeks were slightly rosy, eyes a little red, and I guessed he'd been drinking for a while now.

I'd never seen him like this. The man always oozed so much control, but he seemed a little off today.

Everyone started carrying platters to the dining room, but Easton pulled me over to the side and set his beer bottle down and looked inside the bag. "Can I open it now?"

"Sure."

He reached inside and pulled out the desk plate that I'd gotten him, and he smiled as he looked down at it and read the words. "*Suck Less.* Thank you."

I shrugged and tried to hide my smile. "I figured when people come into your office, they'd at least know what you're thinking."

"It's brilliant. I love it."

He reached inside and pulled out the coffee mug that read: *Evil Genius at Work.*

His head tipped back in laughter. "Damn, you've already got my number, don't you?"

"You're an easy read, Chadwick."

His tongue swiped out along his bottom lip as his gaze

locked with mine. "I don't know about that, but thank you for the gifts."

"Dinner's ready, and I'm hungry. Mom won't let us eat until you two come to the table," Bridger said, his tone flat, and he made no attempt to hide his irritation.

"You know, you have the patience of a toddler." Easton raised a brow, setting the birthday gift on the table, where a bunch of other packages sat.

"I'm fine with that. And I think Melody is also annoyed with you for making us wait. It's a dick thing to do." Bridger's lips twitched the slightest bit, and then he and Easton both started laughing.

"Let's go. This guy gives hangry a new name." Easton led the way to the dining room, where the conversations were flowing.

All at the same time.

This must be how big families communicate. The home I'd grown up in was never loud. Everything was very—controlled. My father was always working.

I basically grew up with the people who my father employed, and when he was home, we'd have dinner, just the two of us.

I wasn't complaining. I'd had a very fortunate life.

I'd just bought a gorgeous house on the water with the money from my trust fund.

I was grateful. I was.

But that didn't mean that I wasn't lonely sometimes.

Darleen had run our home, and she was more like a mother to me than my own mother had been, if I were being honest. I'd only spent summers with my mom most of my life, so Darleen cared for me day to day.

She even traveled with us when my father and I went on vacations. Thomas had been my father's driver since I was a little girl, and he'd always attended all of my tennis matches with Darleen before I left for boarding school.

And once I'd met Lulu, I knew she was family.

But I highly doubted any member of the Chadwick family had ever felt lonely.

You could feel the love in this room.

Bridger took his seat beside his father, and Easton pulled out the chair next to where I assumed he was going to sit, as those were the only two open seats.

"We're so happy you're here with us, Henley. Sunday dinners are my favorite," Ellie said as she looked at me, and all the little side conversations came to a stop at once.

"Yeah, yeah. We're glad she's here. And she's as good as Easton, if not better, at pickleball, so that's also fabulous. Can we eat now?" Bridger asked, and the table erupted into laughter.

Keaton picked up the platter of barbecued chicken and ribs and passed it to Bridger, who I'd just learned was the oldest of the four brothers. His cousin, Archer, was two years older than him, and he set a piece of cornbread on his adorable baby girl's plate before passing it to Easton. There were mashed potatoes and applesauce and baked beans. I'd never seen such a spread before.

"I'm sorry that my oldest son is lacking manners when it comes to dinnertime." Ellie chuckled. "So, Easton tells me that you graduated from Harvard Law School, and you played collegiate tennis at Stanford?"

Clark whistled as if he were impressed. Easton shot him a look, so clearly, they had their inner dynamic that I wasn't privy to.

"Yes. I'd been playing since I was a little girl. I still miss it sometimes, but I started playing pickleball for fun during law school, so that helped."

"Is there anything you can't do, Henley Holloway?" Rafe asked, his tone flirty.

"*Is there anything you can't do, Henley Holloway?*" Easton mimicked him in a dramatic voice, which had the table roaring with laughter again. "Dude. Check yourself. She works with me."

"Ahhh… the birthday boy is finally speaking. I figured a little flirty banter with your coworker would do the trick." Rafe winked at me.

"Yes, it's not dinner without Easton's sarcasm." Clark passed the mashed potatoes to his aunt. "But I agree with Rafe. You're clearly talented."

Easton groaned and kept his tone low so only I would hear him. "Kiss-asses."

I chuckled as the conversation continued. Easton left to get a whiskey, and it was a generous pour, and I didn't miss the looks that passed around the table when he'd returned.

It wasn't judgment if I was reading them correctly.

It appeared to be something softer. Maybe empathy or sadness or even concern.

I wasn't certain, but he tipped his head back and downed the amber liquid in one swift move.

"How many times do you think the Chadwicks are going to be mentioned in 'The Taylor Tea' this week?" Axel asked, before taking a bite of his cornbread.

"Earmuffs." Bridger shot a look at his cousin Archer, and without another word, Archer put his hands over his daughter's ears. She was completely unfazed and eating her mashed potatoes like they were the best thing she'd ever had. Her grandmother, Isabelle, sat on the other side of her, helping her along. "That is some sort of bullshit. What's their obsession with us, anyway?"

"Well, we're clearly handsome and charming and the hottest topic in Rosewood River." Rafe smirked. "I don't have a problem with it."

"You don't have a problem with them insinuating that something happened with me and Desiree Carson? That was a low blow, even for that asshole column," Easton hissed.

"No. Because we know nothing happened, and she didn't actually name you," Rafe said.

"She insinuated as much. The litigation comment was a dig

at Easton." Bridger reached for his beer. "I think it's Emilia Taylor sitting behind her keyboard, judging everyone. She's always had it out for me, and now she's turned her attention to the whole damn family."

"Okay, the earmuffs are off. I'd like to eat my dinner. I don't even read that ridiculous column," Archer said. "And she didn't have it out for you. She had a crush on you. I told you that in high school."

"A crush? She was out for blood. That girl is cutthroat." Bridger shook his head, and everyone laughed once again.

It must be a Chadwick family dinner thing. They just seemed to know one another so well, and there was a comfort between them that was impossible to miss.

I envied it.

And I was just happy to be part of it, even if was just for one night.

eleven

. . .

Easton

WE'D HAD DINNER. We'd had cake. We'd celebrated my birthday, which had become my least favorite day of the year, aside from the fact that my sister, Emmy, had come into the world two minutes and twenty-three seconds after me.

For that reason, I wouldn't completely curse this day.

My mother had taken Henley out to see the horses, and Archer and Melody had gone with them, as well.

I'd indulged in too many whiskeys, which wasn't something I did often, but it was the only way for me to get through my birthday celebration every year now.

My mother was not going to let it pass without at least a dinner.

So, I numbed myself the best I could.

But this year was different because Henley was here.

Why the fuck did my mother think it was a good idea to invite my coworker, a woman I was mentoring, into our family home?

And she'd brought a goddamn gift.

Not to mention my family had taken to her like they'd known her their whole lives. I took the last sip of whiskey before turning to hug my aunt and uncle goodbye. Melody had fallen asleep on my lap before Archer scooped her up and had taken her home about twenty minutes ago. Clark and Rafe had taken off, and Bridger and Axel were just saying their goodbyes now. My mother was talking Henley's ear off, and I couldn't even get annoyed with her because I knew how much she missed my sister, even though my parents had just been in Magnolia Falls last weekend to visit Emmy, Nash, and Cutler.

Perks of having a rich brother. Bridger had a helicopter and a private plane, so when we wanted to go visit Emmy, we could be there in less than an hour.

"This has been so fun. I really appreciate you having me, but I should get going," Henley said as she hugged my mother and then my father goodbye.

"It's a standing invitation, sweetheart. We'd love to have you every Sunday," my mother said.

"Mom," I groaned, moving to set my bar glass in the sink as my father pulled me into a hug.

"Easton." My mother chuckled as she hugged me next.

"Don't make her feel obligated."

"I hardly think she feels obligated," Mom said as she rolled her eyes, but I didn't miss the tease in her voice. "Henley, do you feel obligated to have dinner here again?"

Henley flashed that fucking award-winning smile at me before turning to my parents. "Absolutely not. I'm so grateful for the offer, and I will definitely be back because that was the best dinner I've had in a very long time. And the company was equally wonderful."

I blew out a breath. "What is she going to say? *Yes, Ellie. I feel pressure to come back*? I've had a terrible time, and your cooking will probably give me the shits."

My father burst out in laughter, and my mother swatted him with the back of her hand.

"Stop being such a lawyer," Mom teased as she stepped closer to me, and I wrapped my arms around her.

"Fine. Then you need to stop being so charming and nice to everyone." I kissed the top of her head.

My mom looked up at me and placed a hand on my cheek. "I love you, Easton."

Her eyes were wet with emotion. She didn't know how to handle the fact that I struggled this time every year.

Memories flooded.

Grief weighed on me.

Most days I was fine, but for whatever reason, the week of my birthday was always the worst. When I kept busy with work, things were better. Parties and celebrations were the opposite for me.

"I love you, Mom." I glanced up to see Henley watching us. "Should we head out? I can walk you. It's on the way."

My father clapped me on the shoulder and gave me one more hug. I told them I'd stop by tomorrow to grab the gifts, as I didn't drive here tonight.

We said our goodbyes and made our way outside.

My buzz was still there, but it was starting to wear off.

"Your family is really great," Henley said as we started walking.

"They are. But they can be a lot sometimes."

"I think that's better than the alternative," she said, as she looked out at the river that was on our right.

"What do you mean?"

"I mean, living in a house that doesn't have that kind of life. Or that kind of love."

Her voice was quiet, and I glanced over at her as we walked side by side. The sky was dark, but the light from the moon illuminated her, allowing me to make out her pretty face.

"I don't take my family for granted, and I know a lot of people don't have what we have. I'm lucky, because they are the absolute best."

"But?" she pressed. "It sounds like there is more you want to say."

We turned down the street we both lived on, my house being just a few doors down. "It means that my family is fabulous, and I love them. But, once a year, I'd like to get a pass on my birthday, and they refuse to allow that to happen. So, sometimes they're just—a lot."

She came to a stop and turned to face me after we'd made it up the steps to her front porch.

"They want to celebrate your birthday. It's hardly a criminal offense." She threw her hands in the air like she was annoyed with me.

Why the fuck did she care if I didn't want to celebrate my birthday?

What was everyone's obsession with birthdays anyway?

This was ridiculous.

"If someone doesn't want to celebrate their birthday, they should be allowed to voice that. They should not be forced to do something they don't want to do."

I started walking backward, waiting for her to step inside because I was done with this conversation.

She chuckled, but it wasn't genuine. It was laced with contempt and irritation, which pissed me off.

"They made you a nice dinner and a beautiful homemade cake, which your mother made from scratch," she huffed, and her voice was getting louder now. "And everyone got you presents and sang to you. Poor Easton. What a horrible family you have."

I gaped at her as she whipped around and put the key in the door. She had some fucking nerve. She didn't know what the fuck she was talking about.

This is why you don't bring coworkers to family dinner.

"Whoa, whoa, whoa!" I shouted, as I moved back up the steps to her front door, stepping in the way just before she slammed the door in my face. "You don't get to judge me."

"Why? Because you're my mentor? You judge everyone. Hell,

you judged me when I walked through the door the first day that I met you."

"Well, you didn't exactly walk through the door. You set off the fucking alarm and alerted the entire town, which you followed by dumping scalding hot lava on me, remember?" I asked.

Her back was pressed against the door now, and I had one hand resting on each side of her head, caging her in. Her lips were plump, and her blonde hair fell all around her shoulders, and I didn't know what the fuck I was doing.

I'd watched her all night. The way she'd sat on the floor and read three books with Melody. The way she'd listened to my father's lengthy story about growing up in Rosewood River, and he'd literally started from birth until the present day. And she'd nodded and laughed and appeared interested. The way she'd handled my brothers and my cousins like she'd known them her entire life and then shifted easily to girl talk with my mom and my aunt.

Henley Holloway is pissing me the fuck off.

She was a distraction that I didn't want to deal with.

I didn't get distracted anymore, and for good reason.

But here I was, staring down at her like I'd die if I didn't kiss her right now.

"I remember because you were a complete asshole to me afterward. And I get it—I'm Charles Holloway's daughter. I just got handed a job and an office, and you had every right to be annoyed by that. But your family is what dreams are made of." She chuckled softly. "They're what everyone strives for, you know?"

"I wasn't mad that you got an office. But I knew you'd be judged for it, so I just gave you a heads-up." I cleared my throat. "But I did judge you, and I was wrong. You're brilliant and talented, and the firm is lucky to have you. I had it all wrong."

"Had what all wrong?"

"I thought you got this job because you were Charles Holloway's daughter. But the reality is, the firm was lucky to get you, and they were only able to get you because you're Charles Holloway's daughter."

Her eyes widened, and she looked stunned by my words.

"Thank you for saying that." Her hands moved to my chest, fisting my tee, and I moved closer. I wanted to kiss this woman so badly, I could barely see straight. "I know you love your family, Easton. So why don't you tell me why you were downing whiskey like it was water and why you hate your birthday so much it's bordering on irrational."

I hated that she was so observant.

That had always been my job.

I stepped back and ran a hand through my hair. "Goodnight, Princess. I'll see you at work tomorrow."

I jogged down her steps, needing to get away from her. She was getting too close. Asking too much.

Making me feel things that I didn't want to feel.

"I didn't take you for a coward, Chadwick."

"Maybe I'm not as easy to read as you think I am." I held my hand up to wave goodbye as she slammed the door.

Good. Let her be pissed. It was better that way. Kissing her would be a horrible idea.

And I sure as hell couldn't have a one-night stand with a coworker. I had a strict rule about not mixing business with pleasure. And I highly doubted she'd go for a one-and-done deal anyway.

So I'd take a shower when I got home, fuck my hand once again, and blow off some steam.

But when I walked through the door, that's not what I wanted to do. I paced around the living room and poured myself another whiskey.

How dare she call me a fucking coward.

I tipped my head back and downed the liquid.

And then I stared at my phone for what felt like hours, but in reality, was probably about ninety seconds.

I picked up my phone and sent her a text.

> Call me a coward again and I'll file a complaint with HR and get you written up.

It was funny, but I wanted her to know that I was annoyed with the comment.

PRINCESS
> What would they write me up for? Telling the truth?

The fucking nerve of this woman.

> Well, now I could have you written up for being combative with your mentor.

PRINCESS
> All I asked was why you hate your birthday.

> What are we, girlfriends?

I poured myself another drink because I hated that I couldn't talk about it. I hated that I still had moments where I was drowning in grief. All these years later.

PRINCESS
> Definitely not. Girlfriends don't give one another whiplash.

I drank the booze and set my glass back down before moving to the couch and leaning back.

> How, pray tell, am I giving you whiplash?

PRINCESS

Don't try to "pray tell" me and throw out fancy words. You know exactly how.

Tell me.

PRINCESS

Why should I? You won't answer a simple question.

For fuck's sake, Princess. Tell me how I'm giving you whiplash.

PRINCESS

Hmmm… we swam in my pool in our undies, and then you ran out of here like someone had a gun to your head. You seemed like you were going to kiss me tonight, and then you quickly took off. You're a game player, and I don't play games. So, you don't need to worry about any of it, because you are one big walking red flag.

Red is my favorite color, so I can live with that.

PRINCESS

Goodnight, Chadwick. I'm done going in circles with you.

I scrubbed a hand down the back of my neck and dialed her number.

"I say goodnight and you decide to call me? Another example of giving me whiplash," she said, when she answered the phone.

"Stop talking." I walked to the counter and poured myself one more drink.

"Okay, I'm hanging up on you. This is the kind of game playing that I'm talking about. You called me, and now you're telling me to stop talking? Goodnight."

"Don't hang up." I drank the whiskey and slammed the glass down. "I'm going to tell you something, and I don't want you to ask any questions or pity me or say anything, for that matter."

"So this isn't a conversation even though you called me?"

"Henley."

"Easton."

I groaned. "I don't want to be a fucking coward. So I'm going to tell you why I don't like my birthday. But then we aren't talking about it after that. Got it?"

"Got it, Evil Genius."

"I was with Jilly for three and a half years. I thought I'd marry her after I graduated from law school. I thought I had my whole future figured out." I moved back to the couch. It was unusually quiet. "Are you still there?"

"Yes."

"You didn't say anything."

"You told me not to talk, so I'm listening."

I blew out a breath. "Jilly went on a college graduation trip with her girlfriends. She wasn't due back until the day after my birthday. I teased her about missing it, but it was a fucking joke. I wasn't serious."

"I can see how that could be a joke," she whispered.

"But she came back early. She wanted to surprise me. We were having a big family dinner with me and Emerson and the whole family. Hell, Jilly's family was there, too."

"Oh, God." Her voice cracked on the other end, and she sniffed like she was trying not to cry.

"She got into a car accident on the way to my fucking birthday party. A truck crossed over the freeway, and she never saw it coming. So, I don't like my birthday anymore because it just reminds me of the worst memory of my life. And everyone wants me to celebrate—and trust me, I've worked hard to get my life back—but I just want to have a pass on the day that I have to relive every year. Is that too much to ask for?"

"No. And I'm really sorry, Easton."

Steal My Heart

"No pity, Princess. I just wanted you to know that I'm not a coward."

"I'm sorry I called you that," she said, and her voice wobbled.

"Don't be nice to me now. That makes it worse."

"Okay. You're not a coward, but you are an Evil Genius. Thanks for telling me."

I chuckled, but it was forced and laced with pain. "Goodnight, Princess."

And I ended the call before she could respond.

95

twelve

· · ·

Henley

WHEN I GOT to work Monday morning, I wondered how it would be with Easton. I'd tossed and turned most of the night, thinking about what he'd shared with me. The weight of it all.

I knew that he would most likely be cold to me today because the man was completely unpredictable. Hot one minute and cold the next.

But he'd opened up to me, and it meant something. I knew he wasn't that guy, and he didn't share often, so I was grateful that he'd trusted me with it.

I got to the office early and was surprised to find Rosie and Joey there before me. They were in Easton's office, hanging streamers.

"What's going on in here?" I asked, my tone light, but my heart raced because I knew he'd hate it.

"It was Easton's birthday on Friday, and you guys were in court in the city, so we figured we'd celebrate today. He's always such a grump about his birthday," Rosie said, shaking her head.

"Why do you think that is?" I didn't know what they knew. He was from a small town, so obviously people knew about Jilly's accident all those years ago, but they might not realize the timing of it all.

"Maybe because he's a twin? And Emerson doesn't live here?" Joey said, as he tried to tape his end of the streamer to the ceiling, and it fell. Clearly, they didn't know the reason for Easton's disdain for his birthday.

He was a private man, and I understood it.

"That could be it. Or maybe he's just not a birthday guy. Not everyone likes getting older." I chuckled.

"Yeah, we do this every year, and he's always annoyed about it. But he always gives me a big bonus for my birthday, and he has me order a cake for every employee's birthday every year," Rosie said. "I can't just do nothing for his. He runs this place, and he works hard. So we just want to celebrate him once a year."

"I totally get that. But doesn't he have that Zoom call today with Bruno King? Streamers in the background might not go over well."

She came to a stop. "Oh, I forgot about that. Shoot. Should we just decorate half of his office?"

Joey came down from the stepladder and looked between us. "I don't know. The dude is annoyed with me most of the time, so I really don't want to piss him off."

"Well, you're tall, and I needed help to hang things." Rosie sighed.

There were three bags from the party supply store on the chair, and I knew she was coming from a good place.

"What if we decorate the staff lounge so he can go in there and be tortured for a little while, but he can go back to his office when he wants to leave?" I asked.

"Oh, that's a brilliant idea. Yes! Let's decorate the staff lounge. We can make him come in there for cake," Rosie said, gathering up the bags as Joey and I followed her down the hall.

We spent the next thirty minutes covering every inch of the staff lounge in streamers and party décor. Rosie had brought a large birthday cake, and we sprinkled glittery confetti all over the table.

He would hate it, but at least it wasn't in his office this year.

When we heard the sound of the front door opening, Joey almost tripped over a chair while hightailing it out of there. "I did not help with this," he whisper-hissed.

Rosie and I both laughed and waited until Easton filled the doorway of the staff lounge. He raised a brow and took it in.

"Looks like a Disney princess puked in here," he grumped, but I noticed the corners of his lips turning up the slightest bit.

"Happy Birthday, boss," Rosie said.

"I told you not to call me that." He walked over to Rosie and wrapped one arm around her and gave her a little squeeze. "But thank you."

She raised a brow. "Thank you? I didn't expect that."

"Well, I'm not a complete asshole. So yeah, thank you for refusing to respect my wishes and ignore my birthday year after year." He smirked and turned to see the box of bagels that she'd brought as he moved toward the counter and popped one into the toaster. "Thanks for the bagels. I didn't have breakfast, and I had one too many whiskeys last night."

"This is like a Christmas miracle in August. You're so— friendly and not yourself today." Rosie handed him the knife for the cream cheese, before grabbing a plate and a donut for herself.

"What can I say? I'm a year older and a year wiser." He winked before grabbing his bagel from the toaster and adding some cream cheese before he turned to me. "Grab some food and meet me in my office. I want to go over this meeting with you."

"Got it." I moved toward the toaster and made myself a quick bagel as Rosie gushed about what a good idea it had been to move the party into the staff lounge because he'd handled it much better.

I made my way down the hall and into his office, setting my plate and coffee mug on his desk and sitting in the chair across from him.

We sat in silence for the first few minutes as he stared at his monitor. When he finally looked up, he raised a brow. "How'd you get them to move it out of my office?"

"I'm a savvy litigator, remember? I have my ways."

He nodded. "Thank you. You didn't tell them anything, did you?"

"Of course not."

"Good. I don't need a pity party."

"I don't think anyone would pity you for having a hard time on your birthday if they knew the reason." I paused and thought about my words carefully. "But, it is possible to grieve for Jilly and still celebrate your birthday. You know that, right?"

He reached for his coffee mug. "I thought we agreed that if I told you what happened, we wouldn't discuss it further."

"That was before I knew what you were going to tell me. And I just thought an outside perspective might be helpful."

"Are you my therapist now?" He feigned annoyance, but he had this sexy smirk on his face, and I squeezed my thighs together because when Easton Chadwick looked at me like this, I could barely contain myself.

"I was a double major. Pre-law and psychology." My teeth sank into my bottom lip as he studied me. There was something different about him today.

He was lighter.

More relaxed.

"That's an interesting mix."

"Well, I think they go hand in hand. I want to be able to understand the clients that I'm representing. And if I'm being truthful, I've had the same therapist since middle school. She's brilliant, and I respect what she does for a living, so I was interested in learning about it."

His gaze softened. "Okay, good doctor. Tell me your theory."

"Well, Evil Genius," I said, leaning forward and resting my forearms on his desk. "It's important to know that celebrating your birthday does not make you an asshole."

He barked out a laugh. "That's what you learned at Stanford and Harvard?"

"What I'm saying is that I think you feel guilty about celebrating your birthday because you think it means you stopped grieving the loss of someone you loved. And that's not true."

His face hardened with my words. "How is that not true?"

"For starters, the accident was not your fault, so there is nothing to feel guilty about in the first place. It was an accident. You didn't cause it, and you couldn't have stopped it. Guilt and grief are not the same. So yes, it's fair that you grieve this time of year because you lost someone who was important to you. But it's also okay to celebrate your birthday and have a good time with friends and family." My gaze locked with his. "She wanted to be there for you on your special day. I'm guessing she would not want you to never celebrate your birthday again. You're still here, Easton."

His lips parted for a moment, and then he narrowed his gaze. "You think I'm not living? I've been living every goddamn day. I went to law school weeks after the accident, and I work for one of the best firms in the country."

"I know you did. And you're a brilliant attorney. But I'm just saying, it's okay to have fun on your birthday, too. Grief doesn't have to consume you. And obviously you've moved forward, and that's great. But your birthday doesn't have to be ruined forever."

"Well, this is the first time in eight years that I've eaten cake and not been a complete dick at the office when they decorated for me. Let's call that a win." He leaned back in his chair.

"That's very mature of you. And you didn't even bite off the head of your therapist. This is progress." I chuckled.

"That's because I need a favor."

"Getting the streamers out of your office wasn't favor enough?" I teased.

"It's pickleball night at the club again. These assholes from Colton County are coming to play, and Archer has a work emergency and can't make it again. That's twice in a month that he's missed. I'm ready to kick his ass off the team."

"So you need my pickleball skills?" I tilted my head and smiled.

"I do. Can you sub for him again tonight? You'll be officially listed on the Chad-Six team because you've subbed twice."

"I feel like he should be the sub at this point." My head tipped back in laughter. "But yes. I will play pickleball with you, Chadwick."

"Don't let it go to your head, Princess."

"You just told me you needed me. How can it not go to my head?"

He smiled a wide, genuine smile. "All right. Let's get ready for the meeting. This could potentially be the biggest client this firm has ever signed."

"This could get your name on the door."

"That's the plan." He tossed me a file, and we spent the next hour reviewing the case. King Hotels, one of the most famous luxury hotel chains in the country, was being accused of favoring male over female employees, and Bruno King, the president and CEO, was adamant that this was a smear campaign.

This case would draw even more attention to the firm. My father was a bit of an egomaniac, and being on a list that named his firm in the top three in the country wasn't enough. He wanted to be number one. He'd always been that way.

We spent the next few hours going over all the paperwork, the notes from human resources they'd sent over, the documentation of both the male and female employee salaries for the last ten years, and it did appear that this was pointing in the direction of a smear campaign.

Easton allowed me to sit in on the Zoom call with Bruno King, and things couldn't have gone better.

"I look forward to meeting in person and making this official with a handshake, but I do believe that Holloway, Jones, and Waterman is the firm for me. I've met with Charles a few times, and he said that you would be the man in that courtroom standing beside me. You'll start your investigation tomorrow in the city, so as long as you'll be staying at the hotel, let's just have dinner there."

"That sounds great, Mr. King."

"Please. We're about to be spending a lot of time together, so call me Bruno." He nodded. "And bring your pretty assistant, too."

My shoulders stiffened, and I didn't miss the way Easton's hand fisted on the desk. "My apologies if I wasn't clear. I thought I'd introduced you to Henley Holloway, our newest attorney at the firm, and she will be assisting me in court if we don't end up settling."

He had *introduced me.*

Bruno had apparently just decided to ignore the fact that I was an attorney.

"My apologies, Ms. Holloway. Such a pretty little thing. It's hard to believe she could be both brains and beauty."

Seriously? This pompous ass needs to learn some manners.

"Henley graduated first in her law school class at Harvard. She's brilliant. So I'd ask that you show her the respect she deserves."

Well, I hadn't expected that. We wanted to sign this client, and pissing him off would be the kiss of death. But Bruno didn't appear offended in the slightest.

"Not a problem. I have a lot of respect for beautiful women." He laughed harder now, and his face was red as he started to cough. "All right. So how about dinner tomorrow night at 7:00 p.m. I'll meet you at the steakhouse, and your rooms will be ready for you when you arrive."

"That's very generous. Thank you," Easton said. "We'll be there."

He ended the call and turned to look at me where I sat beside him.

"What a dick," he hissed.

"Well, he's an important dick, right?"

"Let me ask you this, they are being accused of mistreating women, and he just insulted our female attorney on the call. Is that a bit of a red flag to you?"

"Yes," I said. "But your favorite color is red, remember?"

"I'm serious, Henley."

"Well, everything in those files line up. So Bruno King can be a pig and still not mistreat female employees when it comes to fair compensation, right?"

"I don't know. But I guess we're going to find out, aren't we?"

"My father and the other partners are going to want to sign him regardless of what we find out when we start interviewing employees. You know that."

He pushed to his feet. "I do. But they aren't the ones going to court with him. We are. So we'll decide if this is a good move or not."

"Yes, we will. But first, we must dominate at pickleball tonight," I said, my voice was all tease.

"Get back to work. I'll pick you up on my way to the club tonight."

He was back in business mode and rushing me out the door once again. But when I glanced over my shoulder on my way out, I found his heated gaze on me.

And I didn't mind it at all.

thirteen

. . .

Easton

MY IRRITATION WAS at an all-time high. The office had sung "Happy Birthday" to me at lunch, and I'd pasted a smile on my face because I was trying to take Henley's advice to heart. It made sense.

I could grieve and still let people wish me a happy birthday.

Even if it was the last thing that I'd felt like doing.

But now I was playing pickleball with two dickheads from Colton County who were relentlessly hitting on my partner.

And it pissed me the fuck off.

But did I intentionally spike the ball that hit Gary Rite in the groin?

I don't think so.

I mean, I sure as shit wouldn't swear to it in a court of law.

I'd definitely plead the fifth.

"What the fuck, Easton?" Gary whined as he lay on the ground, and now Henley was on the other side of the court, helping him up.

His doubles partner, Brendan Williams, was trying not to laugh as he assisted him to his feet.

We'd played them year after year, and they were Colton County's best doubles team, and they were sore losers.

I stood at the net, acting just as surprised as he was. "I can't always put the ball where I want it to go, buddy. Sorry about that."

"I need to take five and drink some water." The motherfucker was holding on to Henley like she was his lifeline, and his partner decided it was the perfect time for a bathroom break.

And then Gary did the most fucked-up thing of all when she offered to walk him to the bench so he could sit and drink some water.

He glanced over his shoulder and winked at me.

He fucking winked.

I should have hit him right in the dick with that ball.

"Easton," Henley called out. "Can you grab him a water, please?"

I rolled my eyes and made my way over to the water station, where my brother, Rafe, was standing and filling up his cup. "How's it going, brother? Things look a little heated over there."

"Gary Rite is a dick," I said as I pulled out a cup and filled it for him.

"You aren't *wrong*," he said, before breaking out in laughter. "Get it… Rite. Wrong."

"Yeah, I fucking get it. But I'm not in kindergarten, nor am I in the joking mood. He's openly flirting with my partner, and now he's pretending to be hurt."

"I don't know. I was watching. You gave him a pretty good shot to the groin. A little to the left, and he wouldn't have use of his schlong." He smirked, just as Bridger walked over.

"He's working it. He just wants Henley's attention. That fucker winked at me after he pretended to be injured."

"Since when do you let people get under your skin?" Bridger pushed Rafe out of the way so he could fill his water bottle.

"It seems our dear brother doesn't like anyone flirting with his coworker. You two seem to spend a lot of time together, huh?" Rafe smirked. "Is something going on there?"

I started walking backward when Henley shouted my name

like I was the goddamn water boy. "Listen, it's about respect. She's my partner, and he's being a douchebag. I'm a gentleman, and I can't stand by and allow that."

"A gentleman who tried to hit a dude in the dick with a pickleball?" Bridger said, as Rafe burst out in hysterical laughter.

I flipped them both the bird.

I walked over to where Gary and Henley were sitting.

"It's about time, man. I'm parched." Gary reached for the water, and then the bastard waggled his brows at me when Henley wasn't looking.

This fucking guy.

Brendan came jogging over and asked Gary if he was okay.

"He's fine," I grumped. This clown was playing everyone.

Henley shot me a look and turned her attention back to the dickhead, who was moving to his feet. "Do you think you're okay to play?"

"Yeah. I'm fine. I've got to go meet my grandmother at her nursing home after this, so I can't afford to be hurt and let my favorite girl down," Gary said with a shrug.

Are you fucking kidding me right now?

I glanced over at Brendan, and he was smiling, because he knew the dude was pissing me off.

"Well, then, let's finish this game so you can go to the nursing home and then volunteer at the Boys and Girls Club after to bake cookies," I hissed.

He smirked and gave me a nod as I stormed around to the other side of the court.

"What is your problem?" Henley snipped as she moved in front of me.

"My problem? That dude is playing you."

"You and I both know that you hit him on purpose," she said, close to my ear so only I could hear her.

Roses and jasmine filled the air around me, and I hit my breaking point.

Enough is enough.

"Why do you wear perfume to fucking pickleball?" I grumped, and her eyes widened.

"You know what, Easton? I think you actually need to see a real therapist to deal with these ridiculous outbursts." She whipped around, getting into position, and I let a loud, fake chuckle leave my lips.

"You could just stop wearing the perfume," I said, as I bounced the ball a few times before serving it.

This was now just a formality. We were already killing them.

The next fifteen minutes were a joke. They weren't making any effort to engage in this game. I may as well be out here on my own because they were barely returning the ball, and Henley had copped a big attitude and was letting the few balls that made it over the net come to me.

"You could pitch in and hit a few," I growled, as I got ready for the final serve.

Game point.

"Why? You're a one-man show."

And that's the way I like it.

I served the ball, and they both attempted to get it, but neither made contact, and the game was over.

See ya around, losers.

Bridger, Rafe, Clark, and Axel all stood on the side of the court, watching, as our little medical emergency had caused our game to go well over the allotted time.

"Good game, guys," I said to Gary and Brendan, and they both glared at me and then said a lengthy goodbye to my teammate.

I walked over to meet the guys, and they were already laughing.

"Good game, but let's try not to injure the opponents so blatantly," Clark said.

"You're a professional hockey player. You hurt people for a living," I reminded him.

"Are you seriously comparing hockey to pickleball? You

don't see a lot of brawling on the pickleball court, brother." He laughed, just as Henley walked over.

"I think I smoothed things over," she said.

"You don't need to smooth shit over. What did you say?" I raised a brow.

"I told them you were frustrated with your erectile dysfunction medication and that you felt like a failure in the bedroom, so you were just flexing your manliness on the court."

Now everyone was laughing hysterically, aside from me. They were all high-fiving her as we started walking toward the parking lot.

"You did not tell them that," I hissed.

"Of course, I didn't. Stop being a baby." She bumped me with her shoulder. "I told them that you were upset because someone at the office found out your secret that you have three nipples. And throw in the fact that you're lactating, and it was just too much for you."

My brothers and Axel were laughing so hard they had tears running down their faces.

It wasn't that fucking funny.

"Did you learn this particular level of humor at Harvard, Princess?" I said, trying not to join in the laughter, even though she had a gift for lightening the mood.

"Nope. This is called street smarts, Evil Genius."

"I don't think anyone can put this guy in his place quite like you do. It's an impressive skill." Rafe gave her a hug and clapped me on the shoulder as they all said their goodbyes.

I opened the passenger door and waited for her to get in the car.

We were quiet on the drive home.

I pulled into her driveway, and she turned to face me when I put the car in park. "Why were you so mad on the court? It was a little ridiculous, even for you."

"Even for me? What does that mean?"

"It means what it means, Easton." Now she was pissed

again? "It's the whole whiplash thing. One minute you're fine, and we're playing a game, and then the next, you're spiking a ball at your opponent. One minute, you're talking to me in your office, and the next, you're abruptly telling me to leave."

"This whole whiplash accusation is getting old, Princess. When I tell you to leave, it's because we're done, and it's time to get to work. And when I hit that jackass with a ball, it's because he had it coming. I don't stand on ceremony. If someone is acting like a dick, I'm going to call them out."

"Or randomly hit them with a pickleball?" She shook her head in disbelief.

"Po-tate-to, Po-tot-to."

She groaned and pushed out of the car, and I jumped out and hurried around. "Don't be a gentleman after you've acted like a complete asshole." She had her hands on her hips. "I don't need you to walk me to the door. I can get there myself."

Un-fucking-believable.

"Are you fucking kidding me right now?" I ran after her up the stairs, just as she turned around with her back pressed to the door.

"No. I'm dead serious. I won't play pickleball again with you if you're going to behave like a child. I'll be on someone else's team."

"I'm the captain. I decide who plays on what team." I raised a brow.

"And I'm the sub, and I can make myself unavailable."

My hands were on each side of her head, resting against the door.

Again.

We were back in this same place.

My face was so close to hers, I could lean down, and my mouth would be on hers.

"I don't think so."

"You don't think so?" she huffed. Her chest was rising and

falling rapidly. I glanced down to see her nipples poking through her tank top.

What the fuck was this?

We were clearly attracted to one another. But I knew better.

"Nope. I think you'll come back and play with me again."

"You underestimate me, Easton Chadwick." She held her chin up, but her chest arched as if she were desperate for contact.

Have I ever wanted to kiss anyone this badly?

My hand moved to the side of her neck, my thumb stroking her jaw.

"I don't underestimate you, Princess. You're misreading me."

"Why'd you hit him with that ball?" she whispered.

"Because he was flirting with you, and I didn't like it."

Her lips turned up in the corners. "Why didn't you like it?"

"I don't know," I said, as my nose traced along the bridge of her nose. "And that's the God's honest truth."

Fuck.

I wanted her so badly I couldn't think straight.

She pushed up on her tiptoes, her lips grazing against mine. My dick was so hard it threatened to tear through the fabric of my shorts.

"Is it because you want me all to yourself?" she asked.

"That's not really my thing. I'm not that guy."

"Maybe I don't want you to be," she said, and I nipped at her mouth.

"Really? You don't want me all to yourself, Princess?"

"Nope. I think you'd annoy me if I had to deal with you all the time." Her words were breathy, and her hands fisted in my tee as she held me there.

"It wouldn't be wise to cross the line." My other hand moved to the back of her head, and I wrapped her ponytail around my fingers.

"Well, it wasn't wise to hit someone with a pickleball, either." Her voice was gruff. "But that didn't stop you. How about we don't overthink it? It's a kiss. Maybe we'll hate it."

"I hope we fucking hate it." I nipped at her ear.

"Just kiss me already, Chadwick."

It was like a gun had gone off at the starting line of a race. My mouth crashed into hers with a startling desperation.

Her lips parted, granting me access, and our tongues tangled. *Desperate and hungry and needy.*

My hands settled on each side of her face, tilting her head slightly as I groaned into her mouth.

Her lips were soft, her mouth was sweet, and my dick was rock hard as she ground up against me.

Her fingers tangled in my hair, tugging me closer.

I couldn't get enough.

We couldn't get enough.

I'd never kissed a woman like this.

A ringing startled me from the haze.

I pulled back, and her gaze was wild with need, her lips pink and swollen.

"That must be the universe telling us to stop," I hissed as I stroked her cheek.

"Don't be dramatic. It's just my cell phone." She pulled her phone from her purse and groaned. "It's my dad."

"Take it. This never happened. I'll see you tomorrow." I walked backward down the steps.

Retreating.

It's what I did best.

fourteen

· · ·

Henley

THAT HAD BEEN SOME KISS. And of course, he'd run off immediately.

I shouldn't be surprised.

The man was a walking red flag.

I should have charged him a dick tax for kissing me like that, and then cutting it off abruptly. In fact, he should just pay a daily dick tax to me for as much as he pissed me off.

I pushed the door open, and the phone continued to ring because my father didn't like being ignored. I dropped my purse on the entry table and put the phone to my ear.

"Hey, Dad."

"Hey, sweetheart," he said. "Why do you sound like you're out of breath?"

Because I just had a hot make-out session with your senior partner on my front porch.

No? Too much?

"I just got home from a pickleball tournament." I made my way to the kitchen, flipping on lights as I moved through the house.

"I'm glad you're getting out a little. I know it's always hard when you first move to a new place."

"Says the man who's lived in the same home since I was born." I chuckled.

"Right. I don't like change."

"I'm looking forward to seeing you tomorrow night. We're going to stay over in the city for a few days so we can start meeting with employees and begin the interviews."

"That sounds like a great plan. Will Waterman is going to join us, and you remember Jamison, right?"

"Dad," I groaned. "Please don't make things more awkward than they already are."

"Sweetheart, he's Will's son and a senior partner. He'll be a managing partner someday. He just got back in town from vacationing abroad, and he heard you would be there. He wants to sit in on the meeting with Bruno, and seeing you is just an added perk."

My father and Will had been best friends my entire life. They'd always tried to push me and Jamison together, and it was awkward as hell. Jamison was a few years older than me and was just not my type. He was pretentious and a little too self-focused for my liking.

"Why is he coming to the dinner? This is Easton's client. I understand why you and Will are joining us, but it makes no sense to have Jamison there."

"He works for the firm. This is potentially the largest client we've ever signed. We want to show up and let Bruno King know that we're a firm that works as a team."

"Just don't play matchmaker again, okay? I'm there to assist Easton and show Bruno King that I'm a valuable member of this firm. This is a big opportunity for me. I don't need my dad trying to set me up with his best friend's son. It's not happening."

"Sweetheart, I would not do that to you."

"You've done it before, Dad," I reminded him.

"We're all going to be professional at the meeting. But I don't know why you've ruled things out with Jamison. You're living here now, and you're out of school, so the timing couldn't be better."

I poured myself a large glass of water and pulled out the premade salad I'd bought at the store yesterday.

"I'm living in Rosewood River, not the city, remember?" It had been an intentional decision to work out of this office. I didn't want to be in the same office with my father because I knew everyone would act differently to me there. Not that it wouldn't happen here, but it would be easier to establish myself without him hovering around me all the time.

"It's a thirty-minute drive, sweetheart. People date people that live on different coasts."

"Aren't you the one who has instilled in me how important it is to focus on my career? And aren't you also the one who warned me to be careful with Easton Chadwick when I came to work here, calling him a legal Casanova?" I laughed at the memory. "Yet you're trying to push me together with Jamison?"

He chuckled. "Easton is a different beast, Henley. The reason I wanted him to mentor you is that he's the best. There are no other senior partners at this firm who are not the legacies of the managing partners. Easton is brilliant, no doubt about it, and that's why we bent the rules and gave him the title that he wanted. But his success is because he's married to his job. We need him. Everyone in this city, in this state, knows who he is. His track record is unparalleled. We wouldn't have landed a big fish like Bruno King if it weren't for Easton. So yes, I wanted you to work with the best."

"And Jamison is also a senior partner, but you want me to date him?" I chuckled, but it oozed sarcasm.

"I'm just saying, Jamison would be a great partner. And it would be the joining of two very affluent families. Imagine what that would do for the firm. Two managing partners and board members voting together on things. There's a power in that."

I poured the dressing over my salad and closed the lid before shaking it aggressively because I was irritated.

"Okay, let me make this perfectly clear." I popped the lid open and dumped the salad into a bowl. "I'm not going to date Jamison. I'm not interested in a romantic relationship with that man."

"Okay, okay, I'm sorry. Let's change the subject. Tell me how working for Easton is going?"

He's sexy and brilliant and by far the best kisser I've ever met.

"It's going well. He's a hardass, but I'm learning a ton. I'm really happy that I get to assist him with King Hotels. It's going to get a ton of media attention, and I'm guessing it'll go to trial, so I'll get to experience all the different aspects from start to finish."

"Yes. This is a huge case. I'm looking forward to seeing you shine." He paused. "Do you think you'll want to come back to the city in a few months, after you've finished shadowing Easton?"

"I bought a home here," I reminded him. I'd researched this town quite a bit before I decided to move to Rosewood River. I hadn't moved here on a whim. I'd thought about it long and hard. "I plan to stay here, Dad."

"All right. It never hurts to have two homes, and you could run the office in the city," he said.

"I'm happy. I'm exactly where I want to be."

"I'm sorry. It's been a long time since I've had you living near me. I know I'm saying all the wrong things, but just know that I'm incredibly proud of you."

I sighed. He was impossible to be mad at. His heart was good, but his words were a different story. "I know. We'll figure it out together. It's new for me, too. So how about tomorrow night, you treat me like any other attorney working at the firm."

"I can do that. I've got a call coming in. Love you, sweetheart."

"Love you, too." I ended the call and made my way outside with my salad and drink. I stared out at the water and found my center again.

It had been a day.

And tomorrow was going to be even crazier.

––––––

I hadn't slept well. I'd made out with the guy who mentored me, and now I was going to be driving with him to the city and working even closer with him over the next few days.

Easton had sent a text last night that he'd pick me up first thing in the morning. He wanted to get to the hotel and start going through all the files that Bruno King was having brought over to us at the hotel. We had our work cut out for us. There were three women suing the company for sex discrimination, and it was our job to prove that it hadn't happened. According to the few things that had been shared with us thus far from their HR files, it appeared there was no wrongdoing on the company's behalf.

There was a knock on the door, and I grabbed my rolling suitcase and pulled the door open. I didn't know if it would be awkward after that kiss last night. But he said hello and took my suitcase, acting completely normal. When we were on the road, he'd told me that he had to take a call from a client just as the phone rang. He probably planned it so he could avoid any conversation with me.

He was clearly horrified that he'd kissed me because he'd run away right after.

"This never happened."

That's what he'd said to me.

My father had mentioned that Easton was married to his job, and he was probably right.

Falling for Easton Chadwick wasn't an option.

I shouldn't have kissed him.

It was unprofessional and a one-way trip to heartache.

I knew better.

But it's all I could think of.

As a girl with some daddy issues buried deep in there, it didn't surprise me that I was attracted to a man who worked crazy hours and didn't do relationships. I purposely tried to date guys like Pete Powers because they were the complete opposite. But that hadn't panned out for me either.

I loved my father. He loved me. But I had always fought hard for his attention.

I hated it.

Yet here I was.

Trying to get the attention of a man who wasn't interested in me.

But what if this was just an attraction?

What if I didn't want to date him, and we kept it casual?

I'd talked to Lulu about it last night, and she'd made me feel much better, reminding me that you could be attracted to a man that you didn't want to pursue a relationship with.

People did it all the time.

I'd never had a fling, and a make-out session on my porch was hardly a scorching fling, but it didn't have to be a big deal.

Maybe this was all part of me evolving as a woman in my twenties.

"You're awfully quiet," he said, pulling me from my thoughts, and I realized he'd ended his call.

"You were on a call."

"And you looked like you were deep in thought." He glanced over at me. "Everything okay? Are you upset about last night?"

I rolled my eyes. "No. That was nothing."

"That was nothing? Don't belittle it. It was a fucking awesome kiss."

I shook my head in disbelief. "You're the one who said it never happened. So why are we even talking about this?"

"Because you're being quiet."

"You are the most aggravating man I've ever met. You're offended that I'm being a little quiet today, which is mostly because you were on a phone call until two minutes ago?"

"I'm just making sure you're okay with everything. I shouldn't have done that. It was my fault," he said, his voice low and deep.

I sighed. "Let me guess… you're worried that I'm going to be upset, and my father is going to find out, and that's going to affect your chances of getting your name on the door."

He pulled off the freeway and didn't speak for a few seconds before he made his way to the side of the road abruptly and put the car in park. "Are you kidding me right now?"

I glanced out the window, shocked that he'd pulled over on the shoulder of the road to discuss this. We'd been in the car this whole time, and now he wanted to talk about it?

"Why are you so offended? It's the truth."

"It's not the truth, Henley. I don't have a problem with the truth. I will always be straight with you, regardless if you think I'm hot and cold or give you whiplash, or whatever the fuck you call it." He let out a huffy breath, motioning his hand between us. "I'm struggling with this."

"You're struggling with what? The fact that we kissed, and you're afraid my father will find out?" I said, not hiding my irritation.

"For fuck's sake, this is not about your dad. I mean, obviously, I work for him, and I'm sure he'd be pissed, but I don't give a fuck. He has nothing to do with me struggling."

"Let's hear it, Evil Genius. Why are you struggling? Once you kiss a woman, you can't stand the sight of them? Or, let me guess, you've got regrets because it happened? It's ridiculous, really," I huffed.

"I don't fucking regret kissing you. I've been struggling because I've wanted to do it for a while." He raised a brow when my gaze met his. "But I'm not that guy, Henley. I'm not going to show up with flowers and ask you to dinner. I don't date because I don't have time."

"What makes you think that I want to date you?" I smirked, and the corners of his lips turned up.

"I thought it was your thing."

"It is, normally. But I was just thinking about it, and it's not like my way has been working out all that well for me. I'm twenty-five years old. I can have a fling if I want to."

His tongue moved along his bottom lip, and I tried hard not to react, but I squeezed my thighs together to stop the ache that was building. "And kissing me, that's your idea of a fling?"

"No. I barely remember it," I said over my laughter.

I was lying, and he knew it.

"It was a damn good kiss, Princess. Feel free to have a fling with me anytime you want."

"I'll keep that in mind if the mood strikes me," I said, as he pulled back out on the road, heading to the hotel.

And I had a feeling the mood would definitely strike again.

fifteen

. . .

Easton

WE'D SPENT the day going over all the files that Bruno had sent over in a conference room at the hotel. Tomorrow, we'd be interviewing employees and investigating every possible angle so we would be prepared.

The way to win cases was to know what you were getting into. What you were dealing with.

You lost a case when you were caught off guard.

I would never be caught off guard.

I did the work, and I prepared for every single angle that could come my way.

But I had the greatest distraction I'd ever faced working beside me, and to say I was frustrated would be a massive understatement.

Henley was definitely fucking with me. She'd bent over the table, reaching for a file multiple times.

Did I mention she had the most perfect ass?

Like if you were to line up the best butts on the planet—those of supermodels, athletes, and women with shit injected into their ass cheeks—hers would stand out amongst them all. It was small but perfectly peach-shaped. Like she'd done thousands of squats just to mess with my head.

And her perfume… it was obviously injected with some sort of sexual stimulant.

I was sure of it. I'd smelled roses and jasmine before, and I hadn't reacted this way.

The worst part? Henley Holloway seemed completely unaffected by me.

But that kiss.

That fucking kiss.

I never should have let that happen because now I couldn't think of anything else.

How many women had I kissed in my lifetime?

Too many to count.

Yet only one was haunting me.

I knocked on her hotel room door, which was directly across from mine. We'd both been put in large suites on the same floor.

"Hey, let me just grab my purse," Henley said, and I stepped inside her room.

It was exactly like mine, only flip-flopped in the layout. She wore a black dress that ended just below her knees, and it hugged her curves in all the right places.

It was a perfectly appropriate dress for a work dinner event, yet all I could think about was hiking it up to her waist, dropping down on my knees, and burying my face between her thighs.

What the fuck is wrong with me?

"Hello? Are you okay?" She waved her hand in front of my face.

"What? Yes. I'm fine. Why?"

"I asked you if you were ready for the meeting, and you didn't respond." She held her purse up and headed to the door.

But my gaze was on the black lace bra that was lying on her bed. I snapped out of it and followed her to the door. "You know, Princess, everything does not require a response. Of course, I'm ready. I'm always ready."

She pulled the door open, and we made our way down the

hallway and toward the elevators. "Did my father tell you that Will and Jamison Waterman were attending the dinner?"

I held the elevator open for her so she could step on. My gaze moved from her nude heels up her legs, before I stepped in beside her. "Yes. I have no idea why Jamison would be coming. He's a wolf in sheep's clothing."

Her head fell back in laughter. "Tell me how you really feel."

"I am." I smirked. "Let me guess, you and him are old family friends."

"Yes. We do go way back, but it's not like we've kept in touch, so you can speak freely." She chuckled.

"He's a rich dude with a last name that carries some weight, so he went to prestigious schools and works at a top law firm in the country as a senior partner," I said, leaning against the wall and studying her. Her hair was tied back in some sort of twist at the nape of her neck, her face flawless, and lips plump and painted pink. She looked sexy as hell. "But Jamison knows very little about the law, and he has no desire to learn. He wants everyone around him to do the work while he sits back and takes the credit. I can't get on board with people like that."

"He's not all bad. He's just had everything handed to him, so he doesn't know anything different," she said as the door opened, and I held it so she could step off.

I leaned down close to her ear and whispered, "Haven't you had everything handed to you? Yet here you are, working your ass off."

And a perfect ass at that.

But before she could respond, her father, Will, and Jamison were waving us over. I shook each of their hands, and while Charles hugged his daughter and told her how beautiful she looked, I didn't miss the way Jamison was checking her out. His eyes roved over her ass.

The fucking audacity.

Sure, I'd checked her out. But not in public and not so blatantly. And definitely not when she was hugging her father.

I don't know, maybe it was jealousy.

I'd never been a jealous man, but I was exhibiting all the signs of it, according to my brothers and my cousin.

I still believed that Gary Rite had a pickleball to the groin coming.

"Gentlemen and one beautiful lady," Bruno King said as he approached. "I'm Bruno, and I appreciate you coming out to see me tonight."

We went around the group, making introductions, and he lingered a long time on Henley. I didn't miss the way Charles moved protectively closer, just as I was preparing to do so.

Meanwhile, the wolf in sheep's clothing didn't notice and was busy kissing our new client's ass.

My new client.

I didn't know why he was here. The partners always joined in on meetings like this when we were just getting started, but Jamison was here because his father brought him. He had nothing to contribute to this meeting. What I couldn't figure out was why he'd agreed to come. The man hated to work. He didn't do after-hours events that were for work unless there was something personal to gain.

And there was a lot of rumbling going on in the firm behind closed doors about Jamison having some major issues with alcohol and drugs. I didn't do company gossip, but Rosie was always in the know on all things happening at the firm.

She'd told me there had been several different episodes that had been covered up by his father.

I didn't give a shit, as I never saw the dude.

Yes, we had the same title at the office.

But he didn't do shit, so no one paid him much attention. I was out here proving my worth.

Bruno escorted us to the table in a private room in the back. I pulled out the chair for Henley, and Jamison quickly hustled to sit beside her.

I settled in the chair on the other side of her as Charles and

Will each took a seat beside Bruno. The table was round, so we'd all be able to speak comfortably.

I began the conversation, thanking Bruno for choosing to work with our firm and assuring him that we would do everything in our power to give him the best representation. Out of my peripheral, I could see Jamison whispering in Henley's ear.

He wasn't listening to anything I was saying, and over the next hour, it was clear why Will's son had joined us for dinner. And it had nothing to do with Bruno King or this hotel.

And everything to do with Henley Holloway.

She appeared notably uncomfortable every time he touched her shoulder or brought up a personal story from their childhood.

She was here to meet a client, not talk about Turks and Caicos, circa ten years ago.

Jamison had ordered multiple drinks and appeared heavily intoxicated.

I shot Charles a few knowing looks, and he gave me a quick nod. He was more than aware that he'd brought an employee who was not here for the same reasons that everyone else was here.

But the wine was flowing. The appetizers and salads had come and gone, and dinner was just being set down. Jamison managed to derail the conversation and the reason that we were here, talking about every fancy hotel he'd stayed at throughout his travels.

The South of France.

Paradise Island.

The Amalfi Coast.

Yeah, we get it, asshole. You're rich.

But so is everyone at this table, and we aren't fucking flaunting it.

Charles was clearly surprised, and I hadn't missed the looks he'd shot at Will, who appeared extremely uncomfortable. I'd always liked Will. He was a good man, and he clearly loved his son. He tried like hell to build Jamison up every chance he had. It had never mattered much to me until now.

Because at the moment, Jamison Waterman was fucking up my meeting.

And that was not okay with me.

"So, we're looking forward to meeting with the employees tomorrow," Henley said as she spoke directly to Bruno, making an attempt to steer the conversation back to the reason that we were here.

"Yes. All the people who work for me have been told to be open with you and give you whatever you need." Bruno cut into his steak. "I'm sure it won't take long to dig through it all. We have nothing to hide."

They never do. Until they do.

"We will keep you updated. We're planning to be here for three to four days, and then we'll be able to do everything else that we need remotely," I said, glancing over to see dumbfuck Jamison swing his hand and knock his cocktail over. He jumped up, and I watched as his elbow connected with the side of Henley's cheek. I was on my feet now and pissed to all hell.

I bent down and met her gaze. "Are you all right?"

She had a hand on the side of her face, and she nodded, but I didn't miss the way her eyes watered. "Yes. Yes. Of course. I'm fine."

She was trying to salvage this dinner, and I was ready to take off Jamison's head.

Charles's gaze landed on mine, and he gave me that knowing look.

Get this guy the fuck out of here.

I was already moving, one arm around Jamison, as I guided him away from the table. The waiter hurried over, and I stopped him and asked him to bring an ice pack to the lady at our table.

And I walked Jamison straight out of the restaurant and into the lobby and turned to face him. "What the fuck are you thinking, getting wasted at this dinner? You just hit Henley in the fucking face."

He shoved me back. "You don't even deserve a seat at this table. You're a small-town hick who impressed Charles Holloway. He'll tire of his shiny new toy eventually."

"Well, I've been here for four years. Longer than you. And by the looks of your father walking this way, I don't think I'm the one who needs to be worried about my job, asshole."

"What the actual fuck is wrong with you?" Will said through gritted teeth.

"I was having a good time, Dad. I think Bruno appreciated it. If I were a betting man, I'd say he's going to be requesting to work with me instead of Easton. Chadwick can't keep up with people of our caliber."

"Shut up right now, Jamison." Will turned toward me. "I'm sorry, Easton. I made an excuse to leave the table, and Charles is doing damage control. Go on back and see if you can work your magic. I'll get our driver to take us home."

I nodded, and he extended a hand, and I shook it. "We'll talk soon."

I turned to leave and glanced over my shoulder to see Will hurrying his son out of the hotel toward their waiting car.

I made my way back to the table, and Henley was chatting with Bruno as if nothing had happened, and Charles shrugged as if he wasn't sure what to do. I slipped into my seat beside her and glanced at her cheek to see that it was red and swollen.

"Did the waiter bring ice?" I asked close to her ear as Charles insisted Bruno let him cover the bill, and Bruno laughed at the idea.

He owned the hotel.

There would be no bill.

"I'm good. I'll ice it when I get to the room," she whispered, before clearing her throat and turning her attention back to our client when he spoke to her.

"I'm guessing that guy won't be getting a date anytime soon?" he said over loud, boisterous laughter.

I didn't laugh.

She'd been hit in the face, and I was fucking livid.

"We're old family friends and coworkers, so there will be no dates in our future." Henley's smile was forced, and I didn't miss the way her father winced when she looked at him.

"We'll touch base with you tomorrow, once we get started, Bruno." I made an effort to move the conversation back to work. This dinner had been a complete shitshow, and I was just grateful that Bruno hadn't left the table and fired us on the spot.

But right now, I didn't even care.

I wanted to get her out of here.

I wanted to get ice on her face and comfort her.

What the fuck is happening to me?

A few weeks ago, I would have sold my soul to sign this client. And now, he was here, and I couldn't get out of this place fast enough.

"Sounds good. I'm going to go meet my lady at the bar for a nightcap, but I'll speak with you all tomorrow." He pushed to his feet, and we did the same.

I saw a napkin wrapped around something bulky where Jamison had been sitting and lifted the fabric to see the bag of ice she'd hidden beneath the cloth. I took it from the table, tucking it inside my suit coat pocket.

We shook hands with Bruno, and he walked with us toward the bar and waved goodbye. Once we were in the lobby, I turned to Charles.

"What the actual fuck was that?" I hissed, anger radiating from my entire body as I turned to inspect Henley's face.

"I don't have a fucking clue." He turned toward his daughter. "Are you all right? I'm so sorry, sweetheart."

"I'm fine. But it was a bad decision to bring him, Dad. He derailed the conversation multiple times and then proceeded to get completely wasted."

Charles shook his head, placing a hand on his daughter's chin and turning her face to see the swollen area starting to bruise on her cheek. "It's inexcusable. I'll be phoning Will immediately. Jamison hasn't been coming to work much, and I guess it's time to sit down and have a hard talk with him."

"You think? He just made a fool of himself and made the firm look like a joke—and then he punches your daughter in the fucking face?" I ran a hand through my hair and tried to tamp down my anger.

Henley did what I least expected, and she laughed. She laughed hard. "Relax, Chadwick. He didn't punch me in the face. You're being dramatic. His elbow collided with my cheek. It was an accident. But yes, he was sloppy, and it's not a good look."

She placed a hand on my elbow, in what I guessed was a gesture to calm me down. I didn't miss the way Charles's eyes tracked the movement.

Did he track the movement when his rich prick lawyer elbowed his daughter in the face?

"All right. Everyone is upset, and I am, too. Let's call it a night. I'll phone Will when I get in the car. Let him know that we need to have a sit-down with his son. You go get ice on your face, and I'll be in touch in the morning."

Henley hugged her father, and I clapped him on the shoulder before watching him leave the hotel. He lived downtown, so his penthouse was only a few blocks away. I placed my hand on her lower back and guided her toward the elevators. Once we stepped inside, I pulled the ice from my pocket and placed it on her cheek.

"You stole the ice pack from the restaurant?" She chuckled, her hand moving over mine.

"I believe ice is free and can't be stolen."

"Nice argument, counselor." She smiled.

When the doors opened, we walked down the hall toward our rooms, and I didn't even hesitate. "I'm coming in with you."

sixteen

· · ·

Henley

I DROPPED my purse on the dresser and paused at the mirror hanging on the wall to inspect my cheek.

You would think there was a golf ball-sized bruise by the way Easton was overreacting. It was a little swollen with some light bruising.

"This is not that bad. I was expecting much worse by the way you were looking at me." I moved to sit beside him on the edge of the bed, and he turned to put the ice back on my face.

"It shouldn't have happened. It took everything in me not to knock his drunk ass out. I just didn't want to make more of a scene than he'd already made."

"He was like that as a teenager, too."

"How so?"

"He doesn't listen. He's sloppy. Loud. He knocked a cocktail on me at his father's second wedding that I attended with my dad. Will and my father have forever tried to broker that deal, but it's not in the cards."

"Broker what deal?" he asked.

"Me and Jamison dating. My father would love to merge the two families, which is never going to happen. I'm guessing after tonight, he'll stop pushing for that."

"One would hope." He shook his head in disgust. "He wouldn't be at that firm if his daddy wasn't a managing partner. He's a train wreck."

"I think my dad was really disgusted tonight. I'm guessing there's going to be some type of consequence after this."

"I hope so. That behavior wouldn't fly at any firm, and if he can't control himself, he has no business attending events." Easton lifted the ice pack to check my cheek.

"I think I'm good. We can take it off for a little bit."

"Does it hurt?" he asked, and the concern in his eyes made my chest squeeze.

"Not bad. I've been hit in the face with a tennis ball, and that hurt a lot more than this." I chuckled.

"You're tougher than you look, Princess." He pushed to his feet and placed the ice pack in the ice bucket sitting on the minibar.

"I hate that nickname, by the way."

"Princess?" He pulled off his suit coat and tossed it on the chair, before moving to stand in front of me with his hands on his hips. I could see every muscle in his shoulders strain against the crisp white fabric. "You don't like it?"

"Do I like that you think that I'm a rich, spoiled princess? Not really." I leaned back on my elbows and kicked off my stilettos.

"That's not why I call you that. Have you never researched the qualities of a princess?" His voice was all tease as he came to sit on the bed beside me.

"Always the attorney." I laughed. "Are you expecting me to believe that you've researched the qualities of a princess?"

"I told you I'll always be straight with you. I don't lie. I have no reason to. If I thought you were a rich, spoiled woman, I'd have no problem telling you that." He lay flat on his back, and I did the same, and before I knew it, we were both turning on our sides and facing one another.

"So tell me the qualities of a princess."

He reached over, his fingers gently tracing along the bruise on my cheek. "My sister, Emerson, loved that movie, *Princess Diaries*, and made me watch it too many times to count."

I smiled. The feel of his fingertips on my skin was so soothing that I struggled to keep my eyes open. "I love that movie."

"Right. Anyway, Emmy reminded me every day for months that princesses are kind and humble. They're good listeners, and they treat others with respect." His lips turned up in the corners. "That's how I see you, and that's why I call you Princess. I don't think you're spoiled at all. I think you're regal and strong. I think your work ethic could hold its own against anyone at the firm, including me. And don't even get me started on how fucking good you look in that pickleball skirt."

My teeth sank into my bottom lip as I processed his words. "You aren't going to mention my actual pickleball skills?"

"You're all right," he teased, as his thumb moved to my bottom lip, moving it from one to the other.

"You're all right, too. And I'm fine with the nickname now that you explained the meaning."

"I'm not a complete asshole, Henley."

"I know you aren't. I don't even think you're an evil genius anymore." I nipped at the tip of his thumb, and he chuckled when he pulled it back to graze my jaw.

"What am I, then?" he asked, and there was something very earnest in his gray eyes when he looked at me.

"I think you're a really good guy, but you don't want anyone to know it."

"Maybe I'm only that way with you."

"Why?"

"I don't fucking know. But I like you. More than I want to."

"I like you, too. It doesn't have to be a bad thing," I whispered, scooting closer.

"I want to kiss you again. But I don't know what it means, so I'm guessing we shouldn't go there."

"Do you know what it means every time you kiss a woman?" I asked.

He laughed, tugging me closer. "Such a smartass. I just don't want to fuck this up and make things awkward. We work together. Your father is my boss."

"And this involves no one but us. You want to kiss me. I want to kiss you. No one needs to know. And if it never happens again, we just look back on it as a fond memory. There are no expectations here, Easton. I know who you are. You've been very honest about it."

His gaze searched mine. "You're so fucking beautiful, Henley."

I didn't hesitate. I pushed forward, my hands tangling in his hair, as I tugged him down and kissed him hard. He rolled onto his back, taking me with him as I moved on top of him. His hands slid from my hair, down my back, and over my ass as he gave me a squeeze, and I chuckled and pulled back. "Did you just squeeze my ass?"

"This ass is a work of art. I think about it all the fucking time. I've wanted to give it a squeeze since the day you walked into my office."

He tugged me back down, his mouth on mine again, as we kissed and made out for the longest time. His hands were everywhere, as if he were trying to memorize every curve of my body.

My neck.

My arms.

My back.

My ass.

I ground up against him, frustrated that I couldn't get traction with my fitted black dress. And then he did the most unexpected thing, and his hands found the hem of my dress. He slowly tugged it up, and I pulled back to look at him. My dress was gathered around my waist, exposing my pink lace panties, and my legs settled on each side of his hips.

"I want to see you come apart, grinding up against my dick while you kiss me."

My breaths were coming fast. "You have a filthy mouth, Chadwick."

"Use my cock, Princess. Get yourself off for me." His voice was gruff, and I nodded slowly.

His hand tangled in my hair as he pulled me down. My mouth crashed into his, my lips parting on instinct as his tongue slipped inside, and I started rocking against him.

He was long and thick and hard beneath me.

I couldn't even believe I was doing this.

I was dry-humping this man with my dress gathered around my waist. My face was swollen and bruised, but here I was grinding up against him.

My mentor.

The man who drove me crazy most days.

And I didn't even care because nothing had ever felt better.

He had one hand on the side of my neck as he took the kiss deeper.

His other hand caressed my butt as I continued moving against him.

Faster.

Harder.

Desperate for release.

My body started tingling, my head slightly dizzy. I pulled back the slightest bit as white lights exploded behind my eyes, and I gasped his name. I went right over the edge as the most euphoric orgasm tore through my body.

I'd never experienced anything like it.

And we hadn't even had sex.

He continued rocking me against him, his hands running over the fabric covering my breasts, as I rode out every last bit of pleasure. I fell forward, my chest pressed to his, and my face nuzzled in the crook of his neck.

His hands ran up and down my back, as my breathing slowed.

I lifted my head to look at him, not feeling one ounce of embarrassment, which was shocking.

We weren't a couple.

We were just two people who were attracted to one another.

This was what people my age were supposed to do, right?

He was a guy who had flings.

One-nighters.

Hookups.

I could get on board with this.

I'd just had the most amazing orgasm of my life.

It was a win-win.

I reached between us for his zipper, but he wrapped his hand around my wrist to stop me. "Not tonight, Princess. Tonight was about you."

I groaned and rolled off of him, lying on my back beside him now, as I pulled my dress down and covered my face with my hands.

The embarrassment I wasn't feeling thirty seconds ago was here with a vengeance now.

"Oh, God. Did that just turn you off?"

"Turn me off?" His voice was deep, and he tugged my hand down and rolled onto his side to look at me. "Are you fucking kidding me? That was the hottest thing I've ever seen. You riding my cock right over the lace of your pretty panties and the fabric of my dress slacks. Needy and desperate for me. I fucking loved it."

"Yet you don't want more?"

"Henley." He paused, as I squeezed my eyes closed. "Look at me. Now."

My eyelids slowly lifted, and I forced myself to meet his gaze. "I loved that. Hell, if I were trapped on a deserted island, I could get off to images of you on top of me, rubbing up against my dick for the rest of my life, and be very content."

"So then, why do you want to stop?"

"Because you and I view sex differently." He tucked the loose strand of hair that had broken free behind my ear. "I don't want to push you or complicate things."

"I wanted to make you feel good, too," I said.

"You don't get it." His lips turned up in the corners. "Watching you get off was a fucking gift that I didn't even know I needed. You made me feel good. But if you unzip my pants right now, I won't want to stop. And one of us needs to think straight. This isn't the norm for you, and if you wake up with regrets, it's going to make things very awkward for us at work."

"You worry too much, Chadwick. I think flings might be my new favorite thing. I loved that. I don't know why I've waited so long to just have a no-strings-attached orgasm. I've been missing out."

He barked out a laugh. "Slow down there, Princess. Let's see how you feel after you sleep on it, and if you want to unzip my pants tomorrow after what happened tonight, you won't even need to ask."

"Yeah? You promise."

"Yep." He kissed my forehead and pushed up from the bed. "I'm going to go take a very cold shower and get some sleep."

I sat forward and watched as he grabbed his shoes and his suit jacket.

I pushed to my feet and followed him to the door. "Thanks for icing my face and giving me the best orgasm of my life."

"It's a gift." He shrugged.

I laughed as he tugged the door open and winked at me. "Let's be ready to go by 7 a.m. Meet me in the hallway."

"Deal. See you tomorrow."

The door closed, and I fell against it, closing my eyes as I processed all that had happened tonight.

I made my way to the bathroom and called Lulu, clicking the button for speakerphone as I washed my face and filled her in on all that had happened.

"In all the years that we've been friends, I've never been surprised by anything you've told me." She laughed. "You're usually so predictable in the best way. But this… this is the best phone call I've ever received from you."

"Come on. I dated a rocker who liked to eat gummies and have sex. That was a detour for me."

"Please. *You* didn't eat the gummies, and the sex was pretty vanilla. He just liked to stay in bed, and that shocked you. But this, this is the makings of great reality TV. I mean, you've got the drunk family friend who elbowed you in the face. The client dinner was a disaster, and then you went back to your room to ice your face and dry-hump your mentor." She was laughing hysterically now. "Welcome to being twenty-five and having some fun, Hen! I'm so proud of you."

"Thank you. I know it takes a lot to shock you, and I'm happy I could do that for you. You said that you had something to tell me."

"Well, my news is lame now, next to yours."

"Tell me, and I'll decide." I turned on the water in the tub because I needed to soak for a while and calm myself down from the excitement of the evening.

"Remember the fancy spa in the city that I told you about?"

"Yes. The one with the very good-looking male masseuse with spectacular hands?"

"That's the one. *Hector.* He has hands like a Roman god."

My head fell back in a fit of giggles. "Yes. I remember him now."

"Well, I had dinner with Elaine Wicker, the woman who lives in my building in 2B. I told you that she asked me to go have cocktails and dinner with her."

"Oh, yes. Elaine. The supermodel who also waits tables at the diner on the corner."

"Exactly. Get this. She goes to the same spa. She calls it the 'happy endings' spa. Drum roll, please." She paused for dramatic effect and made the sound of a drum by pounding on something. "Apparently, Hector does a whole lot more with his hands to Elaine. I couldn't believe it when she told me. He gave her a happy ending."

I gasped and laughed at the same time. "So, are you freaked out now that you know this?"

"Well, I mean, I guess I'm a weird mix of freaked out and offended. He's never made a move on me. I've been naked under that sheet dozens of times, yet all he does is massage me with those manly hands. But he's doing naughty things to Elaine?"

I shook my head in disbelief as I turned the water off and got undressed. "You would lose your shit if he touched you inappropriately, and you know it. He'd end up in the hospital after you karate-chopped him in the throat. You've taken more self-defense classes than anyone I know."

"Hey, a woman can never be too safe. And yes, I would throat-punch Hector if he'd touched me without permission. But I'm also wondering why he hasn't tried, you know?"

"You're insane," I said, placing the phone on the side of the tub and slipping beneath the water. "Imagine if the media got hold of that story, and you were accused of sexual acts at the spa. Your dad would lose his shit."

"Yeah, that would put him over the edge. He told me to keep my dating antics out of the press and find myself a normal man. The last thing I need is to be getting orgasms at the spa."

"Well, I'm getting them after work dinners, so there is that."

"You're a naughty girl, Henley Holloway. Maybe I've corrupted you after all these years."

"Maybe."

"So, you want to have a fling with this guy, huh?"

"I think I do. Look at us. I want to have sex with my coworker, and you need to find yourself a respectable boyfriend. This is so not us." I let my head rest on the back of the tub.

"I think I need a fling. I need something. I'm in a rut," she said.

"No more calls from unknown numbers?"

"I get them every day. I just don't answer. And he leaves these voice messages where he sounds distraught. But thankfully, he's on tour, so he won't be showing up at my door. The man is outrageous. He wants to bang other women on the road and then come back to me and act like it didn't happen?" she said. "I will never forgive him for what he's done and the humiliation he's caused me and my family."

"Nor should you. You deserve much better than a has-been rock star."

"He just sold out a stadium that holds sixty thousand people. He's not really a has-been, but thanks, bestie."

"Well, *he lost you*, and that makes him a dumbass. That's worse than being a has-been."

"I like this new side of you, Henley Holloway," she said.

"What side is that?"

"The one where you have a casual office hookup fueled by a dirty talker who gives you fabulous orgasms." She chuckled, her voice all tease. "Are you smoking a cigarette right now?"

"No. I'm taking a bath. Don't make me regret telling you what happened."

"You better keep me posted. I hope you make a move tomorrow."

"I'm hanging up," I said over my laughter.

"Love you big."

"Love you bigger."

"Make a move on the hot lawyer tomorrow!" she shouted, just as I ended the call.

I closed my eyes and sighed.

Making a move on my coworker was not really my style.

But when it came to Easton Chadwick, I was willing to break a few rules.

seventeen

. . .

Easton

I WAS IN A FOUL MOOD. I'd fucked my hand in the shower last night and again this morning. Yet I still had a bad case of blue balls.

How was that even possible?

I'll tell you how.

My coworker, Henley Holloway, had an evil side to her.

She'd purposely worn a fitted pink dress and some high fucking heels.

It hugged her ass, which was currently taunting me as she bent over the table and grabbed another file.

"Okay. You've got to stop fucking doing that," I hissed.

She'd been all smiles this morning while we ate breakfast. She hadn't said a word about what happened last night, and she seemed completely okay with everything. I'd prepared for it to be awkward.

I'd prepared for her to want to talk about it ad nauseam.

I'd prepared for her to be angry or hostile or something.

But nope. She was happy and calm and unaffected.

Un-fucking-affected.

And I was left with a pissed-off dick and two very angry testicles. Even though I'd given them relief, it wasn't enough.

Not with those eyes looking at me right now. That devious smirk plastered on her face.

"Stop doing what?"

"Bending over the table," I said, making no effort to hide my irritation. "Wearing sexy dresses. Laughing and smiling and acting relaxed."

"You need to take it down a notch, Chadwick." She smirked, coming closer. "I did not bend over the table. I barely reached for the file. My dress is very basic and comes past my knees and shows zero cleavage. And I'm not laughing or smiling. We're having normal conversation."

I groaned. "Whatever. You're pissing me off."

She narrowed her gaze, and then her mouth fell open. "Oh. Ohhhhhh. You're frustrated. You want me, don't you?"

"Don't flatter yourself, Princess. All men get blue balls."

"I thought you were going to take a shower last night. I figured you'd, you know, take care of business." She chuckled. She was enjoying this.

"I did. Twice. But it didn't work."

"Hmmm… what should we do about this?" She glanced down at her phone and then looked up at me. "We have twenty minutes until the first employee is scheduled to meet us here."

"And?"

"Follow me." She moved to the door and motioned for me to step out into the hall.

"I'll remind you that I'm the boss. You don't call the shots."

"Sure. You're the boss." She paused as she led me to the end of the hallway and glanced around. "It's still early, and no one is here yet."

I just stared at her, unsure what she was talking about, when she pushed the bathroom door open, reached for my tie, and pulled me in. It was a private bathroom, and she closed the door and locked it.

"What are you doing?" I asked. My voice was gruff, making it impossible to hide that I was completely turned on.

"You said that if I wasn't having regrets today, I could unzip your pants." She shoved me up against the door, and I raised a brow with surprise.

"You want to unzip my pants?"

"Yes. I do. Do you have a problem with that?"

"Take what you want, Princess," I said, as she dropped to her knees, and I nearly came in my pants at the sight of her looking up at me with those doe eyes and pretty plump lips.

Within seconds, she had my pants unzipped and pulled down, along with my briefs. My dick was swollen and hard as a rock, and her eyes widened as she wrapped her fingers around the base. I didn't miss the slight tremble in her hand, and I reached down and tipped her chin up so she was looking at me.

"You don't need to do this. I'm fine."

Her lips turned up in the corners. "Remember how you said watching me get off was a gift for you?"

"Yes."

"I want to make you feel good. So, this is as much for me as it is for you."

"Don't threaten me with a good time," I groaned just as her tongue circled the head of my dick.

I sucked in a breath when her lips wrapped around me, and she took me in. The feel of her wet, warm mouth along my shaft was almost too much.

My hand tangled in her hair as she worked me up and down. Over and over.

"Fuck, Princess," I said, watching my cock slide in and out of her swollen pink lips. "Such a good fucking girl, the way you take me in."

That spurred her on, and she took me deeper. She liked praise, and I was happy to give it.

Because this woman was good at everything.

I'd had plenty of blow jobs in my lifetime, but nothing like this.

The sight of this sexy woman down on her knees, wearing a

prim little dress with her perfect lips wrapped around my dick. Big sapphire blue eyes looking up at me like she was enjoying it as much as I was.

I gripped her hair harder—a warning that I was close.

But she just kept going.

Faster.

And then she moaned and took me a little deeper, and that was it.

A guttural sound left my throat, and I tugged at her hair one last time, giving her a chance to pull away before I unloaded in her sweet mouth.

But she didn't move.

She took every last drop and continued working me over as I bucked into her silky, warm mouth with fury.

My breathing slowed as I stopped thrusting, and she pulled back and wiped her lips with the back of her hand.

It was sexy and hot, and I just stared down at her in awe.

"Thank you." It was all I could think to say as she pushed to her feet and chuckled. She turned to the sink and washed her hands before patting her hair in place in the mirror.

"Now, will you be a little less grumpy for the rest of the day?" She smirked.

I tucked myself back in and zipped and buttoned my pants.

I tugged her close and held her chin between my thumb and my pointer finger. "Yes. And those fucking lips are magic."

"Really? Well, I'll take that as a compliment because I've never dropped to my knees in a public restroom before 8 a.m. on a workday."

I knew this wasn't the norm for her, which was why I knew messing around with Henley Holloway was a bad idea. But some of the best things in life come from bad decisions, right?

This blow job, for example.

Not my best decision getting a blow job from my boss's daughter in the hotel of our new client, but if I got fired right now, it would be worth it.

"When do I get to taste you?" I asked as I nipped at her bottom lip.

"Repeat hookups aren't really your thing, so how about we use the Easton Chadwick strategy on you?"

"What does that mean?" I asked.

"Let's see how you feel in a few hours, and if you want to unzip my dress after what happened this morning, all you'll have to do is ask."

I barked out a laugh. "Such a smartass. I wrote the book on casual hookups, Princess. I assure you, if you want to lift the hem of that pretty dress right now, I'll be on my knees so fast your head will spin. I'll bury my face between those gorgeous thighs and lick you and taste you until you're crying out my name."

Her face flushed, and I grazed my finger over the slight swelling on her cheek that she'd tried to hide with makeup.

"Pace yourself, Chadwick. We've got work to do. I'm trying to impress my mentor." She waggled her brows and stepped back, and I knew she was right because we had meetings that were starting any minute.

"He's already impressed." I kissed the tip of her nose and went to the sink to wash my hands. "How should we walk out of here?"

"I'll go first. You count to ten and then you can come out then."

"All right." I dried my hands and leaned against the sink and watched her leave.

I didn't count to ten, but I waited a few beats before stepping out and was startled when I heard Charles's voice from down the hallway.

Good Christ.

I needed to pull my shit together. I was definitely more relaxed now than I'd been thirty minutes ago. Hell, I was more relaxed than I'd been in the last few weeks. But I sure as shit hadn't expected to see her father after what had just happened.

"Good morning, Charles," I said, as I stepped into the conference room.

"Easton, good morning. I brought coffee." He handed me the cup. "I couldn't find either of you, and Henley said she'd gone to check on you because you'd been in the bathroom for a while. You all right?"

I kept my composure and glanced over at Henley, whose eyes were wide.

"Yes. That food last night was a bit rich for me." I took a sip of the coffee and patted my stomach. "But I'm feeling like a new man now. Never felt better."

She looked away, but I saw the corners of her lips turn up the slightest bit.

"Well, you always know how to rally when you need to. This man is a machine, Henley."

"Yes. I can see that." She cleared her throat. "So, we're going to meet with seven employees this morning, and then seven more this afternoon. We'll just be going over the basics. Getting a feel for their employment packages and their general feeling for the company. On paper, everything looks perfect."

"Sounds great. I just wanted to stop by on my way to the office and say hello. I'm meeting with Will in a few minutes. Jamison will most likely be taking some time away from the office. I'll let you know what we decide. Check in with me later." He kissed Henley's cheek and shook his head when he studied the small bruised area on her face. He reached for my hand and gave me a quick shake.

After he walked out the door, her head fell back in laughter. "I did not expect my father to stop by this morning."

We were playing with fire.

But for whatever reason, I didn't care.

"I don't think he suspected anything. Obviously, you thought of something quickly."

"I'm a woman of many talents." She chuckled. "Okay. Our first interview is with Cecilia Jacobs. She's worked for the company for fifteen years. She's got a management-level position, and she's being paid the same as her male counterpart."

"Great. I'm guessing this will be fairly easy. If everyone is paid the way they're supposed to be and treated respectfully, I can't imagine those women will have a leg to stand on."

"It's strange, though, isn't it?" she asked, glancing down at Cecilia's file.

"What?"

"Well, the energy and the money and the time that this would take for those women to pursue this. If you know you don't have a case, why go through it all so publicly?"

"Money does crazy things to people. Maybe they think they can make a quick buck." I shrugged. But I'd wondered the same thing, as well, when this case was brought to us. Going up against a big corporation would be costly and get a lot of media attention. The three women suing the company had mid-level positions. They didn't have the money to take this on. And three voices were not going to be heard over the thousands of voices singing the praises of the King Hotel Corporation.

There was a knock on the glass door, and I pushed to my feet as Henley did the same. We greeted Cecilia with a handshake and offered her the seat across from where we both sat.

The interview went smoothly.

Is there such a thing as too smooth?

Yes. Unfortunately, there is. And there were some red flags going off.

"Well, this was super helpful. I'm thrilled that you've had such a great experience working for King Hotels," Henley said as she thumbed through the papers in the file and paused to read something.

"Yes. This is a dream company to work for. Bruno King and his family are the most wonderful people, and they treat us all like family."

I call bullshit.

First, because she sounded like she was reading from a script. Second, because no place of work is always perfect.

"That's great to hear." I sipped my coffee.

"Just one last question," Henley asked.

"Sure. Ask me anything. I'm an open book, as are Bruno King and all the executives at King Hotels." Cecilia chuckled.

Like I said… I call bullshit.

"I'm just flipping through your pay scale over the years. When you were moved to the management position six years ago, it looks like you were paid on the lower end of the pay scale for the position. Your big raise came eight months ago?"

I glanced over at the file to see what she was looking at. That hadn't been in the original files that were sent to us, as there'd only been current salaries listed.

"Oh, yes. I think that's fine. I had to prove myself." She smiled, but I saw the way her hand trembled the slightest bit when she raised her coffee cup.

"Of course. Yes. That makes perfect sense." Henley smiled up at her. "Thank you so much for coming in today and for making this so easy for us."

"Like I said, I feel very fortunate to work for such a wonderful organization." She pushed to her feet, and I noted the layer of sweat covering her forehead.

We shook her hand and thanked her, and she left.

When I sat down, Henley was already going through another file. "This might not be as much of a slam dunk as we'd hoped."

"I'm getting that vibe, yes. Hopefully, there's an explanation for it," I said as the next employee knocked on the door.

Janet Burns had worked for the company for eight years, and she opened with the same line. "This is a dream company to work for. Bruno King and his family are the most wonderful people, and they treat us all like family."

I looked over at Henley, and she raised a brow.

This was definitely not going to be the clean-cut case that we were hoping for.

But for whatever reason, I didn't care.

I didn't mind going into the trenches with this woman on my team.

By my side.

It was a terrifying thought if I allowed myself to go there.

So I wouldn't.

I'd just focus on work.

It's what I did best.

eighteen

. . .

Henley

MY HEAD WAS POUNDING. We'd interviewed a total of fourteen employees on day one. It was a full day. We'd had lunch with Bruno King, who had clearly had his employees coached, but we didn't mention that. We remained neutral because we still had a long way to go.

And he was our client.

Easton and I rode up the elevator, and we were both quiet. It hadn't been what we'd expected today. We thought we'd spend a few days here, get a beat for everything, and start putting our defense together.

But the prosecutor would have a field day with these employees if he put them on the stand.

"What a day, huh?"

"There was only one good thing that *came* out of this day," he said, his voice low. His heated gaze met mine, and I could feel my cheeks flush.

"No pun intended." I shook my head and chuckled. "So, what do we do?"

"We figure it out. We interview more people. Someone will be truthful. But we've got our work cut out for us." He shrugged. "You hungry?"

"I could eat. But I'm also ready to get out of this dress and these heels, so I don't feel like going downstairs to the dining room."

"How about I order room service, and you go put on something comfortable and meet me in my room in twenty minutes, and we can come up with a plan."

"Sounds perfect," I said, as we stepped off the elevator and made our way down to our rooms.

I stepped inside my room and slipped off my dress, finding my favorite cozy sweats to wear. I tied my hair up on top of my head with my favorite peach scrunchie, then washed my face and padded back out to the room.

It had been a day.

There was a knock on the door, and I chuckled at Easton's impatience.

"I thought we agreed on twenty minutes," I said as I pulled the door open.

I didn't hide my surprise that Jamison Waterman was the one standing on the other side.

"Hey, Henley." His words slurred, and I stood in the doorway, blocking the opening so he wouldn't try to come in.

"What are you doing here, Jamison?"

"Well, I got reprimanded today by your father. By my father. Apparently, everyone thinks I'm out of control. They're making me take a leave from work. Your father could barely look at me. He claimed that I hit you in the face, so I came here to see for myself. And guess fucking what?" He widened his eyes dramatically. "You look fine to me."

I internally chuckled at how irritated I'd been when Easton or my father had pointed out the bruise, yet Jamison acting as if it wasn't there irritated me much more.

Denial is not a river, my friends.

"Listen, I don't think you did it on purpose. I'm not even angry at you, but I am concerned. And if you think showing up here drunk again to apologize and then get defensive and deny that anything happened—it's not a good look, Jamison."

"You always thought you were too good for me, didn't you?" He chuckled, ignoring what I'd said. "If you knew how many women want to line up to fuck me, you'd rethink being a bitch to me."

I startled at his words. Jamison had always been pretentious and cocky, but I hadn't seen this side of him. And now I'd been granted a front-row seat to two days in a row of his irrational behavior.

"You need to leave."

"I don't need to do jack shit, Henley. I came here to apologize, and you're going to listen to my fucking apology. You're the reason that I'm in this fucked-up mess. Because your father is making a big deal out of a little bruise on your fucking face." He was shouting now, and my heart raced at not only his tone, but at the look in his eyes.

They were hollow and empty.

Cold and distant.

I stepped back and pushed the door closed, just as his hand shoved against the wood to stop it, and he pushed back.

"What the hell, Jamison! Leave now!" I shouted, as he tried to push his way inside the room.

"You're not calling the shots, bitch!" His words stunned me.

Everything moved in a blur as he shoved my shoulders hard causing me to stumble.

Easton was suddenly there, and he grabbed Jamison by the back of the neck as he towered over him. He spun him around and slammed him against the wall across from my door and held him there.

"If you so much as lay a fucking hand on her, I will bury you so deep in the ground they'll never find you." Easton's voice was calm and deep. "Henley, call the front desk and tell them we need security."

I shoved a shoe in the door to keep it open, because I was

worried about Easton being alone with that lunatic. I dialed the front desk, my voice shaking as I told them we needed security.

When I ran back out to the hallway, Easton had somehow moved Jamison to the floor, face down, and he had a foot resting on his back. It didn't look like he was applying a lot of pressure, just keeping him still.

He looked up to see me. "Did you call security?"

"Yes." My voice wobbled. "They're on their way."

"Okay, grab your cell phone and dial your father and hand me your phone."

"She's a fucking bitch!" Jamison shouted from the floor, and I was completely stunned by his behavior. We'd never had an issue or even an argument in all the years I'd known him. I'd never liked him much, but I didn't know he was so aggressive and angry.

I dialed my father and hurried back out to the hallway while the phone rang, to see Easton applying more pressure and telling Jamison to shut his mouth.

I handed him the phone.

"Charles, it's Easton." He paused. "Jamison just showed up here, and he's extremely intoxicated. He just got aggressive with Henley and tried to push his way into her room. We've called security."

He listened intently as footsteps in the distance had me turning to see four security guards jogging our way.

"They're here. This ends now. I won't allow him to be around her. Do you hear me?" Easton growled into the phone.

"Fuck you, Chadwick. You're a poor man's version of me," Jamison said, as the security guards told Easton to remove his foot, and they lifted him to his feet.

Easton ended the call, telling my father he'd call him back. I recounted what happened, and they informed us that there were cameras in the hallways, and the head of security was looking at the footage from the camera on our floor now.

"If the cameras collaborate your story, he will be leaving this hotel in a police car," one of the men said. Three of the security guards surrounded Jamison as he shouted about getting them all fired and going on about how they didn't know who they were messing with. They escorted him down the hallway and out of sight.

One security guard remained behind and apologized profusely.

"How the fuck did he know her room number and get up the elevator without a room key?" Easton barked at the man. "This is a fucking high-end hotel. How does that shit happen?"

"Sir, we're looking into that now. I'll get back to you as soon as I have more information. I'm terribly sorry that this happened." He held up a hand. "Can you please write down your cell phone numbers, and I'll phone you in twenty minutes?"

Easton jotted both of our numbers down, and I thanked the man for getting here so quickly. He made his way down the hallway toward the elevators, and Easton turned toward me and opened his arms, and I walked right into them on instinct. It was the first I'd noticed that he had no shirt on, as he was wearing a pair of gray joggers slung low on his hips, and his hair was wet. He smelled like mint and sandalwood. I rested my cheek on his chest.

"I'm sorry. I was in the shower, and when I came out, I heard shouting. I'm so fucking sorry I didn't get here sooner. Did he hurt you?"

I pulled back. "No. I just, I don't know what's going on with him. He's out of control. I think he was prepared to push his way into my room, so I'm grateful that you came when you did. What the hell was that?"

"I don't know. I hadn't seen him in quite a while before last night. The dude barely works and is usually remote and traveling, from what I've heard. I don't know why they keep him on. And clearly, he's got issues with alcohol and possibly drugs. He's completely out of control." He led me toward my room as my phone rang in his hand. "Grab your key so we can close your door. Let's go to my room. This is your father, and we need to let him know you're all right."

I nodded and hustled inside and grabbed my key. He didn't leave my doorway. He waited as he answered the phone.

"She's all right. Yes, they have him downstairs." Easton motioned for me to come across the hall, where he had the top door latch opened to keep the door from closing all the way. I pushed inside, and he followed me, letting my door close behind us. "Here, I'm going to put you on speakerphone so you can talk to her."

"Henley, sweetheart, I'm so sorry."

"It's fine, Dad. No one got hurt. He was just—I don't know, he's out of control."

"Yeah. I haven't seen him in several weeks, and I had no idea things were this bad. He works remotely most of the time, and Will had shared that Jamison had been traveling this summer, so I just thought we'd missed one another at the office because I certainly don't go in every day anymore. But after meeting with Jamison today, it was clear that things are not good." He cleared his throat.

"What does that mean?" Easton asked.

I dropped to sit on the bed as Easton paced in front of me.

"It means that Will opened up to me before Jamison arrived at our meeting this morning. Apparently, Jamison has a huge gambling issue, which they've been trying to hide for some time. He owes a lot of people money, and he's taken large chunks of cash from his trust. Will tried to keep it hidden from the firm to protect his son. He and Bethany sent Jamison to Italy for a few weeks, thinking the time away would help. But clearly, he just spent weeks drinking excessively and going further into debt." Bethany was Will's first wife, Jamison's mother, and I'd always liked her.

"Jesus. You don't just ignore a fucking problem and think a luxury vacation will solve it. They sent an addict away and probably gave him a credit card with no limit. That's not going to fix the situation," Easton hissed.

"I think everyone realizes that now. Will thinks he's mixing alcohol with drugs and digging a deeper hole into his gambling problem. But I don't know why the hell he came to see my goddamn daughter. He is no longer employed by the firm as of today, and Will and Bethany have him booked on a flight tomorrow to go to rehab. He needs help."

"Well, he sure seems ready for rehab, considering he just showed up here wasted and threatening your daughter," Easton said, running a hand through his hair.

"I'm sorry, sweetheart. I've got a call into Bruno because this is his goddamn hotel. I want to know how a man was able to go to the front desk and get your room number and make it up the elevator without a room key. It's unacceptable. Un-fucking-acceptable!"

I'd heard my father angry before, but not like this.

"Dad, I'm fine. But I'm glad they are getting Jamison help. He's not okay."

"Will's beeping in. Let me find out what's going on." He sighed. "Easton, can you stay with Henley right now? I don't want her to be alone."

"Yes. We've ordered dinner, and I'll stay with her. Of course, I will."

"I'll talk to you both soon."

I looked into those steely gray eyes and shook my head when he ended the call. "What a mess."

The knock on the door had him moving in that direction, and I heard him speak to the person on the other side. "I'll take it from here."

He came walking in with the room service cart, filled with platters of food, and I chuckled.

"I hope you're hungry. I ordered a ton of food." He studied me as he pulled the silver domes off the plates.

"Wow. You're not kidding around."

He pulled the cart closer to the bed. "What looks good?"

"How about we split the burger to start?"

He cut the burger in half and brought the two plates over to the bed as he studied me. "Eat."

"You don't want to eat at the table?" I raised a brow and took a bite.

"I think you've had a day, and eating in bed is more relaxing."

"Never guessed you to be a caretaker, Easton Chadwick."

"Because I've never been one. I mean, aside from my family, I don't get too invested in people." He shrugged and then devoured his half of the burger.

"Meaning?"

He reached for the pasta and set a fork down on the napkin for me as he started eating the fettuccine.

"It means I'm invested in you."

My eyes widened. "Because you're my mentor?"

"No. Because I like you."

I chuckled because he said it like it was a death sentence.

"Liking me does not have to be a bad thing, you know."

"True." His lips turned up in the corners. "I think it was that blow job that really sealed the deal."

"Stop!" I shrieked, and he just laughed.

"Eat. You've had a long day."

"So bossy."

"You have no idea how bossy I can be, Princess." His heated gaze said more than his words did.

I took another bite of my burger, and he answered the incoming call from security. They informed us that Jamison had gone to the front desk and said that he was my boyfriend. He'd slipped the guy working at the front desk a hundred bucks to get my room number. They insisted he didn't get a key to the room, just a staff key that would allow him to take the elevator up. But Easton was livid.

They also informed us that everything was caught on camera,

and he'd been taken down to the police station, so it was out of their hands regarding what happened from there. Easton ended the call.

"I can't fucking believe that a high-end hotel like this would allow this bullshit to go on." Easton paced some more around the room, as I lay on my back because I was full from our bed picnic and exhausted from the day, especially the last hour.

"I think it goes on everywhere. But I would certainly hope they wouldn't have given him my room key." I shivered at the thought.

My father had called three more times, letting us know Will had picked Jamison up from the police station and he was being admitted into a program in the morning.

Will had called and apologized to me, and even Bethany had phoned and cried and said how terrible she felt about the whole mess.

I was over it and exhausted and done talking about it.

I lay on Easton's bed, listening to the sound of his voice as he blasted every single person who called, including Bruno King for allowing a breach in security at the hotel that he owned.

When the room was quiet, Easton turned off the lights, and I felt him crawl onto the bed and pull me against him. "I'd burn this fucking place down if something had happened to you."

Had anyone ever come to my defense like this before?

Not that I could think of.

He is definitely invested.

And I wrapped my arms around him and moved closer.

Because I was invested, too.

nineteen

· · ·

Easton

I'D MEANT what I said. I felt protective of this woman in a way that I hadn't felt in a very long time.

I hadn't known her for more than a few weeks.

But for whatever reason, I wanted to keep her safe. I wanted to be around her. I wanted to make her world a better place.

"You don't need to burn anything down," she said, and I could feel her smile against my chest. "I've taken care of myself for a very long time, Easton. But I'm glad you're here."

"Stay with me tonight," I said, sounding like a desperate pussy.

I was not that guy. I didn't do romantic gestures or long-term relationships.

Not anymore.

Hell, I hadn't spent the night in bed with a woman since Jilly.

I always had an exit strategy.

"Okay," she whispered as she tipped her head back and grazed her lips against mine. "You've got me here. What are you going to do with me?"

Her voice was all tease, and my dick responded by springing to life on command.

"What would you like me to do with you?" My voice was gruff. "Because I'd like to make you feel good."

"Yeah? That sounds like a nice end to the madness of this day."

That's all I needed to hear. My mouth was on hers. My hands moved from her waist to her neck to her face. I wanted to memorize every single inch of her.

She reached for my joggers, attempting to shove the waistband down.

"Such an eager girl, Princess." I chuckled against her lips before flipping her onto her back.

She smiled up at me, eyes wild and full of need. "I want you."

"You sure about that?"

"I'm positive. I know what this is, and I want it." She sighed. "Please, Easton. No more waiting. No more holding back."

I nodded and pushed up on my knees, sliding her joggers down to find she wasn't wearing any panties, and my fingers traced over her pussy, and she shivered. "Look at you. Bare and ready to be fucked."

She sucked in a breath and raised her arms over her head so that I could tug her tank top off.

Holy shit.

These tits.

"Fuck me. Look at you lying here bare, just for me." I tossed her top on the floor beside the bed and just stared at her. My dick throbbed at the sight of her, and I leaned down and covered her mouth with mine. My lips moved from her mouth to her jaw to her neck. Nipping and licking and wanting to taste every inch of her. My thumbs grazed over her hard peaks before I covered her breast with my mouth, taking my time as I moved from one to the next as she writhed beneath me.

"Easton, please," she begged, and I pulled back to look at her.

"Goddamn, you're beautiful. I know what you need, and I'm going to give it to you, okay?"

She nodded. "Now."

I chuckled. "All right. But I'm going to make you come on my lips first. And then you can come on my cock next."

Her eyes were wide, as if no one had ever spoken to her like this. And I fucking loved it, because I knew it turned her on.

"Okay," she whispered.

My tongue moved along my bottom lip as I shifted down on the bed a little bit. "Spread those pretty little thighs for me, Princess."

She did as she was told, and I buried my face there. My tongue moved along her most sensitive area as she gasped.

Fuck me. She was so damn sweet.

So damn perfect.

I licked her until she was panting and gasping, and then I sucked her clit as I slipped a finger inside her.

She was wet and warm and tight. I pumped in and out a few times as my mouth sealed over her clit and continued sucking hard.

I slipped another finger inside as her hips moved up and down, and her chest arched toward the ceiling as I took her right to the edge.

I moved quickly, knowing she was close, and replaced my fingers with my tongue, because I wanted all that sweetness on my lips.

I was a greedy man. And she liked it, because her thighs locked on each side of my face as she started to shake.

She rocked harder and faster against me. Her fingers tangled in my hair as she held me right where she wanted me.

Needed me.

And she cried out my name as she went right over the edge.

I continued fucking her with my tongue until she rode out every last bit of pleasure.

When she stopped moving, and her breaths slowed, I raised my head.

She was on her back and chuckling now, and I moved forward to hover above her. "Something funny, Princess?"

She shook her head. "No. That was just—wow."

"Wow?"

"Yeah. I've never, you know, finished with a man—er, doing that."

"You've never come with someone going down on you? Is that what you're telling me?" I nipped at her bottom lip.

"Yes. Has anyone ever told you that you have a filthy mouth?" She raised a brow.

"Absolutely. And you fucking love it." I puffed my chest up as I pushed the hair out of her face. "Don't be embarrassed to tell me what you want. I'll bury my face between your thighs and make you come any time you want."

She looked up at me. "I want you naked right now."

Atta girl.

I pushed to my feet and shoved my joggers down. She pressed up on her elbows, her teeth sinking into that juicy bottom lip as she watched me. "You like what you see?"

She nodded. "Do you have condoms with you?"

"I do." I walked over to where my wallet sat on the desk and pulled out the foiled packet.

"I want to put it on you," she said. "I've never done it before."

I loved that she was telling me what she wanted. I tore the foil packet open and handed it to her as I stood in front of her and stroked myself a few times. She rolled the latex over me before moving back to lie on the bed.

I moved toward her, hovering above, as her chest rose and fell quickly. She was nervous. "Hey, there's no pressure here. If you want to stop, all you have to do is tell me, all right?"

"I don't want to stop. I want this so much." Her words were breathy and sexy as hell.

I settled between her thighs as she spread her legs wide for me.

I reached down, sliding the tip of my dick along her entrance, teasing her a bit before my mouth covered hers. I wanted her so fucking bad that it took everything I had to take this slow.

I slid in the slightest bit, and she gasped.

I was large. She was tight. This was going to take some time, and I needed her to be patient. "We're going slow, Princess. I want you to adjust to me first so it doesn't hurt. I want to make you feel so fucking good that all you'll think about for days is my cock."

Her fingers tangled in my hair as she pulled me down to kiss her.

We kissed, devouring one another's mouths, and I moved slowly. Inch by inch, and I groaned into her mouth, because nothing had ever felt so good. She urged me on, and I continued to slide into all that sweetness.

Slow.

Taking my time, torturing us both.

Once I was all the way in, I pulled back, squeezing my eyes closed as she gripped my cock like a fucking vise.

I looked down at her, and she was just staring up at me—needy and sexy and ready for more.

"You all right?"

"Never better. Stop holding back," she said.

I reached for her hands, pinning them above her head with one of mine. I pulled back slowly and then drove back in as her head fell back on a moan, and she arched her tits toward me. I leaned down and sucked one hard peak between my lips as I pushed back into her. And we found our rhythm.

She met me thrust for thrust.

Over and over.

Faster.

Harder.

Needier.

I couldn't see straight as everything started to blur.

I will not lose control.

"Easton," she said my name on a gasp as she tightened around me. My hand moved between us, knowing just what she needed. My thumb barely grazed her clit when she exploded.

She shook and trembled, and I couldn't look away. She was so fucking beautiful. I pulled back and drove into her.

Once.

Twice.

Bright lights exploded behind my eyelids as I came harder than I'd ever come before.

I continued pumping into her as my forehead fell forward.

When we slowed our movements, I lifted my head to look at her.

Her hands pinned above her head.

Her sapphire eyes glowing in the moonlight.

Half-mast and sated.

Her lips parted and cheeks flushed.

Fucking gorgeous.

It surprised me how much I liked having her in my bed. I kissed her as I pulled out of her slowly before moving to my feet. I walked to the bathroom and pulled off the condom before tying it off and dropping it in the trash.

I turned to look in the mirror.

What was I doing?

I wanted to keep her here.

But that wasn't the plan.

I knew better.

I didn't do this.

One and done.

That was my motto. It was safer that way. And I was a busy man. I didn't need any more people relying on me.

I am not that guy.

My breathing escalated, and this overwhelming sense of panic surged through me.

"You all right in there?" she called out from the bed, and I splashed some water on my face and pulled my shit together.

I moved toward the bedroom, leaning against the wall. "I'm great. How about you?"

"I thought maybe you were having some kind of panic attack because you just slept with your boss's daughter, and now you don't know how to ask her to leave." She chuckled as she pushed to her feet with the sheet wrapped around her. "No need to worry, Chadwick. I know what this was. And it was amazing. But I was planning to leave. I like to take a bath before I go to sleep anyway."

She was looking around for her clothes when I rushed her and tossed her back onto the bed.

She was laughing hysterically now as I looked down at her. "You're not going anywhere. I asked you to stay the night, and I meant it. Don't even think of getting dressed."

I pushed back up and made my way to the bathroom before turning on the tub. I glanced around and saw some bath salts, and I poured them into the water. I walked back into the room, and she was scrolling through her phone.

I marched toward her and took the phone from her hand and tugged the sheet away. She raised a brow, her gaze raking over me as I stood naked in front of her.

I scooped her up in my arms, cradling her against my chest, and she burst out in laughter. "Oh, my gosh. I'm naked. What are you doing?"

"I'm carrying you to the bathroom," I said, setting her down on her feet in front of the tub.

"You ran me a bath?"

"You said you like to take baths before bed." I studied her, my brows cinched together because I wanted to get this right.

We had one night together, and I wanted it to be good for her. I turned off the water and waited for her to speak.

"I do." Her eyes were wide as she glanced over at the water and then back at me. "What are you going to do?"

"I'm going to take a bath with you." I climbed into the hot water and winced before I sat down and spread my legs for her

---

to get in. She pulled the scrunchie from her wrist and tied her hair up in a knot on top of her head.

Her lips turned up in the corners, and she took my hand that I'd extended to her. "You take baths?"

"No. I haven't taken a bath since I was three years old."

She settled her back against my chest and moaned as she sank lower. Clearly, the woman liked baths.

She rolled onto her stomach. "So, why are you taking a bath now?"

I shrugged. "Don't overthink it, Princess."

"I'm not overthinking it. I'm asking a question, Chadwick." She smirked.

"Well, I'm guessing that blow job this morning wasn't something that you enjoyed as much as I did. But you did it because you knew I would enjoy it."

"Did you just compare a bath to a blow job?" She chuckled.

"I know that this isn't the norm for you—having a no-strings-attached fuck."

"Wow. You have a real way with words, counselor." She said.

"What do you call it?"

"A fling."

"Okay. Well, I know that flings are not the norm for you. I wanted to make it nice."

She smiled. "The orgasms were plenty impressive, but I've got to say, the bath is a nice finish to the one-nighter. Thank you."

"Did you take a lot of baths with the stoner or the Harvard wannabe?" I inquired. I wanted to know more about Henley.

I wanted to know everything, if I were being honest, and I shouldn't. I really shouldn't.

"No. Houston thought baths were disgusting. And Pete had eczema, so he was very particular about how much time he spent in the water."

I barked out a laugh. "They both sound like assholes. First, they don't know how to please their lady. They never made you come when they went down on you. And then they wouldn't sit in a goddamn tub of water if it made you happy. What the fuck is wrong with them?"

"Well, when you put it that way." She chuckled. "Thank you for sitting in a tub of hot water with me after rocking my world, Chadwick."

"Happy to oblige, Princess."

And I meant it.

twenty

. . .

Henley

EASTON WRAPPED me in a towel after we got out of the bathtub and carried me to the bed. For a noncommittal guy who only had casual relationships, he'd surprised me.

Maybe this was how it was with flings.

It was a night full of surprises, and then you said goodbye.

He'd convinced me to sleep naked, since we'd agreed we'd only have this one night together, and tomorrow, we'd go back to normal. All in all, the night was what I needed after nearly being accosted. Being with Easton almost wiped that from my memory, and I'd needed that.

The room was dark. Quiet. I was pressed against his body. I could feel every hard line and muscle as I stroked his arm with the tips of my fingers.

"Have you gone rafting yet on the river?" he asked, and I smiled at how random the question was.

"Yes. Lulu and I went when she was in town. We'd gone once before, but the river here is better. But that's really all I've done. I haven't explored the town yet, because I've just been working so much. I mean, I've been to Rosewood Brew for coffee several times on my way to the office. And I ordered takeout from Honey Biscuit Café a few times, but I haven't been in."

He made a tsking sound. "You are missing out. You don't want to order takeout from Honey Biscuit Café because you're missing the whole experience of being there."

"It's that eventful?" I chuckled.

"Yes. You'll just have to trust me. I'm not going to ruin it for you. You'll know what I'm talking about after you go. And you've got The Green Basket grocery store and Randy's Razor and Booze & Brews to yet experience."

"Ah, yes. Booze & Brews. That's where you *blow off your steam*, right?" I teased, as his fingers traced along the base of my neck.

He leaned forward and nipped at my ear. "Don't be a smartass. You need to get out and explore downtown. You'll love it. It's the heart of Rosewood River."

"Your father told me that you all grew up there, huh?"

"Yes. I heard him telling you about his life in real time," he said dryly, but I could feel his smile against my cheek.

"I loved it. My dad was never real chatty, so it's refreshing that your family likes to talk and listen." I shook my head with a laugh. "It seems so basic, but not everyone has that."

"Yeah? My parents are the best."

"What was it like growing up in a small town?" I asked, because I was curious.

"Well, I have four siblings, and my cousins grew up in the house next door, so we had built-in entertainment with that. And when we were teenagers, we spent our summer days down at the river. I love going river rafting and became a rafting guide in college. But all in all, it was a pretty amazing childhood, if I'm being honest, though we got into our fair share of trouble growing up."

"And you grew up with Jilly?" I asked, because he'd mentioned that her parents were at his birthday dinner.

"Yeah. We didn't date until college. We'd always just been friends," he said, his voice quieter now. "So I'd known her most of my life."

I ran my fingers through his hair, desperate to comfort him. "I'm sorry. I know how hard that must be to lose someone you love."

"Yeah. But you move on. It's been a long time. I threw myself into law school and focused on that." He let out a long breath. "Let's talk about you for a little bit."

I nodded, understanding his need to change the subject. "What do you want to know?"

"So, your mom left with the tennis pro and moved to France when you were young. And you stayed with your father most of the year, spending summers with your mom, right?"

"Yes." I didn't hide my surprise that he'd actually listened and remembered.

"I know you said your dad worked a lot, so what was your childhood like?"

"Well, my nanny, Darleen, was wonderful. She was my main caretaker. She'd take me to tennis. I practiced six days a week from the time I started playing. And most days, I would wake up after my father was gone, and I'd be asleep when he arrived home from work. But Sundays were my favorite," I said, remembering how excited I'd be when I'd go to sleep on Saturday nights, knowing what the morning would bring.

"What happened on Sundays?"

"That was my one day off a week from tennis. And my dad would take that day off, as well. Every Sunday, he'd surprise me with a cake donut and a chocolate milk. He'd bring it into my bedroom in a little bag from the bakery up the street from us."

"That was nice. I can't even picture that side of Charles," he said. "And what would you do?"

"He'd have a donut for himself, too, and a coffee. And we'd eat them together and decide what we wanted to do. It was always spontaneous, and he'd let me pick. Some days, it would be to walk down to the wharf and explore. Other times, we'd go to the country club and have lunch, and he'd drive me around on the golf cart. Sometimes, we'd take the boat out, just the two of us. It's my fondest memory of my childhood. Those Sundays with my father. Because the rest of the time, he was in work mode. But on Sundays, he was just a dad, hanging out with his daughter, you know?"

"That sounds nice. And it went on for years?"

"Yeah. From as early as I can remember until I left for boarding school my freshman year of high school."

"Did you want to go to boarding school?"

"I don't really know. It was just always known that I'd go. My father went to Westcliff, and he'd talked about me going for so long that I never really considered an alternative." I tipped my head back to look at him, and even though the room was dark, the light from the moon illuminated his handsome face. "Most of the kids I went to middle school with were going off to boarding schools, as well, so I didn't know anything different. But I'm glad I went. I came into my own and met my bestie there."

He wrapped his arms around me tighter. "It sounds like it was a good experience."

"Yeah. I'm guessing you went to high school in Rosewood River and had that quintessential high school experience."

He let out a puff of air. "What does that mean?"

"You were probably prom king, and your superlative was…" I paused to think about it. "Most likely to take over the world?"

"Lucky guess. I *was* prom king, actually. And my superlative was most likely to be a celebrity." He laughed. "What about yours?"

"My high school was an all-girls high school, so no prom for us. And my superlative was most likely to win Wimbledon. Clearly, I was best known for my tennis skills, not my social skills."

"Well, you should have been named most likely to give the best blow job, because your BJ skills are remarkable."

My head tipped back in laughter. "Thank you. And thanks

for today. I think tomorrow we should probably go back to normal, okay?"

His body shifted a little at my words. "All right. Did I do something to piss you off?"

I thought it over. Easton was a straight shooter. I should do the same. "This was great. Amazing, really. But I know myself. I can handle a fling, as long as I know what it is. And honestly, I've never taken a bath with a guy, even one that I've dated for a long period of time. And I don't normally talk and share this much in my relationships either. So I just think at this rate, this fling could get confusing for me if it continues. Does that make sense?"

"Yes. Of course." He cleared his throat. "If it's any consolation, this is the best fling I've ever had."

"Yeah. We were pretty amazing. All the orgasms, the hallway drama with Jamison, talking about our childhoods, and then the bath. This fling is one for the record books, Chadwick."

"Well, we are both overachievers. We shouldn't be surprised. And tomorrow, we'll go back to normal. Like this never happened."

"Deal," I whispered, as my eyes grew heavy. I breathed him in, and a small part of me wished this night would never end.

But all good things came to an end.

And I knew better than to let myself fall for an unattainable man.

———

The next two weeks were a blur since we'd returned to Rosewood River after spending three days in the city interviewing employees before wrapping things up there. We'd been honest with Bruno that there were some holes in his case that were going to make it challenging.

We'd returned to the office and decided we'd conduct the rest of our interviews remotely. We'd met a few people who didn't seem to be so scripted, and they were fairly convincing. But several of the people we'd met with had said the exact same things we'd heard in many of our interviews, which was a huge concern.

Were they covering for Bruno and the company they worked for?

Were they just nervous about the idea of going to trial?

"Henley. My office now," Easton barked from his doorway as I worked in my cubicle.

We'd stuck to the deal and agreed that morning after we'd had sex that when we left the hotel room, we would never speak of it and it would never happen again. It was a one and done. We'd remained professional ever since, made small talk on the drive home, and acted completely normal.

But I'd be lying if I said that it hadn't been more challenging for me than I'd expected it to be. Lulu had decided that me having my first fling with a guy that I had to see every day was probably not the best idea.

Hindsight, and all that.

I missed our flirty banter. I missed the way he'd looked at me before we'd crossed the line.

The way he'd kissed me and touched me.

The way he'd made me feel.

That was the thing about flings—they had an expiration date, and you had to respect that.

I wasn't upset that it had happened.

I was upset that I couldn't stop thinking about him.

I was upset that I had to pretend that I wasn't fazed by him every single day when I saw him in the office.

"Coming," I said, as I pushed to my feet.

"Beware. He's in a mood today," Joey said under his breath, and I nodded.

Easton had been grumpier than usual the last few days. It was Friday, and I hadn't been asked to join him at pickleball again. Maybe Archer was back. Or maybe Easton didn't feel comfortable with me being the sub anymore.

I walked into his office and took the seat across from him.

"Hey," I said, crossing my hands on my lap.

He looked up and studied me. "Why are you so serious now? Where's the smartass that used to give me shit?"

"What are you talking about? You've barely spoken to me in two weeks outside of barking out a few orders. I didn't think you wanted to do the smartass banter thing anymore." I shrugged, tapping my pen against my notebook so we could get down to business.

"I thought we agreed we wouldn't let it be weird." He raised a brow.

"It's not weird for me. I feel fine being around you. You're the one who has been distant and uninterested in chatting. You've called me in three times this week, shot out a few orders, and then told me to get back to work."

He studied me for a few beats. "Have you ventured downtown yet?"

Where did that come from? This man is the most confusing man I've ever met.

"Have I ventured downtown?"

"Do I need to repeat the question, Henley?"

I rolled my eyes. "No. You don't need to repeat the question, and yes, I went to The Green Basket and loaded up on groceries."

"Did you find it odd that there wasn't a green basket in the place? Not a single one. They only have red baskets. So why the fuck is it called The Green Basket?"

I chuckled, because as much as I wanted to dislike this man, I was so drawn to him. "I didn't notice. I think it's just a cute name."

"Did you meet the owner?"

"Yes. I met Josh. He was very nice."

He pursed his lips as if that were an obscene comment. "He's only being nice because you're—you. He's a dick most of the time. His parents own the place, and he started running it a few years ago. But did he tell you his last name?"

"No. It didn't really come up when I was asking him where the cantaloupes were." I shook my head with a laugh.

"His last name is Black. Josh Black. So, they've got red baskets. Their last name is Black. And do they choose to call their store The Black Basket? No. The Red Basket? Also no. They go with The Green Basket. It's ludicrous."

"Perhaps you should suggest that to them."

"Have you gone rafting again?"

"Have I gone rafting since we've been back from the city? Ummm, I've been buried in interviews with employees from the King Hotels. So, no. I've been busy, Easton."

"Maybe you'll get out there this weekend."

What was his deal? "Okay. Maybe I will."

"Just saying, it's great. But you've got to be careful about which paths you take."

"Sure. Thanks." I raised a brow, because I had no idea why we were talking about river rafting. I never knew what to expect from this man.

He strummed his fingers along the edge of his desk. "We've got a pickleball tournament tonight."

"Yes. I assumed so. It is Friday, after all."

"Yes. I told Archer he needs to play, or he'll be kicked off the team if he doesn't show up this week."

"I'm sure he'll be there, then."

He narrowed his gaze. "All right. Get back to work."

"Yes, sir."

"What's with the attitude?" he asked as I pushed to my feet.

"I thought you missed me having an attitude, so I was being nice. Throwing you a bone, per se."

He chuckled as I walked toward the door.

"Hey, Henley."

I turned around to look at him. "Yes."

"Jamison Waterman is still in rehab. He's there for a sixty-day program. I wasn't sure if your dad told you. I didn't want you to worry about it."

"Yes, my father told me, and I'm not worried. But I wouldn't hold your breath, because Jamison will most likely bail on the program early. Sixty days is a long time."

"That's why I call every morning." He cleared his throat. "Just to make sure he's still there. I'll let you know if he leaves early. Just so you'll be aware."

My mouth fell open, and I gaped at him. "You call the rehab place every day?"

"Yes. He attacked you. We need to know when he gets out."

I sighed. He hadn't attacked me. He'd been aggressive, and his behavior was alarming, but Easton was being irrational about it, which only contributed more to him being a complete puzzle.

"Thank you." I nodded.

And I left his office quickly.

Because the urge to move around his desk and lunge myself at him and thank him for caring was strong.

And I'd made enough bad decisions these last few weeks.

I wouldn't make another one.

twenty-one

· · ·

Easton

"WHAT IS YOUR DEAL? You played like shit," Archer said, as we sipped our beers at Booze & Brews. "We almost lost to The Golden Girls, for fuck's sake."

The Golden Girls were a group of women who were all in their sixties and seventies. Obviously, we lightened up when we played them, but they'd actually surprised me with how good they were this season.

"Hey, Marge brought her fucking A game today. That had nothing to do with me," I hissed

Rafe barked out a laugh. "I bet Marge was hot as hell back in her day. She's got that little something about her, you know?"

Clark raised a brow. "Dude. She's as old as Mimi."

Mimi and Pops were our grandparents, and they lived in Rosewood River, but they were currently on a European cruise, and they'd been gone for weeks. They traveled often and were two of my favorite people on the planet.

"I didn't say I wanted to date her. Just that she's a silver fox."

"For fuck's sake. Why are we talking about this?" Bridger grumped and reached for his beer. "I want to know why you're being such a dick lately, Easton."

Axel laughed. "Leave it to Bridger to ask the tough questions."

"What's going on with you, brother? We've all noticed something's up." Clark studied me. The dude was rarely this serious, so even I was concerned about myself.

I scratched the back of my neck. "Something happened between me and Henley a few weeks ago. It shouldn't have happened. But it's fucking with my head now."

Archer leaned forward and clapped me on the shoulder. "It's fucking with your head because you clearly like her. Stop overthinking it."

"Dude. I need to focus on work. I don't have time to be distracted. But we spend every goddamn day together. We work late hours, and it's too much sometimes. I try to ignore her and focus, but it's tough. And now I can't even focus on fucking pickleball because she's all-consuming." I chugged the rest of my beer, grateful that I'd walked here. "So, tonight, I need to get laid, and that's why we're here. I need to get her out of my system."

"Well, I don't know if that's the answer. And you know I'm all about keeping things casual and having a good time. But come on, brother, you aren't going to forget about her if you get drunk and hook up with a random woman. She'll be there on Monday, taunting you once again. I guess this was bound to happen." Rafe held his hand up and ordered us each a whiskey nightcap.

"I can't believe I'm going to say this, but I agree with Rafe. How fucked-up is that?" Bridger said, and the table erupted in laughter.

"Thank you, dicklestiltskin. Glad I could sway you to the home team." Rafe handed Jazzy Leighton his credit card when she brought the drinks over and asked her to close out our tab.

Jazzy and her husband, Ben, owned the place, and it was the most popular local hotspot in town.

"Jazzy, you can open me my own tab. I'm staying," I said as I slammed the whiskey down.

"You got it, Easton. I'll be back around to check on you in a little bit."

"Wow. You really are on edge," Archer said, concern lacing his tone. "Why is it a bad thing that something happened with her? Is it awkward at work? You crossed a line and now you're uncomfortable?"

"I don't think that's it," Rafe chirped, and I flipped him the bird.

"No. It's not awkward. She doesn't even seem fazed. We agreed to one night together. It's not her thing, but she was open to it, because clearly, we're attracted to one another." I shook my head and reached for the water that Jazzy had set down for each of us.

"And she's not pissed at you?" Clark asked.

"No. She seems perfectly fucking fine."

"So, what's the problem?" Axel sipped his whiskey, and I wished I'd done the same, because the booze was hitting hard all of a sudden.

"Come on, fuckers. This isn't rocket science." Bridger downed his whiskey and then slammed his glass down on the table. "He likes her. He hasn't liked anyone since Jilly, and it's fucking with his head."

We all turned slowly to face my grumpy-ass brother, who normally didn't have much to say.

"Thank you, Dr. Phil," I grumped as I scrubbed a hand down my face.

"Is that what it is?" Rafe asked, his voice no longer laced with humor.

"I don't fucking know. I came here to get laid, and I don't want anyone but Henley because all I think about is her. But I just—I don't know if I can go there, you know?" It felt good to say it aloud.

"Dude, losing Jilly was brutal. Unthinkable," Clark said, reaching over and squeezing my shoulder. "But that doesn't mean that you shouldn't ever date again. It was a horrible accident. And I know it hurt like hell, but you can't just fuck random women for the rest of your life because you're avoiding falling for someone."

"Why? Isn't that what *we* do?" Rafe gaped at him.

"No. We just haven't met anyone that knocked us on our asses yet. So we're out there dating and meeting people—not with a rule that we won't get serious if the right woman comes around. There's a difference." Clark shrugged.

"Agreed." Axel smirked and glanced at me. "We're all fine if we get knocked on our asses, it just hasn't happened yet. You're the only one running from it."

"Actually, I'm not waiting to be knocked on my ass, and I'm not running from it either. I just find that people annoy me most of the time," Bridger said, and I barked out a laugh, because he wasn't lying. "But that's not you, Easton. And you can't let fear rule you. That would make you a weak fucker. And the Chadwicks are not weak fuckers."

"Can we put that on a shirt?" Archer smirked.

"I know what our boy needs. He needs to activate his twin powers." Clark pushed to his feet. "Come on. You'll regret it if you're hungover tomorrow. Call it a night. I just sent a text to Emerson. She's calling you in five minutes. You need to talk to her."

"She is smarter than all of us." Rafe stood, and we all followed suit.

I let Jazzy know I wouldn't be needing that tab, after all, because they were right. I didn't want to be hungover tomorrow. And I was clearly not going to get laid, because I only had one woman on my mind.

We all walked in the same direction for a short distance, and my phone rang. We said our quick goodbyes, as I was the first one to veer off down my street.

"Hey, Emmy," I said, my words slurring a bit.

"Hey, brother. I heard you're having girl problems," my sister said, her voice light and filled with empathy.

Emerson was my best friend. The best sister a dude could ask for. She'd always been my sounding board, even though I didn't like to talk about things the way she did.

"I don't know what's happening to me, Emmy. I can't get her out of my head," I admitted, as I walked up the steps to my house. I'd told my sister what had happened in the city. Emerson and I told one another everything. But I hadn't shared that I had been struggling ever since.

"E, it doesn't have to be a bad thing that you like Henley. I mean, of course, the office thing is going to make it complicated, because her father is your boss," she said with a laugh. "But that's not why you're holding back, and you know it. Because you and I both know if it wasn't something you felt serious about, you wouldn't have gone there, seeing as you work with her. You're holding back because you're afraid. And that's not who you are."

I went to the refrigerator and grabbed a bottle of water and chugged it after I sat on the couch. "I've had two pretty intense anxiety attacks this week."

There. I said it.

"What? Were they as bad as they were after Jilly died?"

"Yeah. I have an appointment with Dr. Langford tomorrow. She was thrilled that I called, of course." I oozed sarcasm. "She's been trying to get me to come back for years."

"I think this is saying a lot, Easton. You had panic attacks after you lost Jilly, and you haven't had them since. And now, you have a one-night stand with your coworker, who you are clearly crazy about, and you have two panic attacks after you agree not to let it happen again. It's very telling, brother."

"I'm aware. I wanted to go get laid tonight. I figured I'd get laid, forget about Henley, and cancel my appointment with Dr. Langford because I'd be cured." I sighed. "But I couldn't fucking do it. I don't want anyone else, and that scares the shit out of me."

She sniffed a few times, and I knew she was crying. I swear, Emerson felt my pain when I was hurting. It wasn't the same for me. When she was hurting, I just wanted to beat the fuck out of anyone who hurt her. But when I was hurting, she felt it and carried it with her like a burden. So I hated opening up to her about this kind of stuff.

Not much hurt me, and that was the truth.

But losing Jilly was the most painful thing I'd ever lived through, and I hoped like hell I'd never feel that kind of hurt again.

I'd set my life up in a way that I wouldn't.

"You didn't want to because you've found someone that you want to be with, Easton. What are you afraid of? What is the worst that can happen?" she pressed.

Was she for fucking real?

"Are you kidding me right now, Emmy?"

"No. Just say it. What's the worst that can happen, Easton?"

"I could fall in love with her, and she could die. Is there anything worse than that? Because it fucking happens, Emmy. I fucking lived it. It happens. And it could happen again," I said, my voice harsher than I meant it to be.

"What you went through is unfathomable and sad and unfair. I'm on your side. And loving someone and losing them is horrific. But never loving someone for fear of losing them is also horrific, Easton. Because at least you got to love Jilly for all those years. So you got that time with her. But never allowing yourself to feel that for someone again is not the right way to handle this. You love me. You love Mom and Dad. And Rafe and Clark and Bridger and Axel and Archer and Melody, and—" she said, and I cut her off.

"You don't have to name everyone I care about, Emmy. I get it. But I have no choice with my family. I already love you, so I can't change that," I groaned. "I'm used to being alone now. I don't have to worry about anyone else."

"Well, that's a lame reason not to be with someone." She paused, and I knew I was about to get a life lesson. My twin sister was the queen of life lessons. "You are one of the strongest men I know, Easton Chadwick. You will not let fear deter you from living your life. So how about you put things into perspective with Henley," she said.

"What the fuck does that mean? How do I put things into perspective?"

"You're not marrying the girl. You like her. She likes you. One night was not enough. So just date her. Don't worry about the future and be in the moment. The way you are in every other aspect of your life."

I nodded, leaning back on the couch. "Why do you have to always show off that you're smarter than me?"

"Well, I am a doctor, right?"

"You sure are." I sighed. "How's Nash and Beefcake?"

"They're great. Cutler is looking forward to FaceTiming with you tomorrow."

I'd grown close to Nash and his boy, and I looked forward to our weekly calls.

"Me, too. And you guys will be here for the fall party, right? Everyone will be excited to have you home." My mom threw a party every year in the fall and invited half the town.

"I can't wait. I want to meet Henley, so stop being a baby and ask her out so you can bring her to the party in a few weeks, and I can grill her." She chuckled.

"I'll think about it, Emmy."

"All right. I'll be around if you want to talk more tomorrow."

"Thanks. Love you."

"Love you more," she said as I ended the call.

I thought about what she'd said. Would it be the worst thing to try to date Henley?

And did she even want to date me?

She'd accused me of giving her whiplash one too many times, and here I was, wanting to change up the rules once again.

I lay back on the couch and thought about what I should do.

I didn't want to live my life in fear. The panic attacks had caught me off guard, and that was why I'd been a dick since we'd come home. And this week, I'd had the most severe attacks I'd had to date. I'd had to run into the bathroom at the office to vomit twice over the last few days, and I'd broken out in a cold sweat.

I'd made the appointment with Dr. Langford because she'd helped me through them years ago when they'd started.

I knew that I was letting fear rule me.

And I was ready to change that.

twenty-two

. . .

Henley

THE SUN WAS SHINING, and I was going to venture out today. It was Sunday, and I'd worked all day yesterday, so today, I was going to do something fun. I'd had a slow morning going over some of the transcripts from our interviews and trying to wrap my head around the fact that we might just be on the wrong side of this case.

The three women who had filed the lawsuit were most likely telling the truth.

I'd wanted to believe differently, but at this point, everything was pointing at Bruno King being a liar.

I sipped my coffee, trying to decide what I'd do for the day, when a knock on the door pulled me from my thoughts. I was still in my jammies, and I wasn't expecting anyone. I padded over to the door and looked through the peephole to see Easton Chadwick standing on my doorstep.

I pulled the door open. "Well, this is unexpected. I thought we were taking the day off?"

"We are. Can I come in?"

"Sure." I stepped back, taking in his dark hair effortlessly styled, his jaw peppered with day-old scruff. He wore a pair of black workout shorts and a gray tee. He looked like a professional athlete, and it immediately irritated me that I wanted him. Why did I have to be attracted to this man?

The most unattainable man on the planet.

"Let me guess, you need me to come play pickleball with you because you are desperate to brush up on your skills because you lost on Friday?"

My tone was light and filled with humor, but he paid me no attention as he walked toward the kitchen. It was the first I noticed the bag in his hand, and he sat down at my table and motioned for me to sit next to him.

"Is something wrong?" I asked.

"Nothing is wrong, Princess." He cleared his throat and opened the bag.

He laid a napkin down in front of me and then pulled out a cake donut with pink icing and sprinkles before setting a little container of chocolate milk beside it.

A lump formed in my throat, and I felt my eyes well with emotion.

"What is this?"

"It's your favorite Sunday tradition."

"You brought me a donut and chocolate milk?" I said, my voice wobbling.

He sucked in a deep breath and his steel-gray eyes locked with mine. "I handled things poorly, and I'm sorry."

"Do you bring donuts to all your one-night stands? You didn't handle things poorly, Easton. You handled them exactly how you said you would. You didn't do anything wrong. I'm okay with it. Please don't pity me." Now I was irritated because I hated that he knew I was struggling. I'd tried really hard these past two weeks to act unaffected, yet here he was, bringing me a sympathy donut.

"I'm not pitying you, Henley." He reached for my hand. "I can't stop thinking about you. It's been like that since the morning you left my hotel room. And it scares the shit out of me, more than I can even put into words. I don't know how to do this."

"How to do what?" I asked.

"Well, I brought this donut over to come up with a plan for today. It turns out one night is not enough for me. I would like to date you, Princess. It's obviously been a long time since I've dated someone, so I don't know how to go about it." He shrugged, and he was so damn adorable I could barely breathe.

My teeth sank into my bottom lip, and I tried to get myself under control. "You've missed all the latest trends. Most people just swipe right and meet up somewhere."

"Fine. This is me swiping right."

I chuckled. "You want to date me? That's a leap from wanting a one-and-done."

"It is."

"So, how do I know that you don't just want to sleep with me again?" I quirked a brow.

"I definitely want to sleep with you again," he said, the corners of his lips turning up. "But I would tell you if that was the reason I was here. It's more than that, Henley. I think about you all the time. You're actually making me physically sick."

My eyes widened as I gaped at him. "Thanks a lot. What does that mean?"

"After Jilly's accident, I started having panic attacks. I'd vomit and break out in a cold sweat. I'd get the spins, and I couldn't speak. I'd end up on the floor, trying to work through it."

"That's awful," I said, moving to my feet and climbing into his lap. He was opening up to me, and I wanted to be closer to him. "I'm so sorry. What did you do to stop them?"

"I saw a therapist. I worked through it, and they've been gone for years. But they've come back with a vengeance. I had two big ones this past week, and I saw my therapist yesterday. She's convinced it's because I knew that I was making a huge mistake by letting you go. Not telling you how I feel about you."

"How do you feel about me?"

He tucked my long hair behind my ear. "I don't know how to put it into words, but I think about you when I'm not with you. I miss your laugh and your smile and your snarky comments. I look forward to you coming to my office, and I'm pissed when I see Joey Barker hanging all over you."

"So you're jealous?" I smirked.

"Fuck yeah. But not because I think you like him. I'm jealous because I want to be hanging all over you. I want to hear what you're saying, and I want to show you around Rosewood River, and I want to be the guy you kiss at the end of the day."

The breath caught in my throat, and I placed a hand on his cheek. "You don't have to wait until the end of the day to kiss me."

"It was a metaphor. I was trying to be romantic and deep."

"And I'm trying to tell you that I want you to kiss me right now," I said with a chuckle.

His fingers tangled in my hair, and he tugged me down. His mouth crashed into mine, and I finally felt like I could breathe again.

My lips parted in invitation, and his tongue slipped inside.

I'd missed him.

How do you miss someone who was never yours?

I didn't know how, but I knew that I did.

Because Easton Chadwick felt like mine.

When he pulled back, his gaze locked with mine. "Princess. You need to get dressed. I'm taking you out before I take you to bed again."

"Wow. You're obsessed with me, aren't you?" I teased, as I pushed to my feet.

"Don't get a big head." He smacked me on the ass. "Get dressed."

"Come with me. We can chat while I get dressed. It's not like you haven't seen the goods." I waggled my brows.

He chuckled and took my hand as I led him down the hall.

"So, you're agreeing to date me," he said, as he dropped to sit on the edge of the bathtub, and I sat down at the vanity and brushed my hair, pulling it into a long side braid.

"That depends. What do you have in mind today?" I applied some tinted moisturizer, a little blush, and some mascara before dabbing some pink gloss on my lips. I moved to the closet off the bathroom and pulled my little black T-shirt dress off the hanger and slipped on some cowboy boots, as the dress ended mid-thigh.

"I'm going to take you downtown and show you all the best places."

"Am I dressed okay for what we're doing?" I asked, as I came out of the closet and moved in front of him.

His hands wrapped around me, gripping the backs of my thighs as they slipped beneath my dress. "You look fucking gorgeous."

He turned his cheek so it rested against my stomach, and his hands moved up further, until his thumbs teased the lace of my panties.

"Easton," I whispered.

I was already breathing heavily, just from the way this man touched me. His thumb slipped beneath the edge of my panties.

"Damn, Princess. You're so wet."

I leaned forward and kissed him as he continued stroking me, before his finger slipped inside. I tugged at his hair as his tongue explored my mouth, and I ground against his hand. He continued to pump his finger in and out as his thumb found my clit, and my entire body started to shake.

My legs were barely stable as I groaned into his mouth and shattered with a gasp.

He stayed right there, waiting for me to ride out my orgasm.

And when I pulled my mouth away from his, he freed his hand and tugged me onto his lap, wrapping his arms around me.

"Great date so far," I said as I looked up at him, and he laughed hard.

"Same." He kissed the tip of my nose and then my cheeks and my forehead. "I think you missed me as much as I missed you."

I nodded. I wanted to give him more, but I was hesitant. Easton had been so hot and cold with me so many times. How did I know that he wouldn't wake up tomorrow and change his mind?

I moved to my feet and walked over to the sink to fix my hair and adjust my dress.

He moved beside me, placing his finger between his lips and sucking before turning on the water and washing his hands.

"So, how will we handle this with work?" I asked, suddenly realizing we were going out in public, and this was a small town.

"I was thinking I would call your father on Monday morning and let him know that I want to date you." He placed his hands on his hips and faced me.

"What is this? The 1800s? You don't need to call my father."

"Henley, I work for your father. He's also been my mentor, and he asked me to mentor you. I think he should be the first call," he said.

"Listen. It'll be a whole thing. He'll want to talk it out. Everyone in the office will find out. That's a lot of pressure when we haven't even been on a date yet."

"I don't do things casually, Princess. I know I've confused you in the past, but I have not said that I want to date a woman in many years. I know what I want, and I'm not ashamed to say it."

I moved closer, taking his hand in mine. "Nor should you be. But, in all fairness, this could be a disaster. It's new for you, and if the whole office finds out and then you decide it's too much, everyone will know that you dumped me. That would make for a very uncomfortable office experience."

"You clearly don't trust my intentions."

"I want to. And I will after some time. But this came out of left field, sort of like everything that you do." I shrugged. "And I'm okay with it. With seeing where this goes, because I'm really happy that you showed up this morning and that you want to give this a try. Because I feel things when I'm with you, Easton. But I am already Charles Holloway's daughter. I do not need to be Easton Chadwick's girlfriend until I know that we are going to go the distance, you know?"

He huffed and ran a hand over the back of his neck.

"You feel things, huh?" He smirked.

I couldn't hide the smile on my face. "I do. But I don't want to get hurt either. So how about we keep this a secret for now until we know that you aren't going to bolt the minute you feel like it's too much?"

He nodded. "Fine. We'll go downtown as friends, and I won't be inappropriate until we're behind closed doors."

"How very mature of you." I pushed up on my tiptoes and kissed him.

"I'm going to surprise you, Henley. I'm not fucking around with this. I'm all in." He held my chin between his thumb and pointer finger before placing one more chaste kiss on my lips.

"Promises, promises. Now, show me your favorite places in town, and then bring me home and have your way with me."

"I think I might up the stakes." He took my hand and led me out of the bedroom and down the hallway.

"What does that mean?" I asked.

"It means no sex until you agree to date me and make it public."

My mouth fell open. "You're kidding."

"Nope. I kid you not, Princess. This dick is off limits."

"I already agreed to date you, you stubborn ass." I marched out the door and down the driveway because he hadn't driven here, so apparently, we were walking.

"I don't want to be your dirty little secret." His voice was all tease.

I whipped around, and my chest slammed into his. "You're the king of no-strings-attached relationships, and now you're refusing to have sex with me until we tell everyone we're dating?"

His lips turned up in the corners. "Yes. It sounds crazy, but that's the plan. That way, you'll know I'm not just in it for the sex."

"What if *I'm* in it for the sex?" I quirked a brow and tried hard not to laugh.

"Then you're shit out of luck. Me and my dick want to date you."

"You're so infuriating," I said, as we started walking. "Is this negotiable?"

"Wow. You really like my dick, don't you?" He chuckled. "Sure, it's negotiable. Let me hear your argument, counselor."

"Well, there are other things we can do without having sex, right?"

"Correct. What did you have in mind?" His finger wrapped around mine as we walked side by side, and then he dropped it when we turned down Main Street with all the shops.

"Baths and showers," I said. "I want to take them together."

"I can agree to those terms. I love being anywhere near you naked."

I laughed and feigned irritation. "How about orgasms brought on by other things besides your penis?"

"Don't ever call it a penis again, Princess. It offends him, and it offends me."

"What would you like me to call it?"

"Dick. Cock. Rocket. Schlong. Big Daddy."

"Wow. You've really thought about it. So, orgasms that don't involve any of those bad boys," I said over my laughter.

"Sure. Fingers. Lips. I'll even allow you to dry-hump me again. I know how much you like that."

"I think you'll crack, Chadwick. The minute we're naked in the shower, you're going to break this ridiculous rule."

We approached Honey Biscuit Café, and he pulled the door open and motioned for me to step inside. But he leaned down, his lips grazing the edge of my ear as he spoke.

"You might be right. Burying myself in all that sweetness is all I can think about."

I shivered, and he chuckled.

This man was determined to do things his way.

But I had some plans of my own.

twenty-three

. . .

Easton

THIS WOMAN WAS ENJOYING torturing me; that much was clear.

But two could play this game.

I'd taken a big step today. I'd admitted how I felt.

To her and to me. And to Dr. Langford.

I wanted to date her. And she felt the same.

I wanted her to be mine. She felt the same.

I wanted everyone to know it. She did not feel the same.

So, I would withhold this magical fucking cock of mine until she knew I meant what I said.

"Easton Chadwick, it's been a while. Nice of you to grace us with your presence," Oscar Smith said. I had always assumed that he was hard of hearing because he shouted every word that came out of his mouth. I gave Henley a side-eye; we'd started communicating without words weeks ago. Oscar and his wife, Edith, owned the place, and they were two of the quirkiest people in town.

"I was here yesterday, Oscar."

"Well, I didn't see you," he grumped. "Which is saying a lot, because my wife likes to fawn all over you Chadwicks when you come in. Like you're goddamn royalty or something."

Oscar basically berated his patrons every time they walked through the door. I was pleased when he wasn't up at the entrance and I could just take my seat. My brothers loved the harassment. Rafe was disappointed when he didn't see Oscar.

"You big ole bully, Oscar. Let the man go to his table." Edith appeared from the kitchen. She was in her mid-sixties and had the tenacity of a twenty-year-old. "You're going to run off all the customers if you shame them every time they come in."

"I don't know how you landed a fish like me, with that mouth on you, woman," he hissed at her.

Henley's eyes were wide, and she just gaped at the two of them. Luckily, the restaurant was fairly quiet this morning.

"Well, who do we have here? You must be the new girl in town. Harley?" Edith asked.

"That's a motorcycle, not a name." Oscar studied Henley, and I just sat back, enjoying the show.

"It's Henley. Henley Holloway. It's nice to meet you both."

"Henley. That's sort of weird, right?" Edith asked. "Did your parents not care much for you?"

Henley's head fell back in laughter. "Henley is my grand-mother's maiden name."

"Ahhh… well, that's better. These Chadwicks all have weird names, too." She flicked her thumb in my direction.

Yeah, we'd endured years of her questioning our names. As if Edith and Oscar were the most common names on the planet.

Glass fucking houses, Edith.

"Well, that doesn't stop you from tripping over yourself every time one of them comes into the place," Oscar said in that loud, deafening tone.

I pinched the bridge of my nose. "Henley and I work together, and I thought I'd show her around Rosewood River. She's been here for weeks and has been working a lot. We wanted to start here and grab some breakfast."

"Interesting." Edith tapped her chin. "I can't remember the

last time you brought a woman with you here, other than your mother or Emerson."

"Are you hitting on him in front of me?" Oscar bellowed.

"For God's sake, you crazy old man. He's not my type. I like my men old and grumpy!" Edith yelled back at her husband. "I'm just pointing out, woman to woman, that this guy is a bit of a workaholic, and from what I gather from the locals, he keeps his relationships very *casual*. That's code for... noncommittal, Harley."

"It's Henley," I snipped. "And as much as I appreciate you warning off a woman that I bring with me to breakfast, I'd like to go to our table now, if the harassment is over. I'm hungry."

"I thought Bridger was the grumpiest Chadwick. Lose the 'tude, dude." Oscar chuckled, and Edith joined in.

That was the thing with these two. Once they'd completely offended you, and you pushed back, they acted like you were the crazy asshole who was being sensitive.

"Follow me." Edith quirked a brow and grabbed two menus. "I heard you bought the big house on the river, Henley. 'The Taylor Tea' was delivering all the gossip when you moved to town. I've been waiting for you to get your butt in here."

We slid into the booth across from one another. "You read that crap, too, Edith? I expected more from you."

"Are you kidding? I live for that crap." She smirked. "Oscar hates it, but I always see him snooping over my shoulder, trying to read it."

"I've been wanting to come in. I ordered takeout the other day from here, and the chicken pot pie was delicious."

"Wait till you try the breakfast. It's what we're famous for. What can I get you to drink?"

We both requested water and coffee, and Edith insisted Henley try the orange juice, even though she hadn't asked for it.

Welcome to Rosewood River.

When she walked away, Henley glanced at the menu, but I already knew what I was getting.

"Guess what you won't see on the menu?"

"What? It all looks amazing," she said, as she looked up at me.

"A honey biscuit. In fact, there is no biscuit at all on the menu."

She tossed her menu aside as Edith dropped off our drinks and took our breakfast orders.

Once she stepped away, Henley studied me. "You have a real hang-up with the way people name their businesses, huh?"

"I just think it's weird. You've got The Green Basket with no green baskets. You have the Honey Biscuit, and they don't even bother to put a biscuit on their menu. I mean, all breakfast places have biscuits. These two decide to serve coffee cake instead of biscuits. It makes no sense."

"And what other businesses do you have an issue with?" She smirked, and she was so sexy it took everything I had not to move to the other side of the booth. I wanted to be near her.

"Well, you've got Randy's Razor. He's my barber. He's everyone's barber. And please, ask me what his name is." I sipped my coffee, and the corners of her lips tipped up in a wide smile.

"I'm guessing it's not Randy?"

"Correct. His name is Max. His father's name was Henry."

"And did his father start the business?" she asked.

"Nope. His grandfather started it." My gaze locked with hers, and I couldn't help but chuckle. "And his name is... Sal."

Her head fell back in laughter, and I fucking loved it.

I loved the sound of her laugh. Loved the way her smile reached her eyes.

"I'm grateful for the Rosewood River history lesson." She paused when Edith set our food down and hurried away, as the restaurant was getting busier now.

She groaned when she took the first bite of her pancakes.

"Don't groan in a public place, Princess," I said, my voice low.

She gave me a devious smile. "Why?"

"Because I'll haul your ass in that bathroom so fast, your head will spin. And then everyone will know our little secret."

"Is it really bothering you that it's a secret?"

I forked my omelet and popped it into my mouth as I thought over her question. "Yes. I don't want to be your dirty little secret."

"It's not that it's a secret, Easton." She chuckled.

"Well, you don't want anyone to know, which, by definition, makes it a secret. This is why my dick is off limits to you."

Her gaze softened. "I know that what you've been through has been tough, and I'm really happy that you want to give this a shot. Because I like you. I like you a lot. But I also don't want to get hurt. And you haven't done this for a very long time, and having everyone at the office know, including my father—that puts pressure on us. And I guess I just feel like…" She paused as she thought about her words.

"You feel unsure if we should even go there." It wasn't a question; it was a statement. I wasn't the safe bet, and I understood that.

"No." She shook her head. "Is that what you think?"

"You wouldn't be wrong to doubt me."

"That's not what this is." She took a sip of her juice and set the glass back down. "I want this to work. And adding pressure means it would have more of a chance of failing. And I don't want this to end because other people are involved."

Damn her. She was fucking right. And of course, I was being an asshole.

"Listen, Princess." I leaned forward, glancing around to make sure no one was watching us. "I really like you. And I haven't said those words in a very long time. Nor have I felt like this. But I understand what you're saying, so my dick is back on the table."

She covered her face with her hands. "Well, that didn't take long."

"What can I say? I'm a sap for my girl." I winked, and the

smile I got in return made me want to say shit like this all the time to her.

"I like the sound of that."

"Me, too. Eat up. I've got big plans for you," I said, and we spent the next hour eating and talking. The more I knew about this woman, the more I liked her.

We left the café and walked the entire downtown. I pointed out Randy's Razor, Booze & Brews, Sweet Scoops ice cream parlor, and she paused in front of The Vintage Rose flower shop, which was connected to Strawberry Dreams, a local boutique.

"Look at those peonies," she said as she looked in the window of the flower shop before turning toward the display next door. "Oh, my gosh, the boutique next door is so quaint."

"Let's go in. My mom's good friend owns Strawberry Dreams." I held the door open and followed Henley inside.

"Easton, this is a lovely surprise." Melanie came around the corner and gave me a big hug.

"Yeah, I was just showing a friend around town. This is Henley Holloway. We work together. Henley, this is Melanie Banks."

"It's lovely to meet you. I heard you were new to town. I'm so glad you've got this guy to show you around. He could be the Rosewood River mayor. Everyone knows Easton." She shot me a wink.

"It's so nice to meet you. I've been here for a few weeks, and I've just been bogged down with work, so I'm thrilled to finally be checking out all the shops down here. This place is adorable," Henley said.

"Let me show you around." She introduced her to Emilia Taylor, who was cutting flowers in the connecting store before guiding her in the other direction. "We've got a whole back room filled with home décor." Melanie led Henley away, and I turned to see Emilia setting the bundle of flowers into a vase as she looked up at me.

"Hey, Easton. How's it going?"

"It's going well. Could you grab me two dozen peonies and wrap them up?" I asked, keeping my voice low.

I had been out of the dating game for a while, but seeing the way she looked at the flowers in the window made me want to get them for her.

This was very out of character for me, and obviously, Emilia knew it, too, because her eyes widened. "Two dozen peonies?"

"They're for a friend." I cleared my throat. "A friend who just got out of the hospital."

I tried to think on my feet as I watched her wrap up the flowers, and I handed her the cash.

"You aren't going to write about this in 'The Taylor Tea,' are you?" My voice was all tease, but she knew that I wasn't happy about that column.

"Well, seeing as I own a flower shop and don't work for my family at the newspaper, I definitely wouldn't be the one writing it. But if someone in town sees you with flowers, I can't help what they choose to print." She shrugged, and I suddenly felt like a dick for giving her a hard time.

I tucked them beneath my arm in an attempt to keep them slightly hidden for now as I gave her a curt nod in understanding.

I made a little more small talk with Emilia before Henley and Melanie came around the corner.

"Thank you so much for the tour. I'm in love with this shop, and I will definitely be back to get a few things for the house." Henley leaned forward and hugged Melanie goodbye, which surprised me. They'd just met, but Henley had a way of warming up to people quickly.

I gave Melanie a kiss on the cheek, and we stepped outside, heading back toward home.

I pulled the arrangement from under my arm and handed it to her.

Her eyes widened. "What are these for?"

"You said they're your favorite."

"I think you might be my favorite, too, Easton Chadwick."
She held them to her nose.

Yeah. You're my favorite, too.

And I hadn't felt that way in a very long time.

twenty-four

. . .

Henley

EASTON and I had been spending every single day together at the office, and every night together at my place or his, for the last month.

He definitely did not hold out on me, as we'd been having more sex than I'd ever had in my life.

I appreciated that this had been kept between us so we could give this an actual try without anyone on the outside getting involved. I knew his family was aware something was going on, because I'd gone to the final pickleball tournament and cheered them on, and I'd also been to several Sunday dinners.

But we'd kept our hands to ourselves in public, aside from him grabbing my thigh beneath the dinner table this past Sunday night.

No one in the office appeared to suspect anything, but we were definitely playing with fire. We worked long hours because this case was all-consuming.

My phone vibrated as I sat in my cubicle.

EASTON

I can still taste you on my lips from this morning.

I chuckled at the text, as he did this all day long. And I loved to feign irritation.

> Highly inappropriate to send during work hours. <eye roll emoji>

EASTON

And you love it, Princess.

> You do keep the day exciting.

EASTON

Do you want me to make it more exciting?

> How would you do that?

EASTON

You could meet me in the janitor's closet. It's Friday, and it would be a nice way to end the week.

> Easton.

EASTON

Henley. You know you're thinking about it. <eggplant emoji>

> There are people working in the file room who could hear something. It shares a wall with that closet.

EASTON

That means you can't make even the slightest noise. I could keep you quiet by putting my tongue in your mouth.

> We shouldn't.

EASTON

> We've got to work late tonight, and we have my mom's party tomorrow, which means you'll insist that we pretend we aren't together. So, I'm following the rules, but I need to have my hands on my girl now.

My girl.

> I'll go in there first. You better not get us caught, Chadwick.

I didn't know why our relationship was even a secret anymore. He'd been completely all in since the moment he'd said he wanted to date me.

No whiplash.

No mixed signals.

I didn't know why I was hesitating. I was head over heels for this man, so maybe it was fear.

Fear that he'd change his mind.

I pushed up from my desk and made my way around the corner. The closet door was easy to sneak into, as the file room was on the other side. I could hear the chatter of the people working in there through the thin walls.

Not two minutes later, the door opened and closed. I heard the lock click behind him, and he moved toward me slowly with a wicked grin on his face. He held up a finger, as if to remind me not to make a sound.

My heart thundered in my chest.

This was risky. I'd insisted on keeping our relationship a secret, and here I was, locked in the maintenance closet.

Loud laughter came from the other side of the wall. Another reminder of how risky this was. Easton raised a brow and smiled.

He liked it.

He leaned down and kissed me.

The minute our lips touched, it was like a fire lit inside us both. This is how it always was with us.

Fiery. Passionate. Explosive.

He tugged my skirt up as I quickly unbuttoned and unzipped his pants, shoving them down as his dick sprung free. He had the foil packet in his dress shirt pocket, and his lips left mine as he tore the top off and quickly rolled the latex over himself.

His gaze was heated as he reached for my hands. He placed them both on the edge of the shelf above my head and gave me a knowing look, letting me know to keep them there. I nodded.

My skirt was bunched around my waist, and he reached for the sides of my hips and slowly lowered my panties down my legs as he bent down and lifted my stiletto-covered foot one at a time and removed my panties. He leaned forward and pressed his nose to my center and breathed me in. I gasped the slightest bit, and his head shot up, and he raised a brow.

Quiet.

He ran his fingers through my slit and then slipped them into his mouth as he pushed to stand, then tucked my panties into the pocket of his dress shirt.

His mouth covered mine as my feet lifted off the floor. His arms moved beneath the backs of my thighs, and the tip of his erection teased my entrance. Without hesitation, he thrust inside, and my head fell back at the sensation.

So good.

Too good.

I wanted more.

My hands gripped the shelving unit as he pulled out and then drove back in.

I flexed my hips, meeting him thrust for thrust, as we found our rhythm.

Faster. Harder. Desperate for more.

I focused on controlling my breathing, and Easton's mouth never left mine.

The sensation of him. The pace. My hands gripping the shelves. The fact that we couldn't make a sound.

It was so erotic.

My body started to tingle, and I knew I was close. My hands fell from the shelf, tangling in his hair, as I kissed him harder.

I stifled my groan as I squeezed my eyes closed and went over the edge.

The orgasm was still ripping through me as Easton thrust harder.

Once.

Twice.

And the slightest sound left his lips as he continued to kiss me.

And we rode out every bit of pleasure until he finally slowed. He pulled back and studied me, as if it were the first time he was seeing me.

His hand was on my cheek as he leaned forward and rested his forehead against mine.

He slowly lowered my feet to the floor and removed the condom before tying it off and pulling a handkerchief from his suit pocket, wrapping the condom inside, and slipping it into his coat pocket. He pulled up his briefs and pants as I just stood there, watching. I was still coming down from an amazing midday orgasm, and my legs were wobbly.

Easton startled me when he dropped to his knees and pulled out my panties, slipping them on one leg at a time, just as he'd taken them off. But then he turned me around so my backside was facing him, and he kissed each one of my butt cheeks, which almost made me laugh. I covered my mouth with my hand and gaped at him over my shoulder before he tugged my skirt down and smacked me on the ass. Then he turned me around, kissed me hard, and pointed to the door.

I patted my hair in place, let out a long breath I hadn't even realized I'd been holding, and cracked the door open. I looked back at him, letting him know that it was clear, and I walked out.

I stopped in the bathroom to wash my hands and make sure I didn't look like a woman who'd just had sex in the maintenance closet, when Katrina came out of the stall.

"Hey, Henley," she said in her usual upbeat tone. Katrina Larson was Carver's executive assistant. I didn't see her often, as her desk was outside Carver's office on the other side of the building, but occasionally, she'd come into the staff lounge for lunch. She had an air about her and had never been very friendly to me.

"Hi, Katrina, how's it going?"

"It's going. Do you have any fun plans this weekend?" she asked.

"Yeah, I'm going to the Chadwicks' party. How about you?"

"Me, too. I purposely found myself in the staff lounge with Easton this morning before most people arrived, so I could make sure he knew that I was coming to the party." She was whispering now, and my breath hitched in my throat at the way she was looking at me. Like she had a secret, and my gut was telling me that I wasn't going to like it. I had gotten here late this morning because I'd spent the night at Easton's house, and I'd had to go home and shower and get ready. "I was flirting hard with him. I told him that his brother, Rafe, had invited my friends and me when we'd run into him at the country club last week. And I made sure Easton knew that I was coming, and I told him that I hoped he'd save me a dance. Apparently, they have a live band and everything out there."

I wiped my hands off on a few paper towels and turned to look at her. "That sounds like so much fun. Did he say he'd save you a dance?"

"He did. I've had a crush on him forever, and I feel like this is my opening." She shrugged and then dabbed on some pink lip gloss. "I know he's a bit of a playboy, but I got the vibe that he was into me when I was talking to him."

"Well, that's really great," I said, making every effort to sound genuine when I was seething on the inside.

This was exactly why I didn't want to make things public. This man had just convinced me to have sex in the maintenance closet, and he'd been agreeing to meet up with Katrina tomorrow on the dance floor.

And since when did Easton Chadwick dance?

"It really is. I'll see you there tomorrow." She skipped out of the bathroom, and I could barely contain the anger boiling up inside me.

I marched down the hallway and whipped his office door open without knocking. He looked up, brow raised as if he were surprised. "You got a minute?"

"Of course," he said, and I closed the door and moved to the chair across from him.

"Are you all right?"

"Am I all right?" I chuckled, and it was laced with sarcasm. "No. I'm not okay. What kind of game are you playing?"

He leaned back in his chair, arms crossed over his chest. "You're going to need to be more specific. I don't play games."

"Really? You could have fooled me."

"Didn't we just have a really great time in the closet? I was not expecting this kind of hostility from you."

"You're unbelievable," I hissed.

"I think so, too. And you seemed to think so just a few minutes ago. What could have possibly changed in the last five minutes?" He was making no attempt to hide his irritation now.

He probably knew that I was on to him.

"I'll tell you what happened, you pompous ass," I said, keeping my voice low so no one could hear us.

"I'm waiting." He pursed his lips.

"I was just in the bathroom with Katrina Larson."

Let's see you weasel your way out of this one, Casanova.

"Carver's executive assistant?" he asked, as if he barely knew who she was.

"The one and only."

"Did she hear us in the closet?" He leaned forward as he folded his hands on the desk and suddenly seemed concerned.

"What? No. She didn't hear us." I squeezed my eyes closed. "This is exactly why I didn't want anyone at the office to know what was going on with us, because I knew this would happen. I knew you weren't ready for this. You just fed me a bunch of horse shit."

He pushed to his feet and came around his desk, standing in front of me, as he leaned against the desk. His legs were crossed at the ankles, and he looked pissed off. "What are you accusing me of, Henley?"

"You tell me."

"I can't, because I haven't done anything. I've been with you at work and at home every single day since we decided to give this a go. I'm the one who didn't want secrets. I'm the one who wanted everyone to know that we were together, including your father. But I respected your wishes and agreed to the ridiculous rule of keeping things quiet. So whatever you think I did, you best go ahead and tell me, because I don't have a fucking clue."

"Katrina told me that you were flirting with her, and you agreed to save her a dance at the party at your parents' house," I said, and suddenly, I felt unsure about my accusation.

Because he wasn't acting like a guilty man.

He was acting like a pissed-off man.

"Carver's assistant? That's what this is about? You think I flirted with her?" His lips turned up in the corners. "You're jealous, aren't you, Princess?"

"This is not funny. You're playing me for a fool, and I'm calling you out."

"This is fucking madness," he hissed, and I pushed to stand because I was done listening. "Sit back down. You don't get to accuse me of something and not hear the truth."

"So, what's the truth?"

"Well, you won't believe me anyway, will you?" He moved to

the office door, pulling it open before shouting. "Joey. In my office now."

"Why are you bringing Joey in here?" I whisper-hissed, as I didn't want to involve anyone else.

"Hey, Easton. What's up?" Joey said, sounding a bit out of breath as if he'd run the short distance to Easton's office.

"Take a seat, please," my boyfriend said, as he closed the door and walked back around his desk to settle in his chair.

Joey glanced over at me nervously, and I shook my head as if I didn't know what he was in here for.

"Joey, were you in the staff lounge with me this morning when Katrina came in there?" he asked.

"Yes. We were all getting coffee at the same time," he said, looking between Easton and me with confusion.

"Did I hit on Katrina?"

He started laughing. "No. I felt kind of bad for her, because she was shooting her shot for sure."

"Can you tell Henley here what happened? Because that's not the story that she heard."

Joey narrowed his gaze as he looked at me, like he was just now putting the pieces together to a puzzle he'd been trying to solve. He cleared his throat. "Katrina told Easton that his brother, Rafe, invited her to the party at his parents' house. I chimed in and said I was going, too, which, by the way, thanks for the invite, Easton," he said, glancing over at him.

"Of course. Continue," Easton said, looking totally relaxed as he leaned back in his chair.

"Well, you know Easton is kind of… annoyed when people make small talk at work—" Joey winced. "Sorry. Just speaking the truth."

"It's fine. Go ahead."

"So he was kind of short and said something like, *yep, it should be a good day for a party.* And she said she'd be looking for him there, and he didn't answer, which isn't really abnormal for him." He glanced at Easton again, and he just nodded and used his hand to motion for him to keep going. "And then he walked toward the door, and she called out to him about saving her a dance. He just glanced over his shoulder like he was uncomfortable with the conversation and left the room. But don't worry, I saved the day and said that I'd save her a dance."

Well, this is a different version of the story.

A much better version.

Easton just stared at me, as if he were waiting for an apology.

"Well, thank you for clearing that up. We wouldn't want an HR mess on our hands, would we?" I said, knowing that me brushing this under the rug was not going to fly with him.

And by the look my boyfriend was giving me, I was right.

twenty-five

• • •

Easton

I WAS NO RELATIONSHIP EXPERT. It had been years since I'd been in one of my own. But I had parents who were a great example.

I had an aunt and uncle who were a great example.

I had a twin sister who was ridiculously happy and in love with her fiancé.

And the one long-term relationship I'd been in had been a solid one.

So, I was fairly certain I'd just been accused of doing something inappropriate with Katrina Larson, a woman I barely knew, and I was owed a big, fat apology.

"Is Katrina telling HR that something inappropriate happened?" Joey gaped at me. "Because that was all her. I've got your back, Easton. You barely acknowledged her. I hope she doesn't turn on me and say I did something inappropriate. I did offer to dance with her at the party because I felt bad that you'd sort of left her hanging. No offense." He shrugged.

The dude was always apologizing.

"None taken. Do you know why I left her hanging?" I asked.

"Because you didn't want to get written up by HR?" He fell

back against his chair on a gasp. "Oh, my God. Am I here because I'm getting written up?"

Henley shot me a look, as if I were making a mess of things. But the truth was, this was on her. And this secret was the reason this shit was happening, and I was done with it.

"Joey, relax. You aren't in trouble. I called you in here because my girlfriend thought I'd acted inappropriately because Katrina had twisted the truth. And none of this would be happening if we weren't keeping secrets."

Joey stared at me, as if he didn't know what I was talking about, and I gave him a few seconds to put it together. His head whipped toward Henley and then back to me.

"Oh. Ohhhhhhh. Okay. You two are together. I got it now." He chuckled. "So I'm not in trouble?"

"You are not in trouble. I appreciate you telling the truth."

Henley sighed. "Thank you, Joey. I'm guessing Katrina just let her imagination get the best of her. I appreciate you clearing that misunderstanding up."

"Well, now that I know the story here, I don't think Katrina was confused." He chuckled. "I think someone else was playing you a little bit, Hen."

Hen? He has a nickname for her?

"What do you mean?" she asked.

"Everyone in the office thinks you two are together. It's been a rumor for a while now. And when Easton walked out of the conference room this morning, Katrina was pissed off that he'd ignored her. She asked me if I'd heard the rumors about you two and if I thought they were true."

"And what did you say?" Henley asked, shaking her head in disbelief.

"I said that I thought they were probably true, but I reminded her that I'd be happy to dance with her at the party, you know, to try to make her feel better about being rejected." He shrugged.

"I can't believe she just did that to me in the bathroom to mess with my head."

"I think she was probably trying to get you to admit it, or maybe she wanted to rock the boat with you two. I don't really know," Joey said.

"Looks like you got played, Princess. But not by me." I leaned back in my chair and turned to the man sitting across from me. "I appreciate you being honest, Joey. You can go back to work."

"Thank you." He walked to the door and turned around. "And congrats to you guys. I'm happy for you. Maybe it's time you just tell everyone so the rumors don't get out of control."

"I couldn't agree more," I said, as Joey left the office, and I crossed my arms over my chest and met Henley's gaze.

"I, um, well, I…" She paused for a few beats. "I'm sorry. I jumped to conclusions. I let her get in my head, and I'm sorry."

I nodded. "She got in your head because she could."

"What does that mean?"

"It means that it's time you trust me, Princess. This is a secret because you're afraid that I'll hurt you. But I'm not going anywhere. I don't want anyone else. I want you. All of you. And I don't want it to be a secret. Once it's out there, everyone will get used to it. People like Katrina won't be able to fuck with you, because she'll know what's going on. So how about we stop with the games and just be honest."

Her eyes widened. "It's not about me not trusting you, Easton."

"It is. And you know it."

Her eyes welled with emotion. "I'm a woman and new at this firm."

"Henley, we're both attorneys here. Yes, I'm technically your mentor for a short time. But you are the daughter of my boss. Your name is technically on the building. This relationship blowing up would hurt me as much as it would hurt you, if not more. There is no power struggle here. We're both in positions of power. But I'm willing to take the risk. The question is, are you?"

A tear moved down her cheek, and it took everything I had

in me not to rush her and pull her into my arms. I was respecting her wishes. My hands gripped the sides of my chair, and I waited.

"I do trust you. I'm just—" She shook her head, and the tears started to fall. I'd never seen her cry, even when that asshole Jamison had elbowed her in the face and then tried to push into her room. She'd never broken down. So seeing her like this caused a sharp pain to tear through my chest with a force. "I have spent my entire life trying to win the love of my father. My mother left to live in another country with her husband. I don't have a family like you do, and I am terrified of going all in and being left alone—I mean *all* alone—in the end." She shrugged.

"Baby. I'm not going anywhere. I'm right here. I want this. I want you. I'm just waiting for you to give me a sign that you want this, too," I said.

She swiped at her cheeks and glanced over at the glass walls before looking back at me. I figured she'd say we'd discuss it later, but instead, she moved to her feet and walked around my desk. She climbed into my lap and placed a hand on each side of my face. "I want this, too."

I tugged her head down and kissed her, and the sound of a few whistles and cheers came from outside the office, but neither of us gave a shit. She pulled back and looked at me and smiled, and I used the pads of my thumbs to swipe her falling tears away.

"I don't like it when you cry, Princess. So let's not do that again."

"Always so bossy." She chuckled. "So we're doing this. We're really doing this."

"Yes. It's about time you got on board. We'll be at the fall party tomorrow night, and I'm just glad I won't have to keep my distance from you. Let me call your father and let him know before he hears it from someone else at the office. It's the right thing to do."

She sighed and leaned forward to grab my cell phone and

handed it to me. "I don't really need to run my dating life by my father, so this is between you and him. I'll just listen quietly."

I nodded and dialed Charles's number and put him on speakerphone.

"Easton, I got your notes on the latest with Bruno, and it's a real shitshow, huh? How do you want to proceed?"

"Well, I've got a plan, and I'll talk to you about that later. Right now, I'm calling about something else."

"All right. What's going on?" he asked.

"I'm here with Henley, and we wanted to let you know that we've been seeing one another quietly, and we have decided to make it public."

"You're dating my daughter?"

"I am. I'm crazy about her. Have been for quite some time."

"I thought you didn't date," he said, his voice hard.

"I thought I didn't date either. But then she came along, and everything changed. I didn't jump into this lightly, Charles, and we were hesitant for a multitude of reasons, but I want this. We want this."

He was quiet, and Henley winced as she ran her fingers along the scruff of my jaw.

"You know if this goes south, it's her I'll choose. If you hurt her, and she doesn't want you here, you're out. You're risking an awful lot, Easton. I know how much a partnership means to you. And dating my daughter might be the one thing that keeps your name from ever going on the building."

"I understand. It's a risk I'm willing to take," I said, because it was.

I'd fallen in love with this woman over the last few months, and I just hadn't known how to tell her. Just hadn't known if she felt the same way.

But I made my living off of trusting my gut, and my gut told me that Henley Holloway was my end game.

"You're fine with it?" he asked as he cleared his throat. "This is obviously serious if you're telling me about it."

I looked right at her, her eyes the darkest sapphire blue with the afternoon sun shining through the window. "I didn't expect to ever let anyone steal my heart, because I honestly didn't know I still had one. But here we are. She has it. So it's hers to break. And if it costs me my job, it wouldn't matter. Because losing her would be what I wouldn't get over. I can go to work anywhere, and we both know that. But there's only one Henley, so I'll take that risk all day long, Charles."

"All right. I appreciate you telling me. I hope you don't fuck it up, for your sake and for mine. Because I'd have to hate you, and I don't want to do that."

I chuckled. "I won't fuck it up. I know a good thing when I see it."

"I hope you're right. Nothing would make me happier than to see her end up with a man deserving of her." Her brows cinched together at his words, and he ended the call.

"Wow. You're pretty crazy about me, huh?" she asked.

I put my finger to her lips. It had been many years since I'd told a woman that I loved her, and it sure as shit wasn't going to be in this office while we were working. "Don't say another word. I need to take you somewhere. Let's go."

"We're leaving work early? We have hours of work to do." She looked puzzled, but I lifted her off my lap.

"We're leaving. It'll all be here waiting for us later."

I took her hand and led her out of my office. Rosie was beaming up at us, and I winked at her. Henley grabbed her purse, and there were a few people saying congratulations as I led her right out the door. I insisted she get in my car, as she wouldn't need hers tonight.

"Where are we going?" she asked as I drove to her house.

"It's a surprise. Get changed into something comfortable, and bring a sweatshirt. We're going out on the river. I'm taking you to my favorite spot."

"Aren't we going rafting tomorrow morning before the party?" she asked as I pulled into her driveway.

"Yes. But this is different."

I walked her inside and waited as she slipped into some jeans, tennis shoes, and a hoodie, as October in Rosewood River was starting to get chilly. We were on the way to my house in no time. I quickly changed into a pair of gray joggers and my gray pullover.

I stopped in the kitchen and tossed a few things into a bag, and she just watched me curiously. Then I took her hand and led her out to the backyard. I helped her onto my boat and then climbed on after her. It seated six people comfortably, but that didn't stop me from pulling her onto my lap, as her back rested against my chest, and I drove us out to this spot that I'd found years ago. I'd never brought anyone here.

I pulled the boat into a little cove overlooking the falls. The sun was just going down, and the surrounding trees created a canopy around us.

"Oh, my gosh, what is this place?"

"It's a spot I found when I was in a bit of a dark place years ago. I'd come here to get away from everyone. Everything. Just clear my mind and be alone," I said, my voice low and quiet.

She turned a bit in my arms. "Is this where you came to grieve?"

"Probably. When I needed to be by myself. I'd go rafting all the time, and I was reckless. My family was worried about me, of course, and Emerson begged me not to go out rafting for a while. I'd given her my word, so I'd take the boat out. The water is where I did my best thinking, and I found this spot. I'd hide out here for hours. I could be angry. I could be sad. I could just work through it, you know?"

Her hands were on each side of my face and she smiled. "I'm glad you listened to Emerson and didn't go rafting to take out your anger. Because I kind of like having you here, Chadwick."

"I never thought I'd get a second chance at this, Henley. That's the truth. So I'm sorry it took me a while to figure it out, but I wasn't lying when I told your dad that my heart is yours. I haven't dated for years because no one made me feel the way that you do."

"How do I make you feel?" she asked, her gaze locked with mine.

"Alive. Like there is more to life than my job. Like there's a future out there that I didn't see before now."

"I see it, too," she whispered. "And my heart is yours, too. It happened before I even wanted to admit it to myself."

"I love you, Princess. I never thought I'd say those words again, but I can't hold them in anymore. I. Love. You."

She nodded. Tears streaming down her beautiful face. "I love you, too."

She leaned down and kissed me. It wasn't frantic or needy. It was different.

As if we knew there was no urgency.

We were both in this.

"Come on. Let's watch the sun go down." I helped her to her feet and led her to the back of the boat, where we settled on the white leather seats. I opened a bottle of wine and poured us each a glass, setting them on the little table in front of us. Henley took out the cheese and crackers, placing them on the paper plates I'd tucked into the bag.

And we sat there eating and sipping our wine and looking up at the sky together. She rested her head against my chest, and I just breathed her in.

"It's so peaceful out here. I see why you like this place," she said, bringing her wineglass to her lips and taking a sip. "Is it hard for you to be here? You know, since this was the place where you grieved?"

"I never thought I'd bring someone here. I never thought I'd tell another woman that I loved her. But when I met with Dr. Langford this week, I told her I didn't want to hold back anymore."

"What do you mean?" She tipped her head up to look at me.

"I don't want secrets from you. I want to share all the things that led me to you—the good and the bad. And yes, I used to come here to grieve, but it doesn't mean that it has to be a place where I grieve forever. Now it's the place that I told you that I loved you. The place where you told me that you loved me. The place where we left our fears in the past and decided to move forward. So now, it's our place."

"I like that. And I'm sorry that I was afraid to tell everyone that we were together. And I'm sorry that I was insecure and thought you were flirting with Katrina. Those are *me* issues, and not *you* issues, Easton."

I stroked her hair away from her face. "You had reason to hold back. I was all over the place with you for weeks because I was afraid. And I understand you being apprehensive. I knew you'd come around, my brave warrior princess."

She snuggled up against me and chuckled. "We're both brave. Giving your heart to someone is a risk. Loving someone is a risk. But I think we're worth it."

"We're definitely worth it. And I'm not going anywhere."

And that was the truth. It had taken me a long time to find someone worth taking a risk for.

And I was going to hold on tight.

twenty-six

. . .

Henley

EASTON and I had gone out rafting this morning on the river. It was exciting, even though he'd taken me on a grade II rapid for the second time, when I'd said I was ready for a little more. Easton had been an instructor for several summers during high school and college, and he'd grown up on the river. It had been a love of his for many years, and I loved going out with him. But everyone in town was talking about this big ride down the river that they did at the end of the season every year, and I wanted to work up to that. It was a grade IV.

"I'm excited to meet your sister and her fiancé and their little boy." He'd shared that Emerson was in the process of adopting Nash's son, Cutler. Easton was the one who'd sought out the birth mother and got the ball rolling. This man acted all broody and gruff on the outside, but when he loved, he loved fiercely. And I felt that love every time he looked at me.

The way he'd buckled the helmet on my head today and secured the life jacket around me, all for a glory ride down the river that barely had any bumps at all. He'd gone over the safety precautions multiple times.

He was fiercely protective, and I'd felt that every time we were together.

"She's looking forward to meeting you," he said. "And you're going to love Nash and Cutler. Man, that little boy is probably the coolest kid I've ever met."

"I'm excited to meet them. So, she knows we're together?"

He turned to look at me, and a wicked grin spread across his face. "There are no secrets in my family, Henley. They're all a bunch of sleuths. The guys knew I loved you before I even admitted it to myself. So, yeah, they all know."

My teeth sank into my bottom lip. We were going to a big party at Easton's parents' house, and we'd be outside. The sun was still out during the day in Rosewood River, but the evenings were now cool. I'd been warned about the winters getting really cold, and apparently, that would happen shortly after Thanksgiving next month. The river had been packed today, as people were getting out on the water as much as possible before it was too cold to do so.

"I can't imagine what it's like to have such a big family." I shrugged. "The only person I've told outside of my father is Lulu. I can't wait for you to meet her."

I'd told Easton all about my best friend. He knew she was more like a sister to me. He'd also been surprised to learn that she was actually the same Lulu Sonnet he'd heard of, as she was somewhat well-known in the press, being born into a very public family and then dating a famous rock star.

"She's still in London on business?"

"Yeah. She's really making a name for herself."

"I look forward to meeting her." He tipped my chin up and kissed my forehead. "You ready for a whole lot of Chadwicks tonight?"

I chuckled. I'd attended many Sunday night dinners, and I'd grown close to his immediate family. But tonight, I'd meet his twin sister and a lot of his extended family, and everyone in town would be there. The Chadwicks were like Rosewood River royalty, and everyone loved them.

"I'm ready."

"You look beautiful. I'm just glad I get to walk in with you, and I don't have to force myself to keep my distance."

"Me, too," I said, and I meant it. "And I won't mind at all making sure Katrina sees us together."

He chuckled. "Just admit that you were jealous."

"Fine. I was jealous."

He smirked like the cocky bastard he was, and I freaking loved it. He looked so good in his white dress shirt, dark jeans, and cowboy boots. I was wearing my cream floral maxi dress with my brown boots.

He kissed my neck and worked his way down, as my off-the-shoulders dress allowed for easy access. "I like you all worked up and jealous."

"Okay," I said, as my breathing picked up. "We're going to be late. We need to be there before it gets dark because your mom said she has a photographer coming to take photos of everyone. I promised we'd get there early."

"Damn. You're such a rule follower, Princess." He pulled back and took my hand, leading me out to the kitchen. I grabbed my purse and denim jacket for later, and we made our way out the door.

Easton carried the two bottles of wine we'd brought, and I held the flowers I'd picked up from The Vintage Rose this morning for his mother.

We walked the short distance to his parents' house, and from the moment we arrived, it was a whirlwind.

His mother ushered us outside to the photographer and insisted we get a picture before things got too busy. Easton surprised me when he pulled me into his arms and kissed me, as the photographer snapped several pictures.

"Well, if that isn't the cutest picture I've ever seen," a voice called out, and I turned to see Emerson standing there, smiling. I'd recognized her from the photos I'd seen.

"Hey, Emmy," Easton said, as he pulled back and took my hand and led me toward his sister.

She was stunning and had the biggest smile on her face as he let my hand go briefly to pull her into a hug. It was hard not to laugh that they were twins, as their size difference was massive in the way he towered over her.

"Enough of that, E. How about you introduce me to your girl," she said over her laughter.

"Henley, Emmy. Emmy, Henley." He motioned between us.

Before I could even say hello, Emerson rushed me, wrapping her arms around me and giving me the warmest hug. "It's so nice to meet you, Henley. I've heard a lot about you."

"It's so lovely to meet you. I've heard so much about you, as well."

When she pulled back, I noticed that her eyes were wet with emotion. She'd known what her brother had been through, and she was happy to see him moving forward. At least, that's how it appeared.

"Uncle E!" a little voice shouted as he ran toward us with a tall man beside him, who I assumed was his father.

"Hey, Beefcake," Easton called out, as the little dude launched himself into his arms.

"Hey, you must be Henley. I'm Nash." He extended his hand to me and then pulled me into a hug.

"It's so great to finally meet you all," I said.

"Well, we're just happy to see the big guy smiling so much," Nash teased, as he turned and hugged Easton, who had just set his son back down.

"Wow. You're real pretty," Cutler said, as I bent down to give him a hug. He was adorable in his jeans and leather coat, with his hair slicked back.

"Well, thank you. It's so nice to meet you, Cutler."

"You can call me Beefcake. Because if you're my Uncle E's girl, that means you're my girl, too." He winked. This little guy had more charm in his pinkie finger than most grown men that I'd met in my life.

"How about a group photo?" the photographer said, and we

all got together and smiled. The property was stunning, with large trees all around us and the barn in the distance.

We chatted for a bit before Keaton called us over, as everyone was arriving. There was a live band playing and a makeshift dance floor. The event was being catered by the Honey Biscuit Café, and the smell of ribs and chicken had my stomach growling. It was like something out of a magazine, with tables and chairs set up all around the backyard. Each table was covered in a pretty tablecloth in coordinating patterns of orange and green and yellow. Some floral. Some striped. Some checkered. There were sage-green linen napkins with little polka dot bows tied around each one at every place setting.

"Wow! Your mom goes all out. This is so cute," I said, as Emerson motioned for us to grab a table together.

"My mom is a natural at this. She loves throwing events, and I've basically given her all the freedom to plan my wedding." She chuckled. "We're doing it together, but she's got a better eye for it."

"You're getting married in the spring, right? Here at the house?"

"Yes. So we're deep into the planning stages now." She paused to glance over at Easton and Nash, who were talking with her brothers and cousins. People were already out on the dance floor, and everyone was having a good time. "I hope you'll come to the wedding."

I smiled. "I would love to. Thank you for including me."

"It's a big deal that he's taken this step, Henley. I know he's told you about what happened with Jilly, and it's been years, so to most people, it wouldn't seem like such a big deal. But for Easton, he really shut down after that. And grief can be very deceiving, you know?" She swiped at her eye as a tear sprung loose, and I startled. "He's out there crushing life. He's an amazing lawyer. He knows how to go out and have a good time, and he can be the life of the party when he wants to be. But my brother has been guarding his heart for years. To the point that I really thought he would just close off any idea of a real relationship again. He was content with being a workaholic and having casual relationships that didn't go anywhere. So this is really big for him. It's a sign that he's moving forward. He held a lot of guilt about Jilly's accident, and it didn't matter how many times we all told him it wasn't his fault, because it wasn't at all. But that didn't stop him from carrying that. But you are a breath of fresh air for my brother, and we all see it. So, thank you for being that light in his life that he desperately needed. But be patient with him. He can be overbearing and protective, but it's a coping mechanism, I think. And when he loves, he loves so deeply. And I can see how crazy he is about you."

I sucked in a breath, fighting back the lump forming in my throat. "I'm crazy in love with that man. He's not going to scare me off. He did give me quite a bad case of whiplash the first few weeks after I'd met him, but I understand it now. Grief is something each person has to work through in their own way."

"Yeah, I know. And thank you for understanding him the way you do. He talks about you like you walk on water," she said with a chuckle. "And Easton usually thinks he's the only one who walks on water."

My heart raced at her words, and I just shook my head and smiled.

"Oh, boy," she groaned before breaking into a fit of laughter. "You think he walks on water, too, don't you?"

"Why do you look like you're up to no good, evil twin?" Easton said to his sister as he came up behind me and kissed my cheek.

"Oh, were your ears burning?" she asked when Nash took the seat beside her.

Rafe, Axel, and Archer found seats at our table.

"Look at Beefcake teaching Melody how to dance," Easton said, wrapping an arm around my shoulder.

"I heard Easton took you out on the water this morning,"

Rafe said with a smirk, like there was some sort of inside joke there.

"I took her on Mayberry Pass," Easton said, as Bridger and Clark brought beers to the table for everyone, setting one in front of me before they took the open seats at the table.

"It was great. Pretty uneventful, but fun."

"You're still new to the sport," he said, kissing my cheek.

"You took her on Mayberry Pass? Come on, dude. She played collegiate tennis. She's an athlete. Mimi and Pops can do Mayberry Pass in their sleep." Rafe was laughing hysterically.

"You should have her come out and do Rocky Mountain with us in a few weeks for the annual last Rosewood River ride. That gives her some time to get out there a few times before then," Axel said.

"I personally don't enjoy it," Emerson said. "These lunatics love it, and I'm always holding on for dear life."

"You got soft with old age, Emmy," Bridger said, shooting her a wink. "It's not that bad. It's a grade IV."

"Although we've been out there a few times where I swear it was more grade V," Rafe said, as he shivered dramatically, and everyone laughed.

"It's between a four and a five. And she's not doing it with us. You've grown up on that river. She's new to it." Easton's voice was harsh, and he gave me a little squeeze.

"I have rafted before moving here. And I did a more difficult pass than what we've done, so I think I'd be fine. It's a few weeks away, and we're going out again next weekend. So how about we just see how I progress," I said, my voice all tease. I'd researched river rafting and was impressed that Easton had been as skilled as he was. But I was athletic and fairly competitive, so I felt confident that I could handle a lot more than what he'd been doing with me.

"Yeah. I heard the girl smoked you at pickleball." Emerson was laughing hysterically now.

"I'm just relieved pickleball is done for now, because Coach is working us hard on the ice. I don't have time for Easton's antics on the pickleball court right now," Clark said.

"Hey, the Chad-Six got the gold again. My antics are what keep you guys coming back year after year."

"I'd like Henley to take my spot next year," Archer said. "I've got too much going on with work and raising Melody. How about I be the sub next year, and you join the Chad-Six?" Archer quirked a brow as he looked at me.

"Well, she's much better than you, so it would be a good move for everyone. What do you say, baby?" Easton asked.

"I'll play with you. But only if you agree to take me out on the river on a more challenging pass next weekend."

His brows cinched, and he studied me before he nodded. "I can do that. Slowly. The river can be a beast."

"A beast that I believe you referred to as your bitch many times," Rafe said, and Easton flipped him the bird.

Someone rang a bell, and everyone was on their feet and heading to the buffet table. Easton offered to grab me a plate so I could stay and visit with Emerson.

"Damn. My brother is ridiculously cute with you. He's never been like this. Not even with—" She stopped herself from saying her name, and I glanced up to see Katrina walking our way.

I groaned internally as she came to stand beside my chair. She crossed her arms over her chest and raised a brow. "Congrats. I heard you and Easton are officially together."

"Yes. Thank you." I forced a smile. "But you already knew that, didn't you?"

"I suspected, but hey, if you weren't going to claim your man, he's up for grabs, right?" She chuckled as she took a sip of her beer.

"Well, lucky for me, he's not up for grabs," I said dryly, my voice completely lacking any humor.

"Hey, ladies!" Joey walked up behind Katrina and made a face at me as if he were apologizing for her. "Great party, isn't it?"

"Joey, can you get me a fresh beer, please?" Katrina held her bottle out to him, and he glanced over at me. He was trying to help me, and she was completely using him.

"How about this? I'll go with Joey to grab that because I think Emerson and I could use another." I gave Emerson a look that said I needed to get away from this woman, and she thanked me for grabbing us drinks.

When Joey and I walked away, I linked an arm through his. "Why are you being so nice to her? She's so rude."

"I'm only doing it to help you and Easton out. You've both been really decent to me." He shrugged.

"Hey, Joey," the cute woman who appeared to be in her mid-twenties and was working the bar said. I didn't miss the way her cheeks pinked when she looked at him, and he looked very happy to see her.

"Hey, Pippa!" he said. "I didn't know you moved back to town."

"Yes. I just got back two weeks ago. I gave Hollywood a try, but I didn't have any luck, so I came home with my tail between my legs." She handed us each a couple of beers. "But I do have that college degree, and I'm ready to put it to work. I just need to find myself a job here in town."

"This is my friend, Henley," he said. "This is Pippa. We grew up together."

"Hi, Henley, it's nice to meet you."

"Nice to meet you, too," I said. She smiled before turning away when someone came behind the bar with a case of booze.

"We're hiring," I whispered to him, and he nodded.

When Pippa turned around, she apologized for the interruption.

"Don't worry about that. I just had a thought. We're hiring at the firm. I'm a lawyer now." He shrugged, and it made me chuckle how humble he was about it. "I don't know if administrative type of work is what you're looking for, but Henley here is an attorney, too, and we could put in a good word for you.

Actually, Easton Chadwick runs the office. I know he was a few years older than us, but you probably remember him."

"Yes. Oh, my gosh, I would be very interested. I heard you went to law school. That's amazing. Um, how should I reach out to you?" she asked, and her cheeks flushed again.

She clearly liked him.

"You can come by the office next week and fill out an application," he said, and I stepped on his foot, and he startled.

"It might be better to just call Joey directly, and he can set up a time for you to come meet with Easton."

"Oh. Yes. Here, let me get your number." Joey was smiling as he handed her his phone, and I glanced around to find Easton standing at our table, looking for me.

Our eyes met at the same time.

He smiled, and I told Joey I'd meet him back at the table.

I hurried back, and Katrina was standing there trying to talk to him, but his eyes were on me.

I didn't look at her when I handed a beer to Emerson, and Easton wrapped an arm around my waist.

"Hey, Princess. Glad you're back."

And then he leaned down and kissed me.

Making sure everyone there knew we were together.

Knew that I was his.

And I loved it.

twenty-seven

. . .

Easton

ARCHER

Melody, who obviously has a limited vocabulary as she's barely three years old, just asked me if she has boobies. Where the fuck did she hear that?

AXEL

My money is on Rafe.

CLARK

Same.

RAFE

Is boobies a bad word now?

BRIDGER

It's better than asking if she has titties.

RAFE

I love me some titties.

CLARK

ARCHER

Hey, I'm trying to raise a little girl over here. Watch your fucking mouths when you're around her.

BRIDGER

I always call "earmuffs" before I say anything offensive.

AXEL

Well, you barely speak half the time, so it's slightly easier for you.

BRIDGER

Maybe you all should take a lesson in the joys of quiet time. You're all so fucking chatty.

Rafe used to get written up at school for talking during quiet time. He can't help himself.

ARCHER

I'm being serious here. My daughter just said boobies.

RAFE

Don't get your panties in a wad. Boobies are great. She didn't say fuck. Or titties. Or pussy. Or dick. You're making a mountain out of a melon.

It's molehill, you jackass.

RAFE

I know. But all this talk about boobies and titties has my mind going to a nice set of melons.

CLARK

I will never look at a cantaloupe the same again.

ARCHER

<middle finger emoji>

> Relax, Archer. You're doing a great job. She's got to call her parts something, right? Boobies is better than the alternative.

RAFE

Agreed. You're overreacting. It's not a big deal.

CLARK

Why don't you ask Emerson what to call them? She's a doctor.

> For fuck's sake. You don't need to ask a doctor what to call boobies.

ARCHER

I'm in over my head lately. I just taught myself how to French braid her hair because some pain-in-the-ass kid at camp wears these fancy fucking braids every day, and Melody keeps pointing them out to me. This parenting gig is no joke.

RAFE

Dude. I love a good French braid. Did you watch YouTube videos?

ARCHER

The fuck are you talking about?

RAFE

Remember Susie Jolly? I dated her sophomore year of college. She had long blonde hair and would ask me to braid her hair all the time. She showed me a few YouTube videos.

CLARK

I don't remember you knowing how to braid hair.

RAFE

I didn't say I figured it out. Just that I watched the videos. Good for you, Archie.

ARCHER

Thanks for that NOT helpful tip.

BRIDGER

Can't you ask your nanny to braid her hair?

ARCHER

Mrs. Dowden has arthritis. She can't move her fingers that easily.

RAFE

That's because Mrs. Doubtfire is a hundred and seven years old. Hire a young, hot nanny like every other single dad raising a kid on their own would do.

AXEL

Mrs. Doubtfire. <head exploding emoji>

RAFE

She dresses like the dude in the movie. And she's too old.

ARCHER

She's hardly a hundred and seven years old. She's eighty-two, and she counts on that income.

I have to agree with Rafe. Dotty Dowden is a lovely woman, but when I stopped by your house the other day when you asked me to check on Melody, she had me make her a cup of tea and walk her to the bathroom. She can't handle a toddler.

AXEL

You had me stop by last week to check on Melody, too. What's the deal with that?

ARCHER

Sometimes Mrs. Dowden doesn't answer the phone, and I just want to make sure everything is okay.

BRIDGER

Dude.

RAFE

Were you going to say something more, Bridger? Or just the single word is all we get.

BRIDGER

It's time to let her go.

Agreed. She's got her husband, and she's got retirement. She's fine. Melody is more active now. You need someone younger and more active.

ARCHER

I know. I'll talk to her and start putting my feelers out.

You're doing a good job, Arch.

RAFE

Does anyone else notice that Easton is much softer now that he's in love?

Laura Pavlov

BRIDGER

Yes. He's a big, fat pussy now.

CLARK

Agreed. He refuses to let Henley go out with us on the annual river day. She told me she wants to come with us.

I've taken her out two more times. Why are you pushing this?

RAFE

Dude. She wants to go. She talked about it at Sunday dinner AGAIN. She'll be fine. She's smart and athletic. Stop being an overbearing dick.

ARCHER

I usually have your back, but I agree on this one. She'd be fine. We'd all look out for her.

AXEL

Rafe is more of a risk than Henley. He screams like a little girl every year. But for real, E, you're the one manning the boat. She'd be fine.

Stop bringing it up. You're pissing me off. I've got to go. I have a meeting.

I TURNED my phone off and pulled the front door open to Dr. Langford's office. I'd continued seeing her every other week since I'd started coming back around the time of my birthday.

Her assistant greeted me and walked me down to her office. I sat on the couch across from her, just like I always did.

"Easton, it's nice to see you. How are you doing?" she asked. She was in her mid-forties. She wore glasses and had that soothing therapist voice like you'd see in movies.

"I'm well. I've got a meeting to get to from here, so I can't go over an hour today."

She loved to go over the allotted time. I was sticking to my commitment to come, but I didn't need more than an hour.

I was a busy man, after all.

And I sort of hated therapy.

But for whatever reason, I felt like it was good for me. She'd been the one to help me realize that I was crazy about Henley. She'd helped me through my grief years ago and again recently.

There were things that I couldn't talk to my family about, or even Henley, that I could talk to Dr. Langford about.

"Did you take Henley back out on the river?"

Here we go.

It was the topic I couldn't speak to anyone else about. This irrational fear I had about the woman I loved getting hurt.

Not on a daily basis, just with things that I knew were dangerous.

River rafting is dangerous.

I knew this because I spent many years of my life doing it.

Was it too much to ask that she didn't try a challenging pass on the river?

Jamison Waterman is dangerous.

He'd attacked her at the hotel.

So I called every fucking morning to make sure that he was still in treatment.

"I did. She's determined to do all the river runs now. And she wants to go on the annual river rafting run. It's ridiculous."

"You were a guide for many years. You go out with your family every year, and you yourself go out on the water often. Why wouldn't you be comfortable with her joining in?" she asked.

"I don't really have the answer, Dr. Langford. I'm guessing because she didn't grow up on the river." I shrugged, reaching for my water bottle to take a sip.

"So everyone who goes river rafting has to have grown up on the water?"

Dr. Langford loved to poke the bear with her condescending questions.

She already knew the answer. She was just fucking with me.

"Obviously not. But I don't give a shit about everyone else. My concern is Henley." I let out a frustrated breath. "And today, I actually have something I want to discuss with you that has nothing to do with going out on the river."

"Okay. What is it?"

"Is there a rule about moving in with someone? Like a specific timeline you need to follow?"

She chuckled as if I was hilarious, and nothing about what I was asking was funny. "Not everything has rules, Easton. Are you thinking about asking Henley to move in with you?"

"Well, we spend every night together, and I like it that way. So I was going to ask her this morning, but I thought I'd better ask you first in case the idea is offensive. We've only known one another for four months, and I always thought you needed to know someone for years before you shacked up. But I love her. I want her with me all the time. So it's silly to have two homes."

"I don't think any woman would be offended to be asked, but it's up to her if she feels ready or not. And I do think that you have to work through some of these—complications that are coming up for you before you take the next step."

"What complications?" I asked.

"Well, the fact that you call a rehab center every single morning to make sure that your coworker is still there. The fact that you have an abnormal amount of anxiety about Henley going out on the river, even though you would be right there with her."

"Wow. Abnormal is a harsh word, Dr. Langford. I thought that this was a judgment-free zone." I quirked a brow, and she chuckled.

"It is, Easton. And I'm not trying to be harsh. But you've got to deal with these things before you take things to the next level, because they won't just suddenly go away."

"Listen. It's not rocket science. I lost my girlfriend in a car accident many years ago. I haven't dated since. I had no desire to date before I met Henley. And now I meet the love of my life, and sure, there's some anxiety when it comes to high-risk sports. I don't have a problem with her playing pickleball, do I? I think you're making a big deal out of something that is not that big of a deal. I love her. I want to keep her safe. It's as simple as that."

She studied me. "I bet you're a brilliant attorney."

"I like to think so."

"You aren't going to school me on my livelihood, Easton. And you can justify this to everyone in your life if you want to, and they'll probably buy it. You make a good point. But you're trained to make a good point, aren't you?"

"Sure. But I'm not making a point. I'm speaking the truth. You're trying to make this deeper than it is."

"I've been doing this a long time, and I promise you, deep-rooted fear does not just go away. You're managing your feelings right now, but all of this will eventually come to the surface. I'm trying to bring you there before you take things too far."

I shook my head and chuckled, but it wasn't genuine. "I appreciate the concern, but it's really fine, Dr. Langford."

"Are you having nightmares?"

"No. I've been sleeping well." The lie slipped easily from my lips. The nightmares weren't bad, and I'd only had a few. I hadn't had them in years, but I'd woken up in a cold sweat a few times over the last few weeks while Henley slept beside me.

The nightmares were manageable.

Just basic shit, like seeing her in a car accident.

Seeing her falling from a raft and floating down the river.

Running toward her and never reaching her.

You know, the basics of any horrible nightmare. But I sure as shit wasn't going to tell Dr. Freud any of that for fear she'd have me committed.

They weren't a big deal. Henley hadn't heard me wake up.

I'd slipped out of bed and paced around the house for a bit until I got tired again and was able to get back to sleep.

Shit happens. Everything does not need to be analyzed.

"All right." She clasped her hands together. "Listen, I'm on your side, Easton."

It sure as hell doesn't feel like it.

"I appreciate that."

"I think the fact that you told Henley that you loved her— that you admitted your feelings—is huge. It's taken you a long time to get here. But with that comes some of the underlying fears. And you need to work through those as they arise so they don't become bigger issues later." She took a sip of her water, and her gaze locked with mine. "I think asking her to move in with you is a lovely idea."

"Great. That's all I needed to hear."

"However"—she held up her hand to stop me from gloating —"if you are feeling irrationally nervous about her going on the river with your family or anxious about your coworker getting out of rehab early or you start experiencing nightmares again, I urge you to speak to someone. If it's not me, talk to Henley about it. Talk to Emerson. Don't hide from it, because it won't just go away, Easton. And if you want a future with this woman, one that includes marriage and children, those fears will only grow deeper the more you invest into building your family with her."

"I'm just asking her to move in with me, Doc. I think you're getting ahead of yourself."

The thought of children caused my collar to tighten around my neck, and I unbuttoned a button.

Kids were a whole other level of risk. The shit me and my siblings and cousins got into could give any grown adult an ulcer.

"You deserve to be happy, Easton. And what you went through wasn't fair," she said, waiting for me to meet her gaze.

"But it doesn't mean it will happen again. Sometimes life is unfair. It doesn't mean it will always be unfair. Jilly was in a horrible accident. That does not mean that Henley will suffer the same fate."

"I'm aware." I cleared my throat because the topic was starting to piss me off.

My neck was sweating.

My hands were sweating.

I was working hard to control my breathing.

My head started buzzing, and I couldn't make out the words Dr. Langford was saying to me.

She was standing in front of me now.

I was gasping and nauseous, and I pushed to my feet and ran to the bathroom in her office, barely closing the door before I vomited several times into the toilet.

Fuck me.

I heaved multiple times before sitting on the floor for a few beats and catching my breath.

I pushed to stand and went to the sink to splash some cold water on my face. After I rinsed my mouth and washed my hands, I walked back into her office.

She was looking at me with concern. "Are you all right?"

"Yes. Of course. I had tuna for lunch, and it clearly didn't sit well."

"Easton. That wasn't the tuna. That wasn't anything that you ate. That was a panic attack. How often are you having them?"

I scrubbed a hand down my face and glanced down at my phone to see the time.

I had a meeting, and I needed to get back to the office. "You worry too much. It's a stomach bug. I've got to go. I'll see you in two weeks."

But I would most likely cancel that meeting.

Because Dr. Langford wanted to make me her science project, and I wasn't down with that.

Laura Pavlov

I was fine.
All of this would pass.
I'd overcome worse, and this would be no different.

twenty-eight

. . .

Henley

MY STOMACH WAS IN KNOTS. Easton and I had driven to our office in the city to meet with Bruno King. My father would be sitting in on the meeting, and he'd supported our decision to proceed the way that we'd recommended, which had surprised me.

This case would not be considered a win.

We'd spent weeks interviewing employees, as well as meeting with the opposing counsel and the three women who were suing King Hotels.

It was our job to present the information to our client and to represent him the best we could.

When we arrived at Holloway, Jones, and Waterman, we took the elevator to the top floor, and Will Waterman was the first person that we saw.

"Henley, Easton, I was hoping to chat with you for a quick moment before your meeting."

Easton glanced down at his wrist to check the time and nodded. Will led us into his office, and we took the seats across from his desk. It was an old-school design with dark cherry wood covering all the walls and thick crown molding and bookshelves with a small bar in the corner. "Thanks for giving me a minute. That's all this will take."

"Is everything okay?" I asked.

"I went to see Jamison in the program this past weekend. I just wanted you both to know that he's sober. He's horrified by what happened, and he feels terrible. It's the first time in a couple of years where he actually seems like himself."

"I'm glad to hear it," I said.

"I hope this doesn't mean that he'll be returning to work immediately after leaving the program?" Easton's tone was strained, and I glanced over to see his hands gripping the arms of the chair, his knuckles white.

"No. He's in it for the long haul. He's decided to stay for ninety days. He's making great progress, and that's the best we can hope for. We won't bring him back here until he proves that he can remain sober once he returns home. But he asked me to give you this letter, Henley." He opened his desk drawer and pulled out an envelope and handed it to me. "It's part of the program to own the mistakes that you've made, so I agreed to pass this on to you."

"Thank you. I'll read it when we get out of our meeting. I appreciate it."

Easton moved to his feet and shook Will's hand before we left his office. I tucked the letter into my purse, and we made our way to the conference room. My father was already there, and he pulled me in for a hug before shaking Easton's hand.

"You ready for this? It might not go well," my dad said.

"It'll be fine, trust me." Easton clapped him on the shoulder, and the three of us turned when the door opened.

Bruno King waltzed in like he owned the place.

"There's my dream team. I hope you're calling me in to tell me that we're going to crush them in court." He chuckled as we each shook his hand and took our seats across from him.

Easton sat in the middle, and my father and I settled in the chairs on either side of him.

"Bruno, we did a thorough investigation and turned over every stone possible because we knew that's what the prosecutors would do. We have to consider every single person who could be called to testify, so we met with endless employees over the last several weeks." Easton took a sip of his water.

"I expect nothing less from you. You're the shark. This firm is the best that money can buy. And that is proven by the billable hours I've seen." His laugh was loud and husky, and I forced a smile on my face.

"I'm just going to give it to you straight." Easton opened his file and then looked up at our client. "You can't win this case. And that's saying a lot, because I don't lose. But if this goes to court, you will lose. You will lose publicly, and it will be a disaster. You weren't honest with us about everything, and you've got a real mess on your hands, Bruno."

"Come on. Is this a joke? I paid for the best representation, and this is it?" His face hardened, and anger filled his gaze.

"This is the best representation that money can buy. I can't get you out of this without exposing every dirty detail to the public, which could sink your company. So here's what I'm suggesting." Easton pushed a file across the table, which stopped directly in front of Bruno. "Take the settlement. Pay these women, because you and I both know that what they're saying is true. They can prove it, and I can't make it go away. There are too many people with similar stories. If you take this to court, you will be destroyed professionally and financially."

Bruno's fist hit the table hard, and I startled. "This is bullshit."

"You can take our advice, or you are welcome to pursue other counsel. We are not working against you, Bruno. But we like to win cases, and this case cannot be won."

"So you want me to pay them to make this go away? What will the public have to say about that? This case has already gotten a ton of media attention. Those women will speak out."

"Those women have already spoken out. There's nothing

more for them to say that hasn't already been said. This is what we are suggesting," Easton said, glancing over at me to take over.

"You settle with the three women who were paid unfairly. The amount they are requesting covers the back pay they should have received, along with a generous severance package. It's a fair settlement, Bruno," I said, as I reached for my water.

"Is that it?" he asked. "And you think this goes away?"

"This doesn't go away," I said. "This is years and years of paying female employees unfairly. Many of your employees admitted that the pay you shared with us was fabricated. If they were willing to turn on you with your counsel, it would be a disaster in court."

"Disloyal sons of bitches!" he yelled.

"The same could be said about you, Bruno, and the way you've treated your employees. And I'm only going to ask you once to keep your voice down in my office," my father said, his tone even, but his eyes were hard. He'd listened to everything that Easton and I had presented, and he'd agreed with the way we were hoping Bruno would proceed. My dad motioned for me to continue.

"They aren't being disloyal, Bruno. They wanted to be treated fairly. So, on top of settling with the plaintiffs, we suggest that you make a public statement that King Hotel Corporation does not walk away from its responsibilities. You will make a public promise that all current female employees will be paid the same as their male counterparts, and back pay to employees that have been paid incorrectly will be paid as an apology."

"What? How much is that going to cost me?" he bellowed.

"It's going to cost you nine million, eight hundred and sixty-five dollars," Easton said. "And considering this company brings in a yearly revenue that is ten times that amount, this is a better option than losing everything."

He sighed as the words sank in. "And this goes away?"

"That's the final kicker. The only way this goes away is to

pay what is fairly owed, and you'll be getting off cheap because if this goes to court, you'll be buried in lawsuits for the rest of your life. But I'd also suggest that you step down as chairman and CEO and let your sister Lucy take the reins. We've met with her, and she's the obvious choice. She's worked under you for years, and it's time to pass the torch. This will show good faith from the company that you are doing a complete revamp, and I think you'll walk away unscathed."

"Unscathed? You're suggesting I hand over my company?" he growled.

"Bruno," Easton said, folding his hands together. "You treated your employees horribly. They are fighting back. There are too many of them for you to win this. So, you do the right thing. It's a family company. It stays in the family. You continue making a ridiculous amount of money because the company does not go under after this case is settled. It can thrive under new management. And you can sail off on your yacht and enjoy retirement. It's a win for you, trust me. This could get very ugly if we don't settle."

Bruno leaned back in his chair and crossed his arms over his chest and nodded. "Fine. I was ready for retirement anyway."

I blew out a sigh of relief. I wasn't certain Easton could sell this to him. It truly was his best option.

Our firm was not going to go to court to fight this because he'd be decimated. Settling was his best option.

But the client doesn't always agree.

He wasn't happy, and that much was clear, but none of us really cared at this point. He'd treated his employees terribly, and I was happy to see them all get paid the money they were owed.

"We'll set up a meeting with opposing counsel immediately, and we'll have a statement for you to look over that will be released to the media as soon as we sign the agreement," Easton said.

"Fine. I'm not happy, but I don't see another option." Bruno pushed to his feet.

"I'm glad you see it that way, because there isn't one that's better than this."

He didn't offer to shake our hands; he just turned and stormed out of the office.

"Well, I think that went as well as it could have gone," my father said, extending his hand to Easton and then pulling me in for a hug. "I'm impressed with you both. That was good work."

My father got called out to another meeting, and Easton and I made our way to the elevator.

"That went better than expected," I said as he stood beside me once we stepped onto the elevator.

"Really? It went exactly as I expected. He was backed into a corner. He's smart enough to know that he'd be ruined if he were to be exposed. So he took the only way out."

"I just didn't know if he'd see it that way," I said.

"I'm glad that he did, because the alternative would not be good for him. Now let's see this letter that Jamison wrote you." His shoulders tensed as I pulled it from my purse.

I opened the envelope, and he leaned over my shoulder as we both read the letter at the same time.

Henley,

I'm embarrassed by my actions the last two times that I saw you. I was spiraling and out of control. This is not an attempt to excuse my behavior; it is my attempt to apologize that I allowed things to get so bad. I am mortified by the way I spoke to you and treated you, and it is not who I am or who I want to be. I will continue to work hard in the program to make sure that I never do that again. I have known you most of my life, and I have the utmost respect for you, and I only hope that someday you will be able to forgive me.

Best, Jamison

"Wow. That was honest and heartfelt."

"I still don't trust him. They probably make them write these and then check them," he said. "I'm still going to be watching that dude when he gets out."

"Don't be such a cynic. People change, and life is about forgiveness, Chadwick." I tucked the envelope back into my purse.

"Yeah. But he's been a dick for a long time, so it's going to take a lot of work to turn that around."

I chuckled as we stepped off the elevator. "Fine. Let's go meet my bestie."

We walked outside and headed to the restaurant next door, where we were meeting Lulu. Easton had talked to her on Face-Time a few times when she and I were chatting over the last few weeks, but today, they were meeting in person.

Two of the most important people in my life.

He held the door open at Francois Café, and Lulu waved us over. She was on her feet, lunging herself into my arms the minute I approached the table. And then she turned to Easton.

"So you're the guy," she said with a smirk.

"I'm the guy. And you're the bestie?"

"Damn straight. I'm the bestie." She hugged him. "Nice to finally meet you in person. My girl doesn't get smitten all that easily, but she talks about you like you set the sun."

"Yeah?" he replied with a cocky grin as he pulled out my chair. "That's good to know. And the feeling is mutual."

"Just know that if you hurt her, I will hunt you down and cut off your balls and make them into Christmas ornaments."

"Wow. That's very specific." He laughed.

"Anyway, what are your plans for Thanksgiving? Do you have to do the big family dinner again with all the Sonnets? Because you would love Rosewood River. Easton's mom is cooking, and then the next day we're doing the annual Rosewood River rafting challenge."

I glanced over at him when his shoulders stiffened. "Come for dinner. My mom goes all out, and the food is terrific. But I'm not sure about the rafting."

He and this damn river rafting were starting to piss me off. I'd been out on the water multiple times now. And the annual river raft challenge was all everyone in town was talking about, and I was determined to join in.

Why was he being such a stubborn ass about this?

"My rafting skills are as strong as my pickleball skills." I raised a brow as I watched the waiter fill our glasses with Pellegrino, and I squeezed a lime into mine.

"What's the deal with the rafting? Have you seen this girl in action? She's quite the athlete." Lulu studied Easton. "She is small, but she is mighty."

"I was a guide for a long time. The path we take is pretty challenging. But I've grown up on the water, so I know what to expect."

"Well, we grew up in the city, but that doesn't mean we don't think you know how to wave down a taxi," Lulu said, giving him a knowing look.

I'd talked to her about how protective he could be. But he was being a little irrational about the river rafting, and I had no idea why. We hadn't had one issue the times that we'd gone out together.

"Exactly. Come on, Chadwick," I said, my voice all tease. "It's the annual river rafting outing. All of you do it. You don't seriously expect me to cheer from the sidelines, do you? Because you and I both know that I can hold my own just fine."

He smiled and nodded. "All right. We'll see how the weather is that morning."

He kissed the tip of my nose.

But a little part of me wondered if he was just trying to appease me.

It didn't matter. I'd never been one to be told what to do.

And Easton needed to know that.

twenty-nine

. . .

Easton

"CAN'T you just buy pies that are already made?" I asked, as I tossed a few candied apples into the basket because they were my favorite.

We were shopping at The Green Basket, and everyone and their mom were there too. This was the last place that I wanted to be.

"Yes. But they don't taste as good. Darleen and I used to make pies every year together. It's sort of a tradition."

"Hey, Henley. Nice to see you back here," Josh Black said, and the way he was looking at my girlfriend was pissing me the fuck off.

"Hi, Josh. Happy almost Thanksgiving. We just came to grab some stuff to make a couple of pies." She smiled before turning back to inspect the apples.

"Easton Chadwick is going to make a pie? I find that hard to believe." He chuckled like a pretentious fucker.

"Yes, Josh. I'm going to make a pie with my girlfriend because it makes her happy." I quirked a brow, and Henley glanced over at me and shook her head, but I didn't miss the smile on her face. She knew me well.

"I heard you won the pickleball championship again. I'm sure it's bittersweet since our team had to forfeit this year, so you can't technically say you beat everyone. Just giving you a heads-up that me and my boys are coming back stronger than ever next season," he said, tossing an orange in the air and catching it.

"Good for you. I was disappointed to see that you quit mid-season. *Again.* Did that have anything to do with the fact that you were losing?" I asked, because this guy talked a lot of shit for someone who'd never made it through one season. The minute his team lost their first game, he always made up a reason why they had to stop playing.

"Pfft," he huffed. "You wish, Chadwick."

"Actually, you're wrong. I wish you'd finish a season so you wouldn't continually tell me that we didn't really win because you weren't able to compete." I leaned forward. "Let me give you a little tip, Josh. You've got to finish a season before you shit talk."

"Well, I'll be out on the water for the last river raft of the season. I sure don't have a problem holding my own on the water with you, do I?" he asked as he followed me over to the baking aisle.

What the hell kind of pissing match was this? I'd come here for some damn pie ingredients, and this dude was all over my ass.

"I don't know. I'm usually in front of you, so I have no idea if you hold your own. Plus, it's not a race; it's just about finishing. We don't even start at the same time."

Henley turned around, and her gaze locked with mine. "Okay. We need to focus, and I need your help."

"I'm just giving your boyfriend a little shit. I better get back up front," Josh said. "But it was really good to see you, Henley. And you're looking gorgeous today."

What the fuck is this guy's deal?

He walked away, and I flipped him the bird behind his back.

"It's Thanksgiving. Stop being so competitive," she whispered against my ear and nipped at my lobe.

"He's a dick," I grumped. "Can we please get out of here?"

"Yes." She smiled as we made our way to the checkout.

"Did you see 'The Taylor Tea' column that just came out today?" Edith asked, and I groaned because she and Oscar were in front of us in line. We were never going to get out of here.

"This is why I don't go shopping on a Saturday. Everyone wants to talk about that ridiculous column." I glanced at Henley as she flipped through the *Rosewood River Review*.

"It's my favorite. I wonder if any of the Chadwicks will be in the column this week," Henley said with a laugh.

"Oh, you can count on it. It's all about how Easton is no longer the king of the river," Oscar said, and he looked way too happy about it. "Now my lady can stop fawning all over you."

"He's still the pickleball champ and a decent lawyer," Edith said. "Well, according to 'The Taylor Tea,' he didn't win his last case, so maybe practicing law isn't his thing anymore either."

They were literally talking shit about me while I stood beside them.

"I can hear you. You know that, right?" I grumped, and Henley was still laughing.

"Hey, pickleball is still a skill. But you're always the first one to lead everybody down that river. So what's the deal? It sounds like you're getting soft," Edith said, as if this was her defense.

"We're going to be on that raft on Friday. He was just waiting to see how the weather was." My girlfriend was piping in now and sticking up for me, which only made things even worse.

"He's never cared about the weather in the past. But suddenly, the slightly cooler temperatures are making him behave like a big baby." Oscar's head fell back in laughter, and that dick Josh started laughing from behind the counter, too.

"Don't you fret, Easton. You're still easy on the eyes." Edith patted me on the cheek, and I wanted to get the hell out of this place.

I grabbed the paper and read the column.

Hey there, Roses. We've got a lot going on in town this coming week. Oscar and Edith are going to be serving Thanksgiving dinner at the Honey Biscuit, and word on the street is that Edith will be making her famous pumpkin pies and giving a free slice to everyone who comes in.

"You know, Edith. 'The Taylor Tea' is always very kind to you. Maybe you're the one writing this column. I mean, they're practically advertising the fact that you're giving out free pie." I quirked a brow.

"I can't help it if the paper loves me. My food does the talking. Keep reading, pretty boy. You haven't gotten to the good part yet," she said, as Josh stood at the end of the register, watching the cashier check us out.

"You know you have to buy that paper now. You can't just enjoy it in line and then give it back," the asshole said.

"Yeah. I'm quite aware how being a consumer works, Josh," I hissed, before looking down as I continued reading.

Henley was talking away with Oscar about his good ole days on the river and how he misses it now.

The annual river raft is for the most skilled rafters in Rosewood River. But this year, I have on good faith that our favorite Chadwick might not be leading his team in their raft. Apparently, our favorite lawyer is more focused on pickleball than winning cases and rafting on the river. I guess our king of the river is ready to retire his crown because it might be a little too cold outside. I wonder if any of the Chadwicks will show up on Friday morning? Maybe they've all gone soft.

That's okay. Rosewood River's favorite family might just want to chill by the fire with a blanket and some pie while the rest of us celebrate Rosewood River-style and soar down the river in our rafts.

Anonymous

I tossed the paper onto the conveyor belt, and Henley turned to look at me.

"I say we smoke them all on Friday," she said, before pushing up on her tiptoes and kissing me.

My phone vibrated, and I looked down to see a missed call from Dr. Langford. I'd canceled my appointment this week. It was a holiday, and I wanted to spend some time with my girl and my family.

I didn't need fucking therapy right now.

"Go ahead and drop that crown off any time, Chadwick," Josh said with a smirk, and I handed my card to the girl ringing us up when she gave me the total.

"Seeing as it's a metaphor and there is no crown, I won't be doing that."

"Never would have guessed you a coward," he said, and that shit pissed me off.

"Don't get excited, Josh. I rarely back down from a challenge."

"If you need to borrow some fuzzy socks and a parka, just let me know. I can ask my grandmother to loan you hers. It's not even that cold outside. I think you're just afraid to lose." He chuckled and walked away.

"Says the dude who quits pickleball every single season," I whisper-hissed to my girlfriend as we walked out of the store.

"They write about you because you're a hot topic, Chadwick," she teased, as we walked toward home, and I held the two grocery bags in my hand. "I love it here this time of year. The ribbons on the light posts and the twinkle lights at night. It's so adorable and festive."

I nodded, but I was still fuming about the column.

I'd been asked by several people in town if we were going to lead that run this year, and I'd made the comment that I hadn't decided if I was going to do it because of the weather.

It wasn't even fucking cold.

My issue had nothing to do with the weather.

My issue was that my girlfriend wanted to do it, and I didn't want her in the raft with us.

So I was trying to convince everyone that we should skip it this year.

But Josh fucking Black and his red fucking baskets at a store called The Green Basket were pissing me off.

"Whatever. The column is stupid."

"You know the best way to shut up a hater, don't you?" she asked, as we turned the corner toward my house.

"Punch him in the face?"

"You should join us in that raft and stop being ridiculous about the weather. You do it every year." She walked up the steps toward the front door.

"Join you?"

"Yes. Rafe and Axel said they'd lead the raft, and Bridger and Archer are both in. Obviously, Clark isn't going to be able to join us because he's got a hockey game. Which, by the way, I'm excited that we're going to be in the city to cheer him on later that night."

My jaw fell open. "You're doing it without me?"

"I told you that I wanted to try it. I'll be in a raft with a helmet and a life jacket. And I think I'm the reason you aren't doing it, and I don't like that." She walked inside ahead of me, and I set the groceries on the counter.

I stepped up behind her and wrapped my arms around her, nuzzling my chin against her neck. "It's dangerous, baby."

"So is life. You practically castrated a man on the pickleball court." She chuckled.

"He had it coming." I kissed her neck. "You're not going out on that river without me."

She turned around in my arms. "Then it looks like we're going together. Let's give 'The Taylor Tea' something to talk about."

I leaned down and kissed her hard before picking her up and carrying her down the hallway, through the bedroom, and into the bathroom.

I turned on the shower, and she raised her arms for me to pull her long-sleeve shirt off, before pushing up so I could peel her jeans down her thighs.

"You're so pretty, baby." My lips trailed down her neck, to her collarbone before I tugged the straps of her bra down.

I teased her hard peaks with my tongue right over the pink lace fabric, and she arched into me as I unsnapped her bra and tossed it on the floor.

"I want your clothes off," she said, as she reached for my tee and tugged it up and over my head.

I looked down at her, and she studied me. "You're looking at me weird. What are you thinking?"

"Move in with me."

"What?" She smiled, her eyes wide.

"I want to fall asleep with you every night. I want to wake up with you every morning. And I want to fuck you in the shower any time we feel like it."

"That's very romantic," she said over her laughter.

My hand moved to the side of her face. "I want to bring you a cake donut and chocolate milk every Sunday and make plans for our day together. I love you, Henley, and I want every day with you."

A tear ran down her cheek, and she smiled. "I want every day with you, too."

"Yeah? So you'll move in with me?"

"Or you can move in with me." She smirked.

"I don't care where we live. I just want to be with you."

"Me, too. Cake donuts and chocolate milk, Chadwick. Rides down the river and pickleball," she whispered.

"And shower sex. Don't forget the shower sex."

"Why don't you remind me how great it is, then," she said, as she reached for the button and zipper of my jeans.

I shoved them down, along with my boxer briefs, and picked her up, her legs wrapping around my waist as I carried her to the shower.

The bathroom was filled with steam, the water was hot, and I had everything I needed right here.

"Shit. I forgot a condom," I said, setting her down on her feet and turning for the door.

She stopped me. "I told you that I got on the pill a few weeks ago. We've both been tested, and I want to feel you. All of you."

Had a man ever loved a woman the way that I loved Henley Holloway?

I didn't think it was possible.

The water poured down on us, and I tipped her head back and kissed her.

Gently this time.

Something had shifted between us, and through the falling water, her gaze locked with mine when I pulled back.

I lifted her up, and her legs wrapped around my waist as her back pressed against the shower wall. I positioned her just right, one hand supporting her ass and the other on the side of her neck.

My eyes never left hers as I pushed into her.

Holy shit.

Nothing had ever felt better.

I'd never been with a woman without a condom.

This was different.

She was different.

I pulled out slowly and drove back in.

Over and over.

We just watched one another, and her sapphire blues were filled with emotion. I saw it there. All the love we felt for one another.

Her hands pressed against my shoulders as she met me thrust for thrust.

I tugged her head down, my mouth crashing into hers as I moved faster.

Both of us were close now, and I gripped her hips as we found our pace.

Our rhythm.

My tongue explored that sweet mouth as I felt her tighten around my dick.

Her head fell back on a gasp, and I knew she was close.

I thrust faster, and she exploded around me, her gorgeous body shaking and trembling as I pumped into her once more.

And that was all it took. I went right over the edge with her.

And I wanted to stay there forever.

thirty

. . .

Henley

LET'S just say that Thanksgiving at the Chadwicks' was like something out of a movie.

It was chaos and hilarity and the most entertaining holiday I'd ever experienced.

I'd met his grandparents, Mimi and Pops. They were everything I'd expected. Warmth and humor and love.

Mimi was sweet and kind, and Pops was sarcastic and loved to joke around with his grandkids.

Everyone was missing Emerson, as she'd stayed in Magnolia Falls this year, and apparently, she was the only one Pops was soft on.

The food was incredible, and I was seated between Easton and Melody. She'd come out of her shell with me these last few weeks, and when she'd climbed onto my lap, I'd stroked her head until she fell asleep. Archer tried to take her from me, but I wasn't having it.

This little girl smelled like baby shampoo and strawberries. I loved it. I smiled down at that little cherub face as I listened to the endless banter around the table.

"So why not just date her?" Clark asked. "You said she's hot. What's the problem?"

Rafe groaned over a mouthful of mashed potatoes. "She's my boss's daughter. She was all over me at the holiday party. She's looking for a husband, not a good time."

"Oh, for goodness' sake, Rafe Henry," Ellie said and gave him a pointed look.

"Mom's pulling out the middle name. You are definitely in the doghouse." Easton barked out a laugh.

"Listen, I'm not opposed to a relationship. But this girl pushed me into a bathroom at the holiday party last year, and let's just say, she came on really strong." Rafe shivered dramatically, which made the table erupt in laughter. "Joseph Chapman is my boss. Dating his daughter is not a good idea. But she wants to date me, and he wants to give his daughter whatever the hell she wants. He wanted me to take her to his wedding next month, so I had to think of something fast."

"So you lied?" Bridger shook his head with a laugh. "Just say you aren't feeling it."

"Says the man who works for himself." Rafe quirked a brow. "And it wasn't a full-on lie. I said I had a girlfriend."

"Oh, do you have a girlfriend?" Isabelle asked. I'd grown close to Easton's aunt and uncle. Isabelle and Carlisle were hilarious. She was razzing him because she already knew the answer.

"Well, not technically. But I could. I mean, I meet women all the time." Rafe forked some turkey and popped it into his mouth. "I just need to find one who's willing to put on a convincing show at the wedding."

"Dude, you should have just been straight with her," Clark said as he reached for the rolls and placed one on his plate.

"Easier said than done. This woman is a stage-five clinger. She was all over me. I won't traumatize everyone with the details, but she sort of terrifies me."

"You are one dramatic dude," Axel said over his laughter.

"I think I might have to push you out of that raft tomorrow, just for shits and giggles," Rafe said, but he had a wicked grin on his face.

"I heard you decided to go out with them tomorrow?" Keaton asked his son, directing his attention to Easton.

"Yes. Because apparently, we have a bunch of traitors at the table, and they were going to take my girlfriend out on the raft without me." He shot daggers around the table, but it only made everyone laugh harder.

"You do realize she's a grown woman and can go out on her own if she wants to," Rafe said. "So man up and get your ass in that raft tomorrow."

"Says the dude who can't even tell his boss's daughter he's not interested."

"Shots fired!" Clark laughed. "We knew you'd come around. Obviously, we all need you in that raft."

"The wind has been picking up, so it's not going to be smooth," Easton said, and I could feel his shoulders tense beside me.

"You've always loved rough waters out there," Pops said, and there was a quiet that came over the table.

As if everyone knew why he was acting like this, aside from his grandfather.

I was no therapist, but I'd assumed it had a lot to do with Jilly's accident. Easton's fear of losing the people he loved was real, and it was all directed at me right now.

That was why I was insisting on going. Because he needed to see that I could take care of myself.

That I would be okay.

"I can't say I mind if you all take a break from that river this year," Ellie said, winking at her son as if she knew exactly what was going on.

"You can't bench a guy like Easton who thrives on the challenge. The adrenaline. It's not how he's designed." Pops glanced over at me where I held Melody on my lap, and he smiled with sweet adoration painted all over his face.

"Nonsense. You grow up, and you have more to think about than just yourself," Mimi said.

"All right, how about we don't talk about that right now. We've been out there in worse. It's fine. I'm fine. Everything's fine," Easton said, and he made no attempt to hide his irritation.

And he certainly didn't seem fine.

"Well, that was convincing," Bridger grumped, as Isabelle changed the subject and insisted everyone go around the table and say what they were thankful for.

Melody stirred in my arms, and her little hand moved to my cheek as her chocolate-brown eyes opened and met mine.

"Hey there, my love," I whispered. She was like a little Hot Pocket, all warm and cozy.

"Hi, my wuv," she said, mimicking my words, and my heart threatened to explode. We'd grown close at Sunday dinners over the last few weeks. "I need to go pee-pee."

Archer was on his feet and taking her into his arms, even though I offered to take her. He was an amazing dad. I focused my attention back on the table.

Keaton was grateful for everyone being together. Ellie was grateful for her family and good food and good friends. Isabelle and Carlisle were very similar, and the boys groaned and gave them a hard time about being lame with their answers.

Axel said that he was grateful that he got to work outdoors making horse trailers. Rafe said he was thankful for fake girlfriends and thinking on his feet, which made everyone laugh.

Clark was thankful for being traded to the home team and having Thanksgiving off. As a professional hockey player, that didn't always happen. But he wouldn't be in the raft tomorrow because he had a home game that we were all going to.

Bridger said that he was thankful that he had a quiet home to go back to after dinner so he didn't need to listen to all this chatter for the rest of the night.

More laughter.

And then Easton smirked. "Well, I'm grateful that my girl just agreed to move in with me."

Isabelle, Ellie, and Mimi were clapping their hands, and Rafe winked at me. Clark held his glass of water up in cheers, Axel nodded and smiled, and Bridger just studied his brother before his lips turned up in the corners the slightest bit. I wouldn't have noticed the small smile a few weeks ago, but I noticed now.

"How about we see if Henley is thankful for the same thing?" Keaton said with a laugh.

"Don't put the girl on the spot," Pops said as he leaned back and rubbed his belly.

"She said yes, Pops. Thanks for the lack of confidence." Easton was laughing now as he kissed me on the cheek.

"I'm very thankful for this guy next to me and that we are taking that next step." I chuckled because they were all gaping at me now. "And I'm really thankful for your amazing family making me feel so welcome. I've never had a Thanksgiving like this, and now I know what I've been missing."

"Where the hell have you been, girl? You fit right in, like you've belonged here all along," Pops said, before a loud burp escaped his mouth, and Mimi threw her hands in the air and shot him a warning look.

"Thank you." I smiled, and Archer returned to the table.

"How about you, Archer?" Mimi asked. "What are you thankful for?"

"I'm thankful that I get to wake up this little girl with stanky breath and wild hair every morning," he said, as he nuzzled his daughter's neck.

"I'm not stanky, Daddy." Melody's head was tipped back in a fit of giggles.

"I'm just teasing, angel face." He kissed her cheek, and she reached out for me, and I didn't miss the way everyone at the table smiled when he set her back in my lap.

"Like I said, you fit right in." Pops winked at me.

And I pushed away the large lump that formed in my throat.

Because I knew he was right.

We had pie and visited for a while before Easton and I made

our way back to my house. We'd been taking turns staying at one another's homes.

I ran a bath, and he sat there leaning against the counter. He'd grabbed us each a glass of wine and set them beside the tub. He surprised me when he got undressed and said he'd join me.

Most nights, I took a bath, and Easton sat beside the tub and chatted with me.

Once we were both submerged in hot water, my hair tied up in a messy bun as my back rested against his chest, I took a sip of wine.

"My family really loves you."

"Yeah? I love them, too." I set my glass on the ledge beside me. "You were quiet when they talked about going out on the river, and I wanted to talk to you about that."

"I agreed to go. There isn't anything to talk about." His fingers were running up and down my arm.

"We both have things that we're working through, Easton. You know that I have trust issues. I've told you about my need for approval from the people I love. I have a huge fear of abandonment. Of not being enough for someone to stick around. And that's what makes me nervous about the way that I love you."

He startled at my words. "I love you, Princess. I'm not going anywhere."

"I know that. And I believe you. But we've all got fears. And you are not being honest about why you don't want to go out on the raft tomorrow. You're letting fear control you. And it's not fear about what's going to happen to you; it's about your lack of control over what's going to happen to me, Easton. I can see that. But you've got to let that go. Trust that everything will be okay, just like I'm doing with you."

"Sounds like you've been talking to Dr. Langford," he said, his voice laced with humor, even though I knew this was difficult for him to talk to me about.

"I haven't. But I can see what's happening here." I rolled onto my stomach. "Tell me about that day. You've never talked about it. Maybe if you share your grief with me about what happened and what you went through, it'll help."

He shook his head. "It's in the past. I don't need to talk about it. I just want you to be safe. It's not anything more than that." His voice was hard now. This was what he always did when I tried to bring up Jilly.

He'd shut down.

"Our pasts are a part of our present and our future. My father leaving that tennis match because I got second place—the way he made me feel didn't leave with him on that plane. It stayed with me. And I had to work through it. Hell, I'm still working through it. But I told you about it, and it helped me to know that you understand the things that I've been through, just like I want to understand the things you've been through."

"Don't push this, Henley." His gaze was unwavering.

Why wouldn't he talk to me?

I nodded, but it stung that he didn't trust me enough to open up to me.

I rolled back over, and we sat in silence for a bit.

"So, which house do you want to live in?" he asked.

He was changing the subject.

He was good at it. And at some point, I'd have to push him harder, but tonight wasn't the night. Tomorrow, after he realized that he'd made too big a deal out of this, I'd broach the topic again.

He needed time, and I understood that.

"I love both of our homes," I said, my voice quiet. I was exhausted.

"We could live in one and rent out the other."

"That sounds like a good plan," I said, as he pushed to his feet and lifted me out of the water with him before wrapping me in a towel.

He dried me off and then did the same to himself. And after I brushed through my hair, he scooped me up like a baby and carried me to the bedroom. I was laughing when he laid me on the bed and hovered over me as his gaze locked with mine.

"I'm trying, Princess. Just give me time, okay?"

I nodded. "I know you are."

"I love you. Isn't that what matters most?"

"It is." I smiled up at him, and he leaned down and kissed me.

And I knew everything was going to be just fine.

Because we loved each other.

And that was definitely what mattered most.

thirty-one

· · ·

Easton

I WOKE up in a foul mood. Maybe it was the conversation we'd had last night. Maybe it was the hurt I saw in Henley's eyes when I'd refused to talk to her about Jilly.

What was the point of digging up the past?

And I was obsessively watching the weather. The winds were increasing, and I just wanted to get this over with.

"I'm ready if you are," my girlfriend said, as she came out wearing a pair of leggings and a long sleeve tee. It wasn't that cold in Rosewood River considering the time of year, though the gusts of wind would make it feel colder. And the water would be chilly.

"I'm ready." My voice was dry. I couldn't fake the fact that I did not want to do this.

She had her duffle bag with her wet suit, helmet, and river shoes in it. Three things that I'd insisted she have.

I took the bag from her hand and slipped it over my shoulder. I opened her car door and helped her inside before leaning down and kissing her.

I needed to shake this off. A clear mind was important when I was out on the water. Maybe everyone was right, and I was overreacting.

It would be fine.

We'd done this dozens of times.

"So, there are a couple of groups that go out, huh? But it's not really a race, is it?" she asked, as we drove down to the area where we would be starting. It was a much higher point on the river. There would be a good rapid at the start and at the finish. The middle would be calmer.

It will be fine. Of course, it will.

"Yes. The local diehards get in the rafts. And everyone in town comes out to watch from down at the bottom. It's just a Rosewood River tradition. We've been coming out here and doing it for years. Others do the easier courses for fun. This is the more intense group." I chuckled.

I was making a conscious effort to appear relaxed.

"Well, you seem like the leader of the intense group, Chadwick." She smirked.

Her hair was in two long braids, and she wasn't wearing any makeup other than a little lip gloss. She looked fucking stunning.

"Such a smartass." I parked the car near the launch point and found the guys all waiting up top with our raft. I glanced down at my phone to see a text from my mom that said they were already down at the bottom, and she was wishing us luck.

We hopped out of the car and made our way over to the guys.

"Ahhh… you decided to show up," Josh Black said, coming up behind me, and I rolled my eyes. The dude was a wanker, and I had no patience for him today.

He was an insecure asshole, and he'd almost caused us to capsize two years ago because he was reckless and irresponsible on the water.

"How about you just stay in your own lane this year. Worry about yourself."

"You never like it when someone challenges you, do you?" he pushed, and Rafe stepped up and got in his face, but he continued. "So used to winning, you can't handle getting thumped by your opponent."

"Josh, step the fuck off. You're being a dick," Rafe said.

"Ahhh… big brother is fighting your battles now, too. You really have gone soft." Josh barked out a laugh just as Bridger stepped in front of him and bumped his chest into Josh, causing him to step back.

"Move the fuck along, asshole." Bridger was a man of few words, but when he didn't like you, he had no problem letting you know.

"Don't let him get to you," I said, clapping my brother on the shoulder as Henley watched us with concern, and I turned back to the asshole still standing there smirking. "The problem is, Josh, that this isn't a race. It's for fun. It's about getting down the river in one piece. We don't all start at the same damn time. Chill the fuck out."

"Yet they call you the king of the river. Like I said before, it's time to pass the crown, asshole."

What is his fucking deal?

"And like I told you before, there is no fucking crown, Josh. It's just a saying. You're taking it way too seriously. And they say that because we've never capsized before. Not that you didn't do everything in your power to make that happen." I turned my back on him because the guy was ridiculous.

"He's such a jerk," Henley whispered against my ear, her hand sliding into mine.

"Don't give him a thought. He just needs to stay the fuck away from us out on the water." I kissed her forehead. "Let's get you into your wet suit."

I set her bag down and helped her slip into her wet suit, life jacket, and river shoes, before putting her helmet on her head and clasping it beneath her chin.

"Looking cute, Hen," Rafe said with a chuckle.

"How come none of you are in wet suits?" she asked, as her gaze moved from me to Axel, Rafe, Bridger, and Archer.

"We grew up here, so we're used to the cold water," Axel said.

"Rosewood River rafters, let's get ready to ride the river!" Carlton Hobbs, the mayor of Rosewood River, shouted through his megaphone.

"Wow. They don't mess around here," Henley said before pushing up on her tiptoes and giving me a chaste kiss.

"Just keep your eyes up, okay?" I said, speaking close to her ear. "And if for any reason you go into the water, remember to stay on your back. I'll get you, all right?"

"You worry too much, Chadwick. We've got this. It's going to be fun."

Everyone got situated, and I made sure that Henley was placed between Bridger and Archer, and Rafe and Axel were on the other side of the raft. I was at the back of the raft, the stern, as I would be guiding and steering us down the river.

Fuck. My stomach was twisting, which it never did.

I loved this shit. Lived for it most of the time.

But I also knew the risks. I knew if my brothers or my cousins went into the water, they'd be fine.

We were all skilled rafters.

But Henley was a different story.

I didn't know how she'd handle that type of situation. Everyone responded differently when they were plunged into the river and being pulled by the current.

She was a strong swimmer, but that didn't matter. The river was a different beast, and having waves go over your head could be scary if you weren't used to it.

I'd gone over all of these scenarios with her dozens of times.

Each time we'd gone out on the water, we'd talked about situations that could arise.

Nothing had happened yet, and I hoped today would be no different.

We were the first raft up, and we got into position.

Henley glanced over at me, her sapphire blues locking with mine, and I looked at her, communicating without words.

Be smart. Be safe.

She nodded as if she understood me.

"Three. Two. One. Go!" Carlton shouted, and we took off.

I heard him shout for the next raft, and I was not happy because he knew he was supposed to allow time between each one. With the winds picking up and the current being a little unpredictable, time between rafts was a safety precaution. But we were off and moving.

I was shouting out commands as we paddled and paused. The water was high, and the waves were causing us to catch some air as we came down the first dip.

My gaze was trained ahead, but I kept glancing over at Henley. She was sitting too far forward.

"Don't lean over the edge!" I shouted to her, but she couldn't hear me with the wind whipping around us.

She was determined to prove to me that she could do this. She paddled her ass off. Trying hard to keep up with everyone else.

"Dig!" I shouted, because we were traveling through some large gaps. We were approaching the roughest area, and I wanted us to be in a good position. "Hard forward dig!"

Everyone did as I instructed.

We were doing exactly what we needed to do.

My arms burned as I did my best to keep us on track. The large boulder to the right caught my eye. "Bump!"

Everyone leaned into the middle of the boat, pulling their paddles in so we would avoid the rock.

Damn. Henley had it down. She was doing everything I'd taught her.

I'd underestimated her.

She glanced over for a brief second with a wide grin on her face as her gaze locked with mine.

She fucking loved this.

I chuckled as we swerved to the right. Everything was going well as we made our way through the aggressive rapids.

My brothers and cousins howled with laughter, and Henley couldn't wipe the smile from her face.

This was a grade IV, which was for advanced rafters, but it was also somewhat predictable, so you knew what to expect. The wind whipped around us, which we were prepared for, but this last gust was more intense than the others.

A raft approached in my peripheral, and I tried to steer us to one side, as we didn't want to get bumped with the rapids moving so quickly.

"High side!" I shouted. "High right!"

This meant that they all needed to leap to the right side of the boat.

They did exactly as they were supposed to.

But Josh motherfucking Black's raft slammed into us hard, just as we hit a rock, causing the boat to catch air, and everything happened so fucking fast.

Henley's body flew from the raft in slow motion. Like I was watching my life flash before my eyes, and I couldn't do anything to stop it.

She hit the water between the two rafts, and Josh's raft went right over her body—and I swore to fucking God I'd kill this motherfucker.

"She's okay! I've got her!" Bridger shouted, as he was at the bow up front, and he had eyes on her.

"Can you see her?" I shouted, the panic apparent in my voice. Rafe looked at me briefly, and I saw the concern in his gaze.

He knew I was losing it. The rapids were out of control, and we paddled, and I tried everything to get to her.

I couldn't fucking get to her.

I could see her moving up ahead. She was on her back, but

water was going over her head. She was reaching her hands out to grab onto something.

"Get the fucking paddle to her!" I yelled, as all four of the guys were doing everything that they could to reach her.

But they couldn't reach her.

I couldn't fucking reach her.

My heart raced so fast I was sure it would burst through my chest.

I dug deeper into the water.

Frantic.

Panicked.

Desperate.

Bridger's paddle was within reach.

"Grab the paddle, Henley!" he called out.

But just as her fingers wrapped around it, her body slammed into a rock, and she went back under. Now she was moving sideways down the rapid, and I couldn't breathe.

I dug harder into the water. Trying to catch her.

Josh was just ahead of us now, and he reached his paddle out for her, but the assholes on his boat didn't know how to steer and instead, Josh hit her in the side of the head with his paddle.

We caught huge air as we were moving way faster than normal, and we still couldn't get there. We were almost at the end.

She'd been tossed all over the river, and her body didn't react when she hit a rock with her side, and panic surged.

Was she conscious?

"Get that motherfucking paddle to her, Bridger!" I cried out, and he tried.

We all tried.

I was done trying.

I dropped my paddle and dove out of the raft.

I swam hard until I reached her.

The water was freezing, but I felt nothing.

I grabbed her arm, pulling her onto my body as I lay on my back with her back on top of my chest, keeping her head above water.

Her body was slack against mine as we traveled down the river with her in my arms and me praying like hell that she was okay.

After we made it through the rough patch, I knew we were close to the finish, and everything slowed. Bridger, Rafe, Archer and Axel were out of the raft and sprinting toward us. I don't know when it happened, but they were pulling us to the side now, as they were able to stand.

We sat her forward, and I pounded on her back.

She vomited and continued to try to suck in air.

"Breathe, baby," I said, as I unclasped her helmet and tossed it in the water. My voice was unrecognizable.

Bridger was in front of her, unclasping her life jacket. "She needs air."

I unzipped the top of the wet suit, rubbing her back as she vomited again.

And then she fell back against me, her breathing labored.

She was breathing.

Her hand clasped mine as she just lay there, staring up at me.

And then she let out a few short breaths and nodded. "I'm okay."

I'm okay.

I'm okay.

Axel and Rafe pulled her to her feet, and she took a minute to steady herself. I just sat in the water staring up at her.

The lump in my throat made it impossible to breathe.

My head hit my knees, and I fucking lost it.

A loud sob left my throat as my fists hit the water.

"Easton." Bridger's voice was hard, determined.

He reached for my hand and helped me stand as fury took over.

Josh walked toward us, holding his hands up in apology. "Sorry about that, Henley. I lost control."

He wasn't the only one.

I dove through the air, landing on top of him and tackling him in the shallow water. The first fist hit him in the cheek, and I was hoping the next would break his fucking nose.

But someone stopped my arm from connecting with his face again, and I heard shouting all around me.

My mother was there. My father was there.

Bridger and Axel were holding me back as Josh just sat there in the water, wiping the blood from his face as he smiled up at me.

Rafe and Archer were keeping Henley upright as she stared at me with tears streaming down her face.

"Looks like the king of the river lost his crown today." Josh laughed.

He fucking laughed.

I fought like hell to get to him again. "You could have fucking killed her!"

"You're being dramatic. She's fine. She took in some water. It fucking happens, asshole," Josh said as he pushed to his feet.

"Easton!" my mother shouted, her hands on each side of my face. "Look at me. She's okay."

I looked over at my girlfriend, who was still wobbling on her feet.

"I'm sorry," she said, as she swiped at the tears streaming down her face.

I held up my hands in surrender. "We need to get her to the hospital. I want her lungs checked for water."

"I've already called 9-1-1," my father said. "The ambulance will be here soon."

I heard the sirens in the distance, and everyone watched as we got Henley loaded inside, and I climbed in and insisted on riding with her.

I didn't speak one word in the ambulance.

Henley's hand was in mine.
But I couldn't process what had just happened.
She'd looked lifeless.
She'd taken in too much water.
I could have lost her.

thirty-two

. . .

Henley

RIVER RAFTING grade IV rapids had clearly been a bit more extreme than I'd expected, but it wasn't like I'd never been out on the river before. Accidents happened all the time, and thankfully, I was okay.

I was fine, actually. I didn't think I needed to be at the hospital, but there was always a risk of taking water into your lungs and having issues, even after you thought you were okay.

Easton was adamant about me getting checked out.

He'd shut down in the ambulance. I'd watched it happen right in front of me as he held my hand and stared down at me. All the life had left his eyes.

He hadn't spoken one word.

When we'd arrived, Ellie had come back into the room with me, as Easton had suddenly stopped walking inside the hospital and let go of my hand as if he couldn't go any further.

The paramedics had hustled me in back, and Ellie had followed.

They'd given me a pair of dry scrubs to put on, and the doctor listened to my lungs.

"You're going to be just fine," he said. "You probably took in a lot of water, but vomiting the way you did helped you expel it."

"All right." I shrugged. I was exhausted. Concerned about Easton. I'd heard him shouting after we'd made it to the bottom of the river. I'd seen the look on his face when I'd been lying in his arms after I couldn't catch my breath.

"You've got a lot of bruises on you, but they'll heal up soon. I guess you just got your Rosewood River initiation," Dr. Spindle said.

I nodded, and Ellie didn't hide her irritation when he left the room, telling us that we'd be discharged soon. She left briefly to let everyone know that I was fine, and Dr. Spindle was just going to watch me for a little while before I'd be discharged. She returned to the room a few minutes later.

Easton did not come with her.

I swiped at the tears running down my face. "He's not coming back here?"

"Oh, sweetheart. He has a thing with hospitals. Jilly died shortly after she arrived at this hospital. And I don't know that Easton has ever stepped foot in a hospital since." Ellie sat down beside me on the bed and reached for my hand.

"I wish he'd talk to me about it."

"Me, too. But I've seen him make so much progress with you. Don't give up on him, Henley. He's trying."

"I would never give up on him," I croaked. "I made things worse. I shouldn't have insisted on going out with them today. I thought I could show him that his fears were irrational. And I managed to make everything worse."

She wrapped an arm around me. "You can't stop living because my son is afraid of losing you. That won't help him. You did the right thing. And yes, it was scary seeing your body come down that rapid the way that it did, but you are okay. That same thing has happened at least once to each of my boys. And guess what?"

"What?" I asked, leaning my head against her shoulder.

"They all went out there again. Easton has been through it himself. But he just loves you so damn much, sweetheart. And that terrifies him. Because the thought of losing you is just too much."

I nodded and sniffed a few times. "What if this pushes him away forever?"

That little voice in the back of my head was questioning everything.

Have I messed everything up?

Am I enough?

Am I worth the risk?

"Not a chance. He loves you. You need to have faith in that, Henley. He just got scared. Give him time."

I closed my eyes, trying to process everything that had happened today. And that's exactly where I stayed for the next hour. In the arms of the mother of the man that I loved.

"Hey, bestie." Lulu came rushing into the room, her eyes puffy, so it was obvious that she'd been crying.

"Oh, my gosh. What are you doing here?" I sat forward and moved to my feet, wrapping my arms around her before introducing her to Ellie.

"Easton called me and told me what happened. He had your phone," she said, holding it up with a chuckle, but then a tear escaped, and she swiped it away.

I nodded. "Where is he now? Did you see him?"

"I guess his brother Rafe took him to his car once they knew that I was only a few minutes out. He made me text him when I pulled up at the hospital. That man can be very overbearing." She shrugged, trying hard to make light of it.

"He left?" The words left my lips on a cry.

He'd left me because I'd gotten hurt?

Lulu and Ellie both wrapped their arms around me. Probably because they didn't know what to say.

Because the simple truth was—he'd left me.

There was no other way around it.

And I couldn't believe that he would do that.

Sure, I'd expected him to be distant, maybe even pull away from me over the next few days after we returned home from the hospital.

But leave me here without saying goodbye?

The betrayal hurt more than all the rocks I'd slammed into as I'd flown down the rapid on my back.

Easton Chadwick had managed to break my heart.

Just as I'd feared he would.

thirty-three

· · ·

Easton

I'D GOTTEN in the car because I'd needed to get out of that hospital.

I'd let this happen.

She'd fallen out of that boat right in front of my eyes.

Her face going underwater over and over again, until I was able to get to her.

I pulled into the driveway at Emerson and Nash's house and put the car in park.

My twin sister had always been my sounding board.

Emerson knocked on the window of my car, and I opened the door.

"You look like shit," she said.

"Thanks. I feel like shit."

She wrapped her arms around me and hugged me. I patted her back and sighed. I think she was expecting an emotional meltdown, but I felt nothing.

I was numb.

Completely numb.

"Come inside. I made soup and cornbread. Nash and Cutler are at J.T.'s birthday party," she said. J.T. was my nephew's best friend, and I'd met him a few times.

I followed her inside the house. "You could have gone to the party. I don't need to talk. I just needed to get away. Sleep for a day and then pull my shit together."

"Seriously?"

"Yes. I just had to get away from that hospital. From the situation. I'll be fine."

She sat down at the kitchen table and pointed to the chair beside hers for me to sit. "Easton, you watched the woman you love go down the river with the rapids going over her face and a raft running her over along the way. You jumped into the freezing cold water because you thought she wasn't breathing. She was taken by ambulance to the hospital. This is not something you"—she paused and used her pointer and middle fingers on each hand to make air quotes—"*sleep off and forget.*"

I ran a hand down my face and groaned. "Emmy, listen. I don't want to do this. I can get a hotel. I just need to sleep."

I needed to shut down. Get those images out of my head.

The thought that I'd lost her—it was too much.

I glanced down at my phone to see the texts from my mom telling me that Henley had been released and Lulu had taken her home.

There was a text from Lulu letting me know that Henley was fine.

Both asked me to come over and see her.

Henley wants to see me.

But I'd left town because it was all too much.

Too fucking much.

"No."

"No?" I hissed. "I'm fucking exhausted, Emerson. This is not the time for a life lesson or a lecture."

"A life lesson or a lecture? Really? That's what you think this is?"

I pushed to my feet. "Either let me go crash in your guest room, or I'll go to a hotel."

"Sit the hell down right now." I'd never seen my sister so angry.

Fuck me.

Had I not been through enough today?

I sat down, but I made a mental note to leave and get a hotel when she was done with whatever the hell she had to say to me.

I'd called on my way to Magnolia Falls and said I needed a place to crash.

I thought she'd understand.

"Easton," she said. Her voice cracked on the single word. She reached for my hand. "You're in shock. You're shutting down. You thought you were going to lose her. You can't just go to sleep and make it go away."

Tears were streaming down her face.

"Emmy, I don't want to do this right now."

"I'm aware. But we're doing it. You left the woman you love in the hospital and drove a few hours to come here. That's not normal behavior. You're scared out of your mind, and you're running away."

"I waited until I knew she was okay. I called her best friend. Mom was with her." I didn't like her insinuating that I'd left her. Anger pulsed, and I tried to push it away, but it was all boiling up. "I was fucking there, Emerson! I was holding her fucking head above water. I was in that ambulance when they were checking her lungs. I was the one who let her get into that motherfucking raft."

I didn't know when my hands had fisted and slammed against the table.

I didn't know when I'd moved to my feet.

I couldn't suck in enough air.

I couldn't breathe.

I couldn't handle the idea of Henley not being here.

"Easton," my sister sobbed, and somehow we were sitting on the floor in her kitchen, and my head was pushed against my knees. "You need to breathe."

"I can't fucking do it, Emmy. I can't lose her, too. I can't be in a hospital with the woman I love and find out she's not coming home with me." My voice was barely recognizable as my heart raced so fast it felt like it would burst through my chest.

There was this soul-crushing pain that I felt in every bone in my body.

"You're having a panic attack," she whispered. "Just try to breathe. She's okay."

I leaned my head back against her kitchen cabinets and waited for my breathing to slow down.

"You are not losing anyone. And you didn't put her in that raft. She wanted to go out on the river. She fell out of the raft. It happens all the time. She took in some water, and she got checked out at the hospital. She's fine," she said, her voice softer now. "You are reacting this way because of trauma from your past. And you have to deal with it, Easton. You have to talk about it. It won't just go away."

"I have dealt with it." My breathing evened out. "I go to therapy. I've moved on. I have. But it's a normal response to see your girlfriend in distress and get upset."

She turned to look at me. "It's not a normal response to first insist that she not go rafting. And then to punch the guy in the face that knocked her out of the raft while she's still sitting in the water. And then to go to the hospital and flip a table in the lobby, all before getting into your car and driving for hours to get out of town."

"Those asshole's told you about the hospital table?" My brothers couldn't keep a secret if their life depended on it. "I was having a moment."

"Easton, you dove out of that raft because you panicked that she wouldn't be okay. And the truth is, you saved her life. You got her down that river safely. But instead of acknowledging that, you bailed. As soon as she was okay, you left. That doesn't seem illogical to you?"

"No. And I didn't know I'd be coming here and getting a lecture. I just needed a place to crash."

"You have a home in Rosewood River. Two homes, actually, because you and Henley just decided to live together, and you each have a home. So why would you come here? You haven't even showered yet or changed out of those clothes since jumping into that frigid water. You'll probably get pneumonia. But you needed to get away because you were freaking out, Easton. Why can't you just say it? Just say that you're struggling and you're scared."

"I love you, Emmy. That's why I came here. I know that I have issues. I'm more than fucking aware that I'm having panic attacks. But right now, I need sleep. And if you don't want me to stay here, I will go get a hotel." I looked up at her, and her eyes were wet with emotion. "I promise you that I will call Dr. Langford tomorrow, and I'll deal with this. With all of it. I just can't do it tonight."

She nodded and pushed to her feet. "Okay. Do you want some dinner first?"

"No. I'm not hungry. But thank you."

She guided me down the hallway and paused in the doorway of the guest room. I'd stayed here before. "There are clean towels in the bathroom, and I grabbed a pair of Nash's joggers and a clean tee and set them on the bed when you told me you were coming straight from the hospital."

"Thank you. I love you." I kissed the top of her head before she walked out of the room, and I closed the door.

There was such a heaviness in my chest that it was hard to breathe.

I turned on the shower and stood beneath the hot water, letting it burn my skin. Once I'd warmed up, I turned off the water and dried off. My phone and keys were sitting on the dresser in the guest room, and I'd silenced my phone.

HENLEY

Where are you?

> I'm sorry, Princess. I hope you forgive me. I love you.

That's all I could say. I didn't have words for what I was feeling.

HENLEY

Forgive you for what?

For letting you fall out of the raft.

For leaving you.

For not being able to tell you what I'm going through.

I slipped on Nash's clothes and moved beneath the sheets, squeezing my eyes closed.

Desperate to get the vision of her struggling in the water out of my head.

I tossed and turned for hours, and finally, my body gave in to exhaustion.

Mental and physical.

And sleep took me.

————

"Uncle E, come on, buddy. You've been asleep for weeks." Cutler's little voice woke me, as did the fact that he was sitting on my chest, poking me in the face.

"He's been sleeping for hours, not weeks," my sister said, and I forced one eye open and peeked up at him.

"Hey, Beefcake. What's up?"

"Not you. I've been dying to see you, and Mama keeps telling me to let you sleep. But me and Pops decided we should make sure you're alive because it's almost lunchtime."

I shifted him beside me on the bed and sat forward, rubbing my eyes.

"Sorry about that. I had a long day yesterday. I guess I needed the sleep." I ran a hand through my hair.

"Mama told me you went rafting and jumped into the water and everything. That had to be freezing," he said, his dark eyes wide and curious.

"Yeah. It was cold."

"And then you drove all the way here to Magnolia Falls. You didn't want to take Uncle Bridger's 'copter here?" he asked.

He'd flown on Bridger's helicopter a few times.

"Nope. I wanted to drive. Clear my mind a little."

He chuckled just as Nash came around the corner with a coffee mug and handed it to me. "He's alive."

I nodded, and he gave me a sympathetic smile like he knew I was going through hell.

"Pops, did you hear that? Uncle E drove all the way here because he wanted to clear his head." The little dude tossed his hands in the air as Nash sat in the chair beneath the window, and Emerson moved to sit on the bed beside her son.

I guess I was up now. They were clearly not letting me go back to sleep, so I sipped my coffee.

"I heard him. Sometimes we all need to clear our heads."

"Yeah, remember that one time we had to take Bridger's 'copter to Rosewood River to get our girl because you and Mama were clearing your heads?"

I didn't miss the way Nash looked over at my sister like she set the sun, and he winked at her.

"Yep. That was all me. I was making a huge mistake by pushing her away because of my own issues. Could have lost everything if I hadn't figured it out quickly." Nash looked at me now, brow raised.

"Great. Another life lesson," I grumped under my breath.

"Why isn't Henley here with you? Mama said you two are

going to live together, so you must love her, right, Uncle E?" he asked.

If anyone else was firing off these questions, I'd lose my shit. But Cutler Heart could pretty much ask me anything, and I'd answer.

"Yeah, buddy. I love her." I rumpled his hair.

"So, why didn't you bring her here?" he pressed, and Nash chuckled into his coffee mug.

"That's a great question," my sister said.

Cutler just stared at me, waiting for an answer.

"Well, remember your mama told you I jumped into the water yesterday on the river?"

"Yep," he said.

"Well, Henley fell out of the raft, and I jumped in to help her because the rapids were really rough."

His brows cinched together. "Is she okay?"

"Yes. She got checked out at the hospital, and she's going to be fine."

"So, why did you leave her there? Are you mad at her for falling out of the raft?" he asked.

"No. Of course not. I'm mad at myself for letting her fall out."

He looked over at his dad and then at my sister and then back at me, with this confused look on his face. "Did you push her out of the raft?"

"No. The rapid was wild, and another raft bumped into us, and she fell out." I sipped my coffee, saying a silent prayer that he was done with the questions.

"Oh, man. One time, J.T. and I were racing on our bikes, and he popped a tire and wiped out. But he wasn't mad at me that I didn't pop my tire." He scratched the side of his head and then winced. "But he would have been real mad at me if I'd left him there by himself."

"I didn't leave her there. I got her out of the water. I went with her to the hospital, and I left once I knew she was okay," I said defensively, and Nash made a face that said a whole lot without speaking a word.

You really fucked up, brother.

"Oh, man, Uncle E. I wouldn't like it if someone left me at the hospital. Remember when I was there for my asthma that one time?" He looked at his dad. "I would have been mad at you if you left without me, Pops."

"You would have had every right to be mad." Nash quirked a brow and then looked at me. "But I bet I'd have a good reason for leaving if I did that, because that's not like me, right?"

"Like maybe you were hurt, or you had an 'mergency?" Cutler asked his dad.

"Yeah. Something like that."

"Did you have an 'mergency, Uncle E?" He turned his attention back to me.

I let out a long breath, because everything looked different this morning. And I knew I'd fucked up by leaving.

"Actually." I paused and looked at my sister. "I had a panic attack."

"What's a panic attack?" Cutler asked, brows narrowed with concern.

"It means that he loves Henley so much that he got really scared when he saw her hurt, and he couldn't handle it, so his instinct was to run away," Emerson said, as she reached for my hand and squeezed it.

"Oh, man... I think you better run back home and fix this, or you're going to have a panic attack when she doesn't want to talk to you, Uncle E."

Nash barked out a laugh, and I rolled my eyes.

"Yeah. I think you're probably right, Beefcake. You're one smart little dude, you know that?" I set my mug down and pulled him into me for a hug. "Thanks for helping me see things a little more clearly today."

"You're going to fix this, right? Because I want Henley to be at my parents' wedding. My mom said she's part of our family now."

"Damn straight, Beefcake. And I've obviously got some work to do."

But it was deeper than just going back home and apologizing.

That wasn't going to fly after I'd freaked out and left.

I knew what I needed to do.

And it wasn't going to be easy.

thirty-four

. . .

Henley

"ALL RIGHT, you've slept most of the day. It's time to get up. And this was on your doorstep when I got back from the store," Lulu said, holding up the little white bag and handing it to me as I sat up in bed.

She opened the curtains, and I shielded my eyes from the sun and looked inside the bag to see the cake donut and a little container of chocolate milk.

"How did he get this here?" I asked, biting into the donut because I'd barely eaten yesterday, and I was starving.

"Maybe he's back?" Lulu said.

"His mom said that he left the hospital and drove straight to Magnolia Falls. He's not here. Maybe he had someone drop it off." I shrugged. "Which makes no sense, since he's barely speaking to me."

"Listen, Hen, you know I can be a man-hater on command. And if a guy does you wrong, he better run for his life." She chuckled as she sat down beside me on the edge of the bed. "But that man was distraught yesterday. His voice was shaking, and he sounded—"

"He sounded what?"

"Broken. He sounded broken."

She pushed to her feet and walked out of the room before returning with two coffees and the newspaper. She kicked off her cowboy booties and handed me a coffee before climbing into bed next to me.

"Listen, we can't know what he's going through until he deals with it. So, when he comes back, he will not be allowed to give you some lame excuse. The man flipped out and left town. It's inexcusable, so he will either explain himself, or you will kick his ass to the curb." She shrugged. "In the meantime, we're going to drink our lattes, read 'The Taylor Tea' that came out yesterday, because everyone at The Green Basket was talking about it, and then we can binge-watch some movies."

"I'm glad you're here," I said, wincing as I adjusted my back against the headboard. My body was pretty bruised from the beating I took in the river.

But it was my heart that hurt the most.

I couldn't believe that he'd left me.

I mean, first, I couldn't believe that he'd jumped off that raft and kept me above water through the rapids.

He'd risked his own life to save mine.

But then he'd bailed.

He wouldn't tell me what was going on, no matter how hard I pushed lately.

And we couldn't move forward if he couldn't tell me when he was struggling.

If he doesn't trust me enough to open up to me, I can't trust him enough with my heart.

I was all in. I would not be all in on someone who didn't feel the same about me.

"Fine. Let's hear 'The Taylor Tea,'" I said, taking a sip of my coffee and tucking my hair behind my ear.

"Oh, my," she said. "It's really juicy today. And you're quite the hot topic. Which, by the way, that douche tomato that runs The Green Basket was there this morning, and he had a black eye and a bruised cheek."

I couldn't help but smile, even though I wasn't a fan of violence. Josh Black was an asshole, and I doubted this was the first or the last time someone would lose their shit on him. "I still can't believe everything that happened yesterday."

"Well, your man was not having it. But… it makes for interesting tea in Rosewood River. Are you ready?" She cleared her throat.

"I can't wait," I said, not hiding my sarcasm.

My mind was on my boyfriend right now. He'd only texted that he loved me and that he was sorry.

Sorry for what?

Well, I hoped he was sorry for leaving me, because I was pretty pissed off about that. He knew I had my triggers. The fact that I fell out of the raft, and he had to dive in and rescue me, was embarrassing enough. But then he'd bailed at the hospital.

My insecurities were raring their ugly head at me.

"*Hey there, Roses. Well, it's the week we're reminded to be thankful, and one thing you are going to be thankful for is the tea I'm about to spill,*" Lulu read, and she paused to waggle her brows at me. "*Rosewood River's favorite lawyer is at it again. He may be the king of the river, but he's clearly willing to set the crown aside for his queen.*" Lulu squealed and kicked her feet. "Are you kidding me right now? This is freaking gold. Anonymous is speaking my love language."

"Just continue, please." I rolled my eyes, even though I was curious about what it was going to say.

She shook the paper and looked back down as she read more. "*Our local king saw his queen take a spill on the river, and before he allowed her to sleep with dead fish, he dove right over the side, abandoning the other sexy Chadwicks in the raft.*" Lulu paused again, and I groaned. "She's right. I only met Axel and Bridger at the hospital, but damn, they were hot. And I know Clark Chadwick is also gorgeous, because he's on every sports channel I turn on."

"Since when do you watch sports?" I laughed.

"Well, I don't. But when I've been channel surfing, I've seen him. So how about the others? Who am I missing?"

"Rafe and Archer." I stopped her before she started grilling me. "Yes, and yes. Both are gorgeous. It's a hereditary gene. And Easton's twin sister is stunning. So there you go. They're all beautiful. Can you finish reading? You left me on a cliffhanger."

"Yes. Of course. So, where were we? Okay, he abandoned the other sexy Chadwick's in the raft." She paused before changing her tone and getting serious again. "*He carried his fair lady on his body, keeping her head above water, before he helped her purge all that water she'd taken in. Yes, she vomited half the river right there in front of everyone,*" Lulu said, glancing up to find me horrified.

"I could have drowned. She didn't have to be so descriptive," I groaned. "Go on."

"*But apparently, our favorite legal eagle has a problem with a certain grocer extraordinaire, who I shall not name... but let's just say his basket is not green. IYKYK. The king knocked out the man who keeps us all well-fed, and there was some serious hate between them. Several locals said they saw he, who shall not be named, intentionally knock his raft into another raft, causing our queen to spill out into the raging rapids. And to say there is a lot of animosity there now would be a massive understatement. But buckle up, Roses... because the king has left the castle. He left the hospital in a huff, and we can only be left believing that there is trouble on the river, because another little birdie told me the king asked his queen to shack up with him. But now he's nowhere to be found. Maybe he has cold feet... maybe the future queen isn't happy with him throwing fists on her behalf... or maybe this is just the end of their fairy tale. Time will tell. For now... we can all focus on the holidays. The town tree goes up tomorrow, and word on Main Street is our not to be named mayor cheaped out on hiring help, and his team is not happy with him at all. But an insider tells me that it's all because Mrs. Mayor was seen canoodling with Mr. Mayor's smoking hot chief of staff after a few Thanksgiving hot toddies. And you know what they say, Roses... where there's smoke, there's usually fire.*" Lulu fell back against the headboard. "She's such a savage. I love this."

"She just told everyone in town that I puked."

"Please. Everyone in town already knew. You didn't hide it. You did it out in the open. She's just sharing the facts."

"I could have drowned." I raised a brow.

"Well, then she wouldn't have said you puked. So it was actually good news. And Mr. Black Basket did not look happy at all this morning. He slipped on some sunglasses, and he claimed his store was out of the *Rosewood Review.* He didn't have any for sale."

"So, how did you get it?"

"I went to Rosewood Brew for coffee, and there was a guy standing outside the coffee shop selling them." She beamed at me.

"I thought you hated the media. You've been dragged through the mud, yet you support this?"

"Listen, this is not national news. This is small-town fun." She set her coffee cup down. "Or maybe I just like that I'm not the topic."

"Yeah? I get that. Have things quieted down for you now that the election is over? Your uncle won, so at least you can't be blamed for him not being governor," I said.

"Yes. Thank goodness for that. And things are quiet for now. But you know how Beckett is. He never really goes away. But I haven't been stalked by the press lately, so maybe he's moving on with his backup singer after all." She sighed. "One can hope because my father is all over me. And I just signed this huge deal with a company in France, and he had no interest in hearing about it. He just keeps asking if I'm ever going to settle down."

"Maybe settling down is overrated. I haven't even moved in with my boyfriend, and he's already bailed on me." I tried to act unaffected, but I'd never been able to hide anything from Lulu.

She tugged me over to her and wrapped her arms around me, hugging me tight. "He'll come around. He's got some things to work through, but I don't doubt for a minute that he loves you. And that's what matters most. He'll figure it out."

A tear streamed down my cheek. "And if he doesn't?"

"Then I'll cut his balls off and mail them directly to 'The Taylor Tea.' I'll give them something to talk about."

I chuckled, even as the tears continued to fall.

And fall, they did. For the next several hours. Because the truth was, I knew that Easton was hurting. And the only way that I could help him was if he opened up to me.

And I wasn't sure that would ever happen.

I forced myself to get out of bed, and Lulu and I watched two movies before she left to go pick up dinner for us from Honey Biscuit Café.

I'd showered and tied my hair up in a messy bun on top of my head before slipping into some cozy sweats.

I'd checked my phone several times throughout the day, and I hadn't heard a word from Easton.

His parents had both texted me to see how I was feeling.

His brothers and cousins had put me on a group chat to see how I was doing, and though Easton was on the chat, he hadn't commented.

I stared at my phone, trying to decide if I should reach out to him, when a knock on the door pulled me from my thoughts.

"I thought you took a key," I said, as I tugged the door open, expecting to see Lulu.

And there stood a disheveled Easton. He wore a pair of navy joggers and a gray hoodie.

"Hey," he said, his gaze searching mine.

"Hi. I thought you were in Magnolia Falls."

"I was. And then I drove back, and Dr. Langford did an emergency appointment with me today before I came here." I'd known that he'd been seeing Dr. Langford, and I was grateful that he'd seen her today after what had happened.

"Okay." I shrugged. I wasn't going to just act like everything was okay. He'd bailed on me in the hospital, and I needed to know why.

"Can I come in? There are some things I need to say to you."

"Of course," I said, leading him to the living room, where I sat on the couch. He paced in front of me for a few seconds before turning to look at me.

"I'm sorry."

"For what specifically, Easton?" My tone was harsher than I'd intended.

He sighed and moved to sit beside me. "I'm sorry for not telling you what I was going through before now. I'm sorry for being irrational about you going rafting. I'm sorry for losing my shit after we got to shore, when I should have been focused on you instead of punching that dickfuck Josh in the face." He paused and took my hands, his eyes wet with emotion. "I'm sorry for leaving you at the hospital. For not going back in the room with you, and for getting the hell out of town when you needed me most."

I nodded. "That's a lot of apologies. Are you going to tell me why you did what you did? Because I don't want any more excuses, Easton. You asked me to move in with you. We're starting our lives together, and there's this whole side of you that you won't share with me."

"I know. I've held it all in for so long that I didn't know how to say the words aloud. I've used my own coping mechanisms for years. And according to Dr. Langford, everything was working well for me, until I met you."

"What does that mean?"

"Well, I guess it's just been the way I processed things after Jilly's accident. I went off to law school and put my head down and worked hard. I got back to living in my own way. I didn't have a serious relationship, but I hooked up with women over the years, and that had worked well for me. And then I got hired by the firm, and I became obsessed with being the best at my profession. There was no time for anything more," he said, his thumb stroking my palm. "And then I met you."

"And then you met me," I whispered.

"I guess meeting you, loving you, it brought back all those fears that I'd tucked away. I hadn't cared about anyone in a very long time, and then you walked into my life and stole my fucking heart, Henley. I didn't even know it still worked. But it's yours, and I didn't know how to handle the things that I was feeling."

"What kind of things?"

"Nightmares that had come back. Panic attacks that were debilitating at times. Fears about losing you." He cleared his throat and looked away. "I'm a proud man, Princess. I don't like asking for help. I don't like feeling weak. But loving you has made me a weak man."

Tears were streaming down my face. "You're not weak, Easton. You're human. You're allowed to feel vulnerable and scared, but you have to talk to me."

He nodded. "Before we even went out on that water, I was having panic attacks about you getting hurt. Nightmares where I couldn't get to you. I wasn't sharing it with you or with Dr. Langford because I just thought I could push it away. But it didn't work. And all my fears were unraveling before my eyes on that river, and I just couldn't handle it."

"That's why you left the hospital?"

"I left the hospital because the last time I was there, I was told that my girlfriend had died." He blew out a breath. "And even after they'd told me that you were okay, I was overcome by the thought that I could have lost you. Because there's one thing I'm certain of—" he paused to think over his words.

"What?" I whispered.

"I can't live in a world that you aren't in, Princess."

My heart shattered at his words.

Because I couldn't live in a world that he wasn't in either.

thirty-five

. . .

Easton

I WAS FUCKING EXHAUSTED. My appointment with Dr. Langford had been emotionally draining. At the end of the day, she'd said there was no way to move forward without dealing with the past.

I'd pushed it away for years. But loving Henley had brought it all back.

And sometimes there was no way to avoid a storm. Sometimes you just had to open the door and go through it.

"I'm not going anywhere, Easton," she said, pushing closer and wrapping her arms around me.

I breathed in all that goodness.

All that hope.

Henley Holloway was my future.

But we weren't going to have one if I continued to hide what was going on with me.

I pulled back and used the pads of my thumbs to swipe the tears from her cheeks.

"I want to tell you about the night that Jilly passed away. I want you to understand why I am going through what I'm going through."

She nodded. "Okay. I want to know everything."

"I think I avoided telling you because I didn't want to burden you with my shit. I really thought I could handle it, but I think after yesterday, it's clear that it runs deeper than that."

"I agree." She nodded, her hands in mine.

"We were celebrating mine and Emmy's birthday. Jilly's parents were there. We were all having a good time. We had a bunch of friends over, as well, and it was a big party, you know?"

"I can see it. A Chadwick-style celebration," she said, as she sniffed a few times because we both knew how this story ended.

"We'd gotten the call that there'd been an accident. I was confused because I thought she was out of town, but her parents told me that she'd wanted to surprise me. Obviously, we were worried when we'd gotten the call, but we had no idea the severity of the accident. We'd just been told that there'd been an accident, and she was being brought to the hospital." I blew out a breath. "So her family and my family piled into a bunch of cars and got down there as quickly as we could."

"I'm glad they were with you," she said, her voice just above a whisper.

"At first, we were told that she'd been brought in and that she was in a room, and they were waiting for the doctor to come out and update us. So we just thought everything was probably okay." I looked away, because I hated this memory so much. It was one that had haunted my nightmares the entire first year after Jilly passed. It had finally gone away, and I never wanted to go there again.

But here we were.

"And then a nurse came to tell us there had been some confusion because there were multiple people injured in the accident. Some more severely than others. Jilly was actually not in a room. She'd been rushed into surgery, and her injuries were extensive, but she was expected to recover. So we went from thinking everything was okay to thinking things were not great but not dire. Never in a million years did I expect what would happen next."

Henley wiped her tears free and squeezed my hands harder. "Tell me."

"Dr. Wicker came out to see us, and I knew the minute he pushed open the doors. It was written all over his face. After hours of surgery, he looked defeated and devastated and everything you never want to see on a doctor's face." I cleared my throat and said the words he'd said to us all those years ago. *"I'm so sorry. We did all that we could. Her injuries were just too severe."*

I leaned back on the couch, pulling Henley with me as I relived the worst moment of my life.

"I'm so sorry. That is anyone's worst nightmare, Easton," she said, as she looked at me and stroked my cheek.

"I can still hear the horrific cries from Jilly's parents after he'd said those words. My parents were a mess, and my mother was sitting on the floor, holding Jilly's mom. And I couldn't process any of it. I just stood there, dumbfounded, unable to speak or cry or feel anything."

"Everyone deals with grief differently."

"Agreed. And I spent days in bed afterward, doing just that. Every night, I'd lie in the fetal position, shaking, reliving those words. Then I went to see Dr. Langford, and after the summer, I left for law school. And I poured myself into school, you know?"

"Yes. I understand that."

"And everything was good for years. Sure, I'd get drunk once a year on my birthday when I remembered what I'd lost on that day. But I was able to compartmentalize—up until I met you. And everything changed."

"I'm sorry. I wish you would have told me," she said, stroking my face over and over. As if she could take my pain from me, and in a way, she was.

Just telling her was healing. Like this heavy weight was lifting off my shoulders.

"I thought I had it handled. But then the nightmares started. And then the panic attacks came more often. I thought if I could just get you not to go out on the river, it would go away. And then when you insisted on going, I thought if we could just get through it, maybe it would all go away."

"It's trauma, Easton. You lost someone that you love. But that doesn't mean that you will lose me. I'm here. I'm right here. And you are the reason for that. You saved me. You dove out of that raft and you got me down the river. And I want you to lean on me when you need me. I don't want you to suffer in silence."

"It's my burden, Henley. I did not want to put that on you. But when we pulled up at that hospital, I felt like the walls were closing in around me. I couldn't breathe. Even when the paramedic told me that you were going to be okay, I didn't believe it. And then my mom came out and said everything was fine and that you were getting released, and I don't know—I lost it. I told Rafe to give me a ride to my car. He tried to talk me out of it, but I wasn't having it. I texted Lulu and asked her to get to the hospital, and then I got into my car and drove to Magnolia Falls. Away. I needed to be away."

"I'm sorry I scared you." Her words broke on a sob. "I'm sorry I made you relive that day. But I'm grateful you were there for me. You saved me, Easton."

"Baby, do not apologize. You didn't do anything wrong. You were just living your life, which is exactly what you should be doing. Hell, I do it every day. I can't expect you to stop living because of my issues." I kissed her forehead. "But in that moment, when I thought I could have lost you, I couldn't breathe. I couldn't think straight. And I did the only thing I could to survive, which was leave. It's not an excuse, and I know I was wrong. And I'm going to work like hell to do better next time. But telling you everything is a big step forward."

She shifted, climbing onto my lap and placing one hand on each side of my face. "It's a huge step. And we'll figure it out together. It doesn't mean I won't do things that scare you, but it means we'll talk through them, and we'll do it as a team. Okay?"

"Yeah. I like the sound of that. Dr. Langford asked if you'd come to therapy with me next week," I said, rolling my eyes because I couldn't believe I was dragging my girl to therapy now.

"Have you met me? Of course, I'll go. I love therapy." She chuckled. "We've all got our shit, Easton. It takes strength to face our fears, to talk about them."

"I love you, Princess. I want to move in with you. I want this life with you."

"I do, too," she said, just as the front door opened and closed.

"Well, what do we have here?" Lulu raised a brow. "You're back?"

I wrapped my arms around my girl. "I am."

She studied me for a few beats and then looked at her best friend, and her gaze softened. "It looks like we're working things out? You didn't let him off the hook easily, did you?"

"I did not. He was open and honest, and that was exactly what I needed," Henley said.

"Thank God. And lucky for you because while I was waiting for the food, I was researching tools that would be strong enough to cut off a man's balls. But then I thought it over and realized orange is so not my color, and jail time would really piss off my father."

I barked out a laugh. "Well, I guess I'm thankful for that."

"Come on. I've got food. I brought an extra entrée because I heard we might have company," Lulu said, waggling her brows as she moved to the kitchen.

My girl and I followed behind her.

"What do you mean?" Henley asked.

"Edith and Oscar are crazy asses. My stress level is off the charts. They were arguing about Edith swearing she saw Easton drive by out the window. But she was confused because 'The Taylor Tea' said you'd fled town. And then Oscar got all barky and jealous and told her she was too consumed with you." She unloaded the food from the bag, setting three entrées down.

"So you just assumed he'd come to see me and you got him dinner?" Henley laughed.

"I did." Lulu turned to look at me. "I know when a man is in love with a woman, and I didn't doubt that he loved you when he left. He just took a minute to work out his shit."

I passed out the napkins and utensils. "Thank you."

"Sure. But there's a message in your meal, so don't you forget it, Chadwick."

Henley opened her container to find the chicken salad that she'd ordered, and Lulu had a steak and a salad. When I opened my container, there was spaghetti with two large meatballs on top. I glanced over at Lulu, and she was twirling the plastic knife in her fingers.

The table erupted in laughter.

"I get it. My balls are on high alert," I said, as we dove in and started eating.

I looked up at my girl to find her watching me.

And I knew in that moment that we were going to be just fine.

———

RAFE

Glad you figured out your shit and came home, brother.

CLARK

Yeah. I've been worried about you.

ARCHER

You just needed to take a beat and figure it out.

BRIDGER

And fuck 'The Taylor Tea' for calling you out.

Laura Pavlov

AXEL

As much as I hate it, the author does seem to be spot-on with everything. How the fuck does she know what's going on?

Glad to be back. It's obviously someone who knows us well.

ARCHER

Or someone that just observes everyone and everything.

BRIDGER

Wake the fuck up. It's Emilia fucking Taylor. It has to be. She's clearly out to get us. Why is she always writing about our family?

RAFE

Maybe because we're the most exciting topic in Rosewood River? And our boy did punch that assmunch, Josh, in public. So it doesn't have to be Emilia. It could be anyone.

AXEL

Why are you so convinced it's Emilia, anyway? She doesn't even work at the newspaper. She's a goddamn florist, for fuck's sake.

ARCHER

I'm telling you, she had a crush on Bridger when we were young, and he's always misread it.

It doesn't even matter who it is. I don't give a shit. I got my girl back. I'm home. People can talk all they want. I'm tuning out the noise, boys.

RAFE

What the fuck is happening? Who is this, and what have you done with our bitter brother?

It's me. And this is what happiness looks like, fuckface. Maybe give it a try.

CLARK

Happy for you, brother. You deserve this. When is moving day?

ARCHER

Let me guess... you want to know so you can claim you have practice?

CLARK

Moving isn't my favorite thing. I prefer to get a stick to the face. <winky face emoji>

AXEL

That explains a lot about your face. <laughing face emoji> Let me know when you need me, and I'll be there.

RAFE

I wish I could help you move, but I've got a doctor's appointment.

I haven't told you the day, you dipdick.

RAFE

Remind me of the date.

Relax. We're moving into Henley's place. I'll leave most of my furniture at my house, and we'll probably rent it out. There is no moving day. But glad to know some of you fuckers were going to bail.

RAFE

Oh. My doctor just texted. My appointment is canceled. Indefinitely.

RAFE

Am I still good to stay in your guesthouse while I get the renovations done at my place?

Of course. It's got a separate entrance, so we can still rent out the house with you in the back cottage.

RAFE

Great. Appreciate it, brother.

ARCHER

Are we still meeting tonight to see the Christmas tree and the lights downtown? Melody is old enough to enjoy it this year.

BRIDGER

Wouldn't miss it.

RAFE

I swear Melody is the only girl Bridger's ever been soft for.

BRIDGER

Riddle me stupid. She's three years old and the cutest thing on the planet.

CLARK

Can't argue with that. I'll be there.

RAFE

I'll be there. My boss is bogging me down with work right now, and I swear he's being a dick because I told him that I have a girlfriend. Easton, can I file some sort of HR complaint against him?

Sure, buddy. File a complaint that you think your boss is making you work because you told him that you have a girlfriend, one whom you've made up in your head to avoid dating his daughter. They'll have a field day with that.

AXEL

The shark has spoken. You better find a lady before you go to your boss's wedding or the jig is up.

RAFE

I could find a lady in my sleep.

Well, I found mine, and I'd like to stop texting you and go enjoy her muffins.

RAFE

You're a filthy pig.

She made blueberry muffins for breakfast, you trash bag. But... now that you mention it. <winky face emoji>

ARCHER

See you tonight, assholes.

A slew of emojis came through, and I set my phone down as my girl pulled the muffins from the oven.

And I just watched her.

I knew she was the woman I'd spend the rest of my life with. I knew I'd propose to her when we were both ready.

Because she was the one I'd been waiting for.

And forever started the day she'd walked into that office.

So I'd just savor every day, every moment, with the woman who stole my heart.

epilogue

. . .

Henley

"I'M glad you agreed to come back again," Dr. Langford said. "He always wants to cancel these appointments, so the fact that he's still coming is a good sign."

"*He* can hear you." Easton chuckled, feigning irritation. "And *he* was fine with it. Plus, I know my girl is not going to bail on therapy. She lives for this shit. Any chance to analyze me, right, baby?"

"Well, I do enjoy diving into that mind of yours," I said. "We're in this together, Chadwick."

"I'm glad to hear it. So, no panic attacks in the last two weeks?" Dr. Langford asked my boyfriend.

"Nope. And trust me, I worried that they'd come when we moved in together, but I've been more relaxed than ever." His voice was all tease as he winked at me. "Best decision I ever made."

"Me, too." I smiled up at him, and he tugged me against him.

We'd grown even closer now that everything was out in the open. He'd been vulnerable with me, and it was almost as if this invisible weight had lifted from his shoulders.

"And I assume your father is still being supportive, and you introduced him to your grandparents?" Dr. Langford asked.

"Yes. My dad has been very supportive. We just had dinner with him this past weekend with my grandparents. And, of course, they loved him." I bumped him with my shoulder as my teeth sank into my bottom lip.

My grandparents were thrilled for me and Easton, and it meant a lot to me. I didn't have a big family like he did, so I wanted him to know the few people in my life that were important to me.

"You're adorable, Princess. You know that?" He leaned down and kissed my forehead. "I loved meeting her grandparents, and her father seems genuinely happy for us."

Dad was very happy for us, and it meant a lot to me. He'd insisted on some changes at the office, and we hadn't had an issue with it. I was no longer working directly under Easton, and my probation period had come to an end. Easton was still determined to get his name on the wall and make partner, and my father assured him that the partners had already met and agreed, so his promotion would be coming in the new year.

"Jamison is getting out of rehab soon. How do you feel about that?" She steered her question to Easton.

In the past, he would have gotten tense and serious, but he just kept smiling at me. "I feel fine about it. He wrote that letter, and he's done the work, so it seems genuine."

"And," I said with a laugh, "you called and spoke to him."

Dr. Langford raised a brow. "Oh? What did you say?"

"I just asked how he was doing and let him know that Henley and I were together. It was an olive branch."

"It was a warning," I said, and I couldn't stop the smile that spread across my face.

He was working on his irrational fear of keeping me safe, but that didn't mean he wasn't a protective guy by nature. And though he wasn't having panic attacks and nightmares right now, Easton would still punch a guy in the face if he knocked me out of a raft or tried to push his way into my hotel room.

That was who he was.

Laura Pavlov

And I wouldn't change a thing.

"Listen. I'm good with her living her life. We're all going skiing this month, and I feel fine about it. But this guy got aggressive with her, and I'm glad he's seeking treatment, but I want him to know that I'm here. End of story."

"Well, I can get behind that. Protecting the people you love is in your nature. You just have to keep it within reason." Dr. Langford smirked.

"I'm working on that," he said. "Thank you for torturing me week after week, Doc. I'm the happiest I've ever been, and I owe a lot of that to you."

"I appreciate it," she said. "But you've done all the hard work. And life is a marathon, not a sprint. So, I plan to see you both back here in two weeks."

Easton groaned. "Fine. See you then. Have a nice holiday."

I gave her a hug goodbye, and Easton and I both put our jackets on, as it was cold and snowy outside. Easton reached for the white beanie with the large pompom from my pocket and pulled it over my head.

When we stepped outside, we walked through downtown. I loved it here this time of year. The storefronts all had festive window displays, and the streetlights were wrapped in garland with white twinkle lights around them and overflowing baskets filled with red and white flowers.

"We've got a stop to make before we go Christmas shopping," I said, pulling open the door to The Vintage Rose.

"All right," he said, as we stepped inside. We both stomped our feet on the doormat to get off any snow and moisture before moving further inside.

"Hey, Henley, Easton. Nice to see you," Emilia said as she looked up at us from where she was cutting a few roses and wrapping them in paper.

I'd gotten to know her since moving to town, and she was really sweet.

310

"Hi, Emilia," I said, admiring the arrangements on the counter that were clearly ready for delivery.

Easton gave a curt nod and said hello. He was cautious with her because he hated that her family had printed stories about his family. But Emilia didn't even work for the paper, and though Bridger was convinced she was the one writing 'The Taylor Tea,' there was no proof of that at all.

"I've got your flowers all ready for you." She walked to the refrigerator and pulled out a pretty arrangement of red and white florals with fresh greens mixed in.

"Thank you. These are gorgeous," I said.

"I just brought you flowers home yesterday." Easton furrowed his brow.

"They aren't for me," I said.

I'd paid over the phone when I'd called in the order, so I thanked her as we made our way to the door.

"Have a great day," she called out, and we waved goodbye and headed back out into the cold.

"She's really nice. You shouldn't blame her for a paper that her family runs," I said, leading him down the street and to the right.

"Bridger is convinced she's the one writing that column."

"He has no proof. He's just looking to hate someone, and she's an easy target because her family owns the paper." I turned down the street, leading him toward the cemetery.

When we got to the entrance, he came to a stop. "What are we doing here?"

"We're wishing Jilly a happy holiday." I pushed up on my tiptoes and kissed him, as we stood with the snow falling all around us.

"I haven't been here in years."

"I know. Dr. Langford asked you about it in therapy last week, and I just thought it might be nice to come and visit. It's all part of moving forward."

"How'd I get so lucky to find you?"

"I'm the lucky one, Chadwick. Come on," I said, and he pointed in the direction of where she was buried.

I set the flowers down on the grass, and Easton just stared down at her grave. "Hey, Jilly Bean. There's someone I want you to meet."

I smiled. "I think she'd be happy for you."

"Yeah, I do, too." He kissed the tip of my nose. We stood there for twenty minutes, and he told me about one Christmas when she had gotten him an orange sweater that he absolutely hated, but he wore it to dinner with her because he didn't want to hurt her feelings.

He laughed at the memory and said goodbye to her before we made our way out of there and walked toward home.

We'd both learned that the past was just part of the journey. It was what led you to where you were now.

And you didn't have to run from it or hide from it; you just had to keep moving forward.

And that's exactly what we were doing.

Together.

———

Christmas was just a few days away, and we were sitting in front of our Christmas tree, admiring the pretty ornaments. Some I'd collected over the years, and others were ornaments that Ellie Chadwick had given us, as she'd collected some for each of her kids to use on their trees now that they were grown. But most, we'd gone out and purchased together over the last few weeks.

Easton had gotten me a crown ornament that said *Princess* on it. I'd found a pickleball ornament and had the guy at the holiday shop paint *Chad-Six* on it.

He'd bought me a river raft ornament and insisted that we were going to get back out on the river when the weather warmed up.

"I think my favorite is that big-ass shark ornament." Easton turned to look at me. "He's such a badass."

"Well, that's why they call you the shark. You're a badass, Easton Chadwick."

"Love you, Princess." He kissed me and then pulled back. "Thanks for showing me how good life could be."

"Yeah? You don't mind shacking up with your coworker?"

"Never been happier, baby." He kissed my neck as my phone vibrated on the table.

"Me, too," I said, reaching for my phone. "Oh, it's Lulu. She's supposed to be at dinner with her family tonight."

"Take it," he said, sitting back against the couch as I answered.

"Hey. Aren't you at dinner?" I asked.

"Well, dinner ended abruptly. Check your texts. I sent you the photos currently going viral on the internet," Lulu said, her voice calm as I switched her to speakerphone and opened my texts.

I gasped at the sight of Beckett Bane in a rage at a famous steakhouse in the city. The table was flipped. Lulu's family stood there, gaping in surprise.

"Oh, my gosh, Lu. What happened?" I asked, as Easton leaned against me and read the screen with me.

"Hurricane dickhead happened. That crazy ex of mine read an article where my father was recently asked about my relationship with Beckett, and of course, my dad was pleased to say that I was dating someone and was very happy, because obviously that's what I've told him. Beckett, the cheating reptile that he is, flew into a jealous rage. Apparently, his tour was on a break, and he was in the city and somehow found out where we were eating, and he came there. Drunk and sloppy and completely irrational. My God, Hen, how did I ever date that guy? He's fully sleeping with someone else, and he won't leave me alone."

"I'm so sorry. I'm sure your dad is upset."

"Yeah. He gave me another one of those disappointed looks, and my mom tried to soften things by telling him it was not my fault. I can't control a crazed boy band musician who continues to have temper tantrums every few weeks. I've cut him out of my life. I've blocked him. We don't speak. I'm in a very serious fake relationship, according to the press." She laughed.

"So what happened at the restaurant? How are you going to avoid seeing him if he's in town?"

"That's what I'm calling about. The restaurant called the police, so I'm guessing he'll be detained tonight, and I'm leaving town with my family for the holidays tomorrow. But I was wondering, is Easton's house still available for rent? I think I'm going to come to Rosewood River for a few months. I need a break from the city, and I've got to work on some new designs, so what better place to do that than a gorgeous small town with no paparazzi and my best friend right down the street? Apparently, Beckett canceled his tour dates and will most likely be in the city for the next few months, so I'd prefer not to be here."

"Hey, Lulu," Easton said. "The house is yours if you want it. My brother, Rafe, is having his home renovated after the holidays, but he'll just be staying in the guesthouse on the property. It has its own entrance, so you'll barely see him."

"That would be great. I need some time away. I appreciate it." She sounded tired, which was out of character for Lulu. She'd always managed the pressure of being born into a well-known family, dating a famous musician, and running a huge company so well.

But everyone had their breaking point.

"I'm so excited that you're going to be living here for a few months. And we'll practically be neighbors."

"That's right, bestie. So you best behave, Easton. I'm sharpening the knives now." She chuckled, but it sounded forced. "I've got to go. We're leaving early in the morning for the Hamptons, and I need to pack."

"All right. I love you."

"Love you, too, Hen. Bye, Easton."

"Bye," he said. "Have a good holiday."

She ended the call, and I scrolled the internet after typing in Beckett Bane's name, and article after article started coming up. It was all over social media and every major news channel.

The headline for the *San Francisco News Today* read: Beckett Bane Flies into Jealous Rage over Socialite Lulu Sonnet's New Love!

"This guy seems like he's unhinged," Easton grumped.

"Says the guy who's been a little unhinged himself."

He tipped me back on the couch and tickled me. "I didn't flip a table in a restaurant, did I? I prefer to stick to hospital meltdowns."

He hovered over me, and his heated gaze locked with mine.

"You dove out of a raft and beat up that jackass Josh, not to mention the vicious pickleball incident with Gary Rite."

"I can live with that," he said, rubbing the tip of his nose against mine.

"Yeah? Well, I can, too. And I plan to live with you until the end of time."

"You sure you can make it that long? You won't get sick of me?" he asked.

"Never going to happen. I'm all in, Evil Genius."

He chuckled and just stared at me for the longest time. "I love you today. I'll love you tomorrow. I'll love you till I take my last breath."

"I'm going to hold you to it."

And I meant it.

Because I'd found my forever in this tall, broody, cocky, overbearing, protective, brilliant, beautiful man… and I was going to hold on tight.

And never let go.

. . .

Buckle up, Roses... Lulu Sonnet is coming to Rosewood River, and she needs to find herself a fake boyfriend quickly! Pre-order My Silver Lining , a Small Town, Fake Dating Romance HERE:

   https://geni.us/mysilverlining

keep up on new releases

Linktree Laurapavlovauthor
Newsletter Laurapavlov.com

acknowledgments

Greg, Chase & Hannah, Thank you for inspiring me to chase my dreams! I love you endlessly!

Willow, Forever grateful for your friendship! Thank you for always supporting me and encouraging me and making me laugh! Love you so much!

Catherine, Thank you for celebrating all the things with me, for listening, for making me laugh and for being such an amazing friend! Love you!

Kandi, you are such a bright light in my life. Thank you for being the biggest cheerleader and always helping me push through the challenging days. I would be lost without you. Love you!

Elizabeth O'Roark, so happy to be on this journey with you. Love you my sweet friend!

Pathi, I would not be doing what I love every single day if it wasn't for YOU! I am so thankful for your friendship, and for all the support and encouragement! I'd be lost without you! I love you so much!

Nat, I am SO INCREDIBLY thankful for you! Thank you for taking so much, and never hesitating to jump in where you are needed. Thank you for the daily encouragement, taking so much off of my plate and going to signings with me so that everything runs smoothly. I am forever grateful for you! Love you!

Nina, I'm just going to call you the DREAM MAKER from here on out. Thank you for believing in me and for making my wildest dreams come true. Your friendship means the world to me! I love you forever!

Priyal, How lucky am I to get to work with you?! Thank you for believing in my words and helping to get my books out in the world. I am forever grateful for YOU!!

Kim Cermak, Thank you for being YOU! There is just no other way to say it. You are one in a million. I am endlessly grateful to have you in my corner, but most importantly, to call you my friend. Love you!

Christine Miller, Kelley Beckham, Tiffany Bullard, Sarah Norris, Valentine Grinstead, Meagan Reynoso, Amy Dindia, Josette Ochoa and Ratula Roy, I am endlessly thankful for YOU!

Tatyana (Bookish Banter), thank you so much for teaching me all your savvy tricks on social media, and being so kind and supportive! I adore you!

Janelle (Lyla June Co.), thank you for your support and friendship! I'm so grateful for you! Xo

Paige, You make mother proud. I love you so much and I'm so grateful for your friendship!

Stephanie Hubenak, thank you for always reading my words early and cheering me on. The daily chats are my favorite. Love you so much!

Kelly Yates, thank you for being an endless support! So thankful for you!! Love you!

Logan Chisolm, I absolutely adore you and am so grateful for your support and encouragement! Love you!

Kayla Compton, I am so happy to be working with you and so thankful for YOU! Love you! Xo

Doo, Annette, Abi, Meagan, Diana, Jennifer, Pathi, Natalie, and Caroline, thank you for being the BEST beta readers EVER! Your feedback means the world to me. I am so thankful for you!!

To all the talented, amazing people who turn my words into a polished final book, I am endlessly grateful for you! Sue Grimshaw (Edits by Sue), Hang Le Design, Sarah Sentz

(Enchanted Romance Design), Christine Estevez, Ellie McLove (My Brothers Editor), Jaime Ryter (The Ryters Proof), Julie Deaton (Deaton Author Services), Kim and Katie at Lyric Audio Books, thank you for being so encouraging and supportive!

Crystal Eacker, Thank you for your audio beta listening/reading skills! I absolutely adore you!

Ashley Townsend and Erika Plum, I love the incredible swag that you create and I am so thankful for you both!!

Jennifer, thank you for being an endless support system. For running the Facebook group, posting, reviewing and doing whatever is needed for each release. Your friendship means the world to me! Love you!

Rachel Parker, So incredibly thankful for you and so happy to be on this journey with you! My forever release day good luck charm! Love you so much!

Natasha, Corinne and Lauren, Thank you for pushing me every day and being the best support system! Love you!

Amy & Rebecca, I love sprinting with you so much! So grateful for your friendship! Love you!

Gianna Rose, Rachel Baldwin, Sarah Sentz, Ashley Anastasio, Kayla Compton, Tiara Cobillas, Tori Ann Harris and Erin O'Donnell, thank you for your friendship and your support. It means the world to me!

Mom, thank you for being my biggest cheerleader and reading everything that I write! Love you!

Dad, you really are the reason that I keep chasing my dreams!! Thank you for teaching me to never give up. Love you!

Sandy, thank you for reading and supporting me throughout this journey! Love you!

To the JKL WILLOWS… I am forever grateful to you for your support and encouragement, my sweet friends!! Love you!

To all the bloggers, bookstagrammers and ARC readers who have posted, shared, and supported me—I can't begin to tell you how much it means to me. I love seeing the graphics that you make and the gorgeous posts that you share. I am forever grateful for your support!

To all the readers who take the time to pick up my books and take a chance on my words…THANK YOU for helping to make my dreams come true!!

other books by laura pavlov

Rosewood River Series
Steal My Heart
My Silver Lining
Over The Moon
Crazy In Love
In A Heartbeat
Whisper Sweet Nothings

Magnolia Falls Series
Loving Romeo
Wild River
Forbidden King
Beating Heart
Finding Hayes

Cottonwood Cove Series
Into the Tide
Under the Stars
On the Shore

Before the Sunset
After the Storm

Honey Mountain Series
Always Mine
Ever Mine
Make You Mine
Simply Mine
Only Mine

The Willow Springs Series
Frayed
Tangled
Charmed
Sealed
Claimed

Montgomery Brothers Series
Legacy
Peacekeeper
Rebel

A Love You More Rock Star Romance
More Jade
More of You
More of Us

The Shine Design Series
Beautifully Damaged
Beautifully Flawed

The G.D. Taylors Series with Willow Aster
Wanted Wed or Alive
The Bold and the Bullheaded

Another Motherfaker
Don't Cry Spilled MILF
Friends with Benefactors

follow me

. . .

Website laurapavlov.com
Goodreads @laurapavlov
Instagram @laurapavlovauthor
Facebook @laurapavlovauthor
Pav-Love's Readers @pav-love's readers
Amazon @laurapavlov
BookBub @laurapavlov
TikTok @laurapavlovauthor